The Frontiers of Political Theory

The Frontiers of Political Theory

Essays in a revitalised discipline

EDITED BY

MICHAEL FREEMAN
Lecturer in Government,
University of Essex
AND
DAVID ROBERTSON
Fellow and Tutor in Politics,
St Hugh's College, Oxford

ST MARTIN'S PRESS NEW YORK

All rights reserved. For information write:
St. Martin's Press, Inc., 175 Fifth Avenue, New York, N.Y. 10010
Printed in Great Britain
First published in the United States of America in 1980

ISBN 0-312-30920-1

Library of Congress Cataloging in Publication Data

Main entry under title:
The Frontiers of political theory.
Includes index.
1. Political science – Addresses, essays,
lectures.
I. Freeman, Michael, 1936–   II. Robertson, David Bruce.
JA71.F73 1980   320   79-27449
ISBN 0-312-30920-1

FE 12'82

Contents

List of Contributors

Michael Freeman, joint editor of the collection, has been a Lecturer in the Department of Government at the University of Essex since 1968. He has written on the theories of revolution and on the political sociology of Edmund Burke. In 1979 he was a Visiting Professor at the University of North Carolina.

David Robertson, joint editor, was a Lecturer and Senior Lecturer in Goverment at the University of Essex from 1970 to 1979 and is now Fellow and Tutor in Politics, St Hugh's College, Oxford. He has worked mainly on theories of voting behaviour and is still a Director of the British Election Study at Essex. He is now working on the relationship between politics and law. He has been a Visiting Professor in American and Canadian universities.

Benjamin Barber is a Professor of Political Science at Rutgers University. Author of several works on Democratic Theory, he was a Visiting Professor at Essex in 1977. He is also a playwright.

John Gray was a Lecturer in Government at Essex from 1973 to 1976 and has since been Fellow and Tutor in Politics, Jesus College, Oxford. His work has been on problems in Liberal political theory, on Herbert Marcuse, and on Bertrand Russell.

Ernesto Laclau has been a Lecturer at Essex since 1974 and is one of the best known modern Marxist scholars, whose debate with Miliband and Poulantzas is well known. His work is increasingly on problems of ideology in Marxism, but he is also a Latin-Americanist.

Kenneth Macdonald was a Lecturer and Senior Lecturer at Essex from 1970 to 1975, during which time he was also Director of the SSRC Survey Archive. Since then he has been a Fellow of Nuffield College, Oxford. Originally a methodologist with publications on regression and path analysis as well as social mobility, he has always maintained a strong interest in political philosophy and written in the field.

David Miller was a Lecturer at Lancaster University and the University of East Anglia (when he taught also at Essex) and since 1979 has been an Official Fellow of Nuffield College, Oxford. His work has been on theories of social justice, and he now works mainly on problems of the social market society.

Peter Morriss was an undergraduate at Essex, has been a graduate student and Lecturer at Manchester University, and returned to Essex as a Lecturer in Government in 1979. He has worked on the theory of power and on formal theories of politics.

Patrick Riley is Professor of Political Science at the University of Wisconsin-Madison and in 1977 was a Visiting Professor of Government at Essex. Widely interested in traditional political theory, most of his work has been on social contract theory and on the political theory of Leibnitz.

Preface

We hope in this collection of essays to present a sample of contemporary political theory as a creative enterprise. All but one of the essays here have been written specially for this book and do not appear elsewhere in print. They vary enormously in style, concern, technique, and ideological viewpoint because political theory today is more pluralist in all these respects than it has ever been. The editors deliberately made no attempt to put together a homogeneous selection; that would have destroyed the point. Nor did we ask our contributors to write 'surveys' of their fields, for we wanted not to *describe* political theory but to exemplify it, or as much of it as space would allow.

Some organising principle was necessary at first. We took an institutional one. As both editors, at the time the project was conceived, worked in the Department of Government at the University of Essex, we decided to make a connection, though often loose, with Essex the criterion for selection. This made sense because the enlivening trend in political theory we want to demonstrate fits well with the deliberately modern ethos of the Essex political science orientation, and its catholicity allows for the flowering of the theoretical pluralism we comment on. It says a lot of that Department that authors as varied as ours have worked happily in, or been successful and esteemed visitors to, it. As editors we would like this collection to be seen as a tribute to the Department, with which sentiment all the contributors would happily accord.

MICHAEL FREEMAN
DAVID ROBERTSON

University of Essex
August 1979

Introduction: The Rebirth of a Discipline

MICHAEL FREEMAN and DAVID ROBERTSON

THIS collection of nine essays is an attempt to demonstrate the variety and range of political theory today. Naturally no such collection can represent all that goes on under the rubric of political theory and philosophy. There are lacunae of two sorts. First there are those problems, topics, approaches, of which the editors are aware but have excluded. Some we would have included but for space. There is, for example, no essay in the realm of mathematical or formal political theory in this book, though it is clearly an important area, if one that has not lived up to the promise it once seemed to offer.

Others are excluded deliberately. With the possible exception of Patrick Riley's essay on Kojève, there is here nothing from that side of political theory which is the history of political ideas. This is no accident; we neither feel that the history of political theory ought to be represented here, nor that it is necessary, given the preponderance of that tradition in journals and other books.

Then there are those omissions which will be seen by some readers of which we are unaware, because political theory, even more than other philosophical disciplines, is much subject to the varied and often conflicting conceptualisations and categorisations of its practitioners.

It is doubtful that any general definition of political theory can be usefully offered. For the moment we prefer to restrict ourselves to the admittedly unsatisfactory argument that political theory is what political theorists do, and that it is usually possible to agree about any particular suggested piece. That is, within a very general notion that political theory or philosophy is rigorous and systematic thought about the political, one can easily enough recognise some when one sees it. In fact one of these essays, Benjamin Barber's discussion of Nozick, is based on an argument about the essential nature of political theory.

Even if it is necessarily incomplete we think that a book like this, of specially written original essays dealing with a number of substantive or methodological problems, is useful and timely for several reasons.

The first reason is that it is only about twenty years since the death of political theory was announced. The subject did not die, and could not have done so, though it is easy to see why either its murder or its suicide could have seemed an iminent possibility in the late 'fifties. It did not die, but it has certainly changed, and the change, a necessary change to avoid that intellectual morbidity, is demonstrated in these essays. So the first purpose of this book is to offer examples of what has happened to revitalise the discipline.

The second purpose of the book is to satisfy a felt need of many teachers of political theory. There are no real textbooks of political theory (leaving aside textbooks on the history of political ideas) and there could not be any. None of us would willingly trust to one man the writing of a supposedly comprehensive, general and true account of the whole of our subject. Textbooks in other areas of political science are difficult enough but in ours impossible. Yet when teaching, most of us feel that we would like to be able to recommend a book that will give students a good grasp of the different sorts of activity, in terms both of topic and method, that are embraced by the subject.

It seems that a collection of essays such as this is the best way of meeting that need, for it can provide an intellectual pluralism avoiding the dangers of a textbook. At the same time, one wants this teaching material to represent the best creativity of political theory. Thus, we have commissioned original essays on problems, not descriptive 'state of the literature' pieces. This is not meant to be the equivalent of a survey course; it is meant to demonstrate political theory, not to describe it. The essays are thus, in intent and in the belief of the editors, of value and worth in their own right, as well as being signposts and paradigms.

Good political theory essays need no brush, as it were, and there seems no point in further justification. But we wish in this introduction to say something about what we take to be the major themes, in this revitalised discipline, and to account for the renewal of energy, to describe the frontier the title evokes and the paths to it. Above all, we want to say why and how we think the political theory being written now is different in important respects from that of twenty years ago. In so doing we comment on the individual essays and on some striking similarities and communalities amongst them. It is worth remarking, at this point, that the essays were not deliberately planned to contain these communalities. Surely, we felt, any common ground that is really there will emerge naturally, and an attempt to ensure one would be pointless. We were right, as our later comments show.

WHY WAS POLITICAL THEORY SEEN TO BE DEAD OR DYING?

A brief answer to this is the best starting point for a characterisation of its contemporary health. In one sense no-one ever felt seriously that political theory was dead. A common understanding of the term, as we have suggested, has been that political theory, in teaching and writing, means discussion of political theories written some time ago by other men. Quantification may be spurious, but one would guess that even today as much as fifty percent of all writing in political theory is critical scholarship about political theories, rather than actual attempts to solve intellectual or empirical problems in theories of politics. We appreciate that the boundary is vague. Often criticism of one theory is the way we advance our own, and always the surrounding scholarly framework of a problem must be discussed. Yet what had happened in political theory by the 'fifties was not this natural and inevitable use of others' thoughts, but the discussion and criticism of (usually old) theories as an end in itself. While we do not wish to doubt the value, in some ways, of the history of ideas, it is fairly obvious that the writing of histories of political ideas is not in itself the writing of political theory.

A side glance at our cognate disciplines makes the point: sociological theorists, economic theorists, and philosophers all from time to time discuss and criticise their historical stock of ideas, but they do not take that to be the essence of their activity. Philosophers discuss Kant because some of them find his arguments useful to solve problems about the nature of space and time. More rarely economists may study the development of Marshal's ideas of the market, but because they want to understand the contemporary phenomenon of oligopoly. No-one could have thought political theory dead because political theorists used Hobbes' description of the state of nature to analyse the sources of our obligation to obey a modern state, were this what political theorists did. A real example, for instance, may be the difference between John Rawls using, when others merely criticise, Rousseauian contract theory.

One of the problems that seemed so mortal in the late 'fifties then was simply that much of what was done under the label of political theory was no such thing, and should have been done in departments of history. Very little original creative construction of theories about political reality and morality was in fact done between, say, the death of Mill and the (publishing) birth of Rawls. So while a subject persisted in name, it was increasingly a misnaming.

Secondly the writing that was done was often by those committed to one or both of two views which would indeed have been fatal had they persisted. The beliefs were a faith in a rather naive behavioural scientism, principally of American origin, and an acceptance of a doctrine about the nature of philosophy and its tasks that can be laid at the feet of writers like J.L. Austin or the young A.J. Ayer.

The attempt at scientific behaviouralism has too often been too unfairly criticised for us to wish to make much of it. In itself, there is no reason why it should have been antagonistic to political theory. Many of its leaders were actually acutely aware of the need for empirical research to be 'theory-guided'. They were partly responsible for encouraging one of the developments that has made for the rebirth of the subject, by correcting the tendency of political thought to be altogether too remote from empirical connections. However one of the sub-beliefs of the behaviouralists was that science, implying as it does objectivity, meant that normative questions could not be the concern of social scientists, and much, if not all, of the historical tradition of political theory was seen as irremediably 'value laden'.

There was therefore a hostility to one of the very central aspects of anything that could be called political theory, the answering of questions about political morality and the justification of polities in terms of a vision of the good life. This hostility both discriminated against the doing of much political theory by making it seem in many eyes 'unprofessional', and sadly impoverished that which was written. Michael Freeman makes this point in his critique of theories of revolution, many of which were written from the perspective we attack. A second example is the peculiar literature on what was called 'political development', surely a topic crying out for a theoretical treatment which would, amongst other things, be overtly and proudly 'normative'. Yet strangely its practitioners thought they had to defend themselves against what its enemies for some odd reason thought to be a criticism, that its central concepts were value-laden.

A version of philosophical positivism, perhaps best represented by T.D. Weldon's work, was the other belief, which led both to a restriction in the ambition of political theorists, and to a particularly arid formalism in what was left of more philosophically inclined political theory. The difference that has come about in the writing of analytic political philosophy shows clearly amongst some of our essays here, particularly those by Gray, Barber, and David Miller. If behaviouralism with its opposition to normative theory nearly murdered political theory, the acceptance by so many of a restrictive positivist understanding of the methods and role of philosophy was virtually suicide. Weldon believed that little more than ground clearing, abstract conceptual unravelling of empiricists' confusions could be done by political theory. It was the old extreme logical positivism that characterised philosophy as a mere 'handmaiden to the sciences' that robbed political theory of the rest of its vitality.

This movement had other effects too, for it encouraged a technique of analytic philosophy, linguistic philosophy applied to political concepts, that rested heavily on formalism in argument. Keen on the one hand to abolish metaphysics from political thought, admirably enough, it actually made political theory less capable of engaging empirical reality by its stress on analyticity, on the purely formal treatment of concepts. Two essays here at least, Gray's solution to the 'happy slave' paradox and Miller's demonstration of the 'need' basis of social justice, probably could not have been written twenty years ago because they reject formal or linguistic weaponry in favour of substantive arguments about the nature of social life. Barber's essay on Nozick would possibly also have been rejected by readers because he stresses so much the immanence of political reality against the formal truths of philosophical analysis.

Had Weldon-style political theory not been replaced, political philosophy might well have died; what interesting things were there to say in a world where a theorist could aim only for the analytic *a priori*?

What was needed for political theory to live again was a radical rejection of these three conditions – an undue concentration on the history of political thought, a commitment to crude behavioural scientism, and an over-restricted positivist view of the functions and tools of philosophy.

WHERE ARE WE NOW, AND HOW DID WE GET HERE?

No explanation in historical terms can be given, so close are we still to the dying days of the old political theory. However, in discussing the separate contributions to this collection we hope to sketch the current diverse natures of political theory, and give some idea of sources of contemporary political theorists' concerns.

Some major trends can be detected in the intellectual changes of the last two decades of political theory, as represented here. There has been a very strong resurgence of Marxist thought. It is almost as thought Marxism had become intellectually respectable in Anglo-American Politics Departments overnight sometime in the late 'sixties. One is pointing here to a serious and rigorous Marxist theorising, not to some vague resurgence of emotional radicalism. The single most important aspect of the arrival of Marxism has been the emphasis this school has given to the theory of the state, a topic oddly neglected by political theory for a long time. Ernesto Laclau's essay represents this movement and this concentration. Very few people know as much or are as creative exponents of the Marxist theory of the state as Laclau. His essay starts by noting the complaints within that tradition about the lack of a serious study of politics by Marxists.

Although sometimes just, the standard complaints of those unsympathetic to Marxist analysis, that it is jargon ridden and incredibly difficult to read, are usually misplaced. True Marxism, as any other philosophical/political corpus of ideas, has its own language. Why should it not? It conceptualises the world in a different mode from empiricist oriented philosophies, and thus it needs its own terms. Marxist political theory also tends to operate with a different epistemology, a different canon of good argument. These also present difficulties to the unsympathetic. These are all difficulties worth the overcoming, because whether or not one ultimately accepts a Marxist interpretation, one will not find elsewhere at the moment any equally thoughtful critical comprehension of the nature of the state, and its exercise of power.

In the end Laclau's piece demonstrates the changes that have come over Marxist political theory, just as our other contributions show change in their respective traditions. It might well occur to readers to ask by virtue of what Laclau should be labelled a Marxist. The whole thrust of his piece is away from class or economic determinism. His argument for a Marxist political theory indeed concentrates on the need for a generalised vision of the state, the state as the soul of oppression, rather than any view specific to capitalist politics. Even those who find the idea of the 'democratic subject' as outlined by 'interpellations' of ideology, a democratic subject not located in any specified state, too abstract cannot but admit that his analysis reaches to the core of the whole problem of state coercion without requiring us to treat all social conflict as economically determined.

What is specifically Marxist about his approach is the logic of analysis, rather than the substantive assumptions. The economic base may be missing, as perhaps it increasingly must be in all intelligent Marxism, but the dialectic, the interpretation of social problems in terms of logical antagonisms between characterising moments of society, is fully present. This is Marxism as a methodology, and still a highly rationalistic one, rather than Marxism as a concrete doctrine. But it is part of our entire thesis here that the changes in political theory over the last twenty years are crucially methodological.

It was noted in the Introduction to the fourth series of *Philosophy, Politics and Society*[1] that an increasing awareness of ideology had helped political theory escape from the hubris that nearly destroyed it. It is fitting that Marxist analysis, the home in some ways of the whole idea of ideologically distorted perception, should demonstrate this further. One of Laclau's more valuable insights is into the role of ideology generally in shaping not only political perceptions but the very nature of antagonisms in society. For Laclau the individual who is coerced and opposed by the state is a creation of ideology. Some of us may think that the Althusserian language of ideological interpellations is uncannily close to Parsonian role theory. But still he perceptively analyses the way the antagonism between increasing bureaucratic domination and the principle of free citizenship is dependent on ideologies so often constrained by political and economic structures.

Most valuable in this direction may be his comments towards the end of the piece about the way not only 'bourgeois' social theorists, but 'radical' ones too, are led to assume logical or necessary connections between political symbols which have in fact only a contingent connection of common connotation arising from historical conjunctions. So it is worth both sides being reminded that the connection between democracy and the liberal bourgeois state is indeed not a necessary relationship; if this makes the 'ultra-leftists' wrong in opposing democracy, it makes others wrong in assuming that institutions like private property are mutually implied by democracy.

One might, of course, argue that the methodology that makes Laclau's piece ultimately different from all the other essays here is not Marxist at all, but Hegelian. A question very much like this is raised by Riley. For his essay also is a study in methodology, and a study of ideological interpretation. As such his article, though it bears a surface resemblance to the 'critical history of ideas' school that we suggest has too much characterised political theory, is in truth very different. In trying to see how Kojève's 'reading' of various texts works, he is highlighting another, but perhaps not dissimilar, aspect of the Marxist revival, the rediscovery of Hegel. It may well be, indeed, that what we see as a specifically Marxist upsurge is better understood as a general reaching for the post-enlightenment European tradition of political and social thought. It is worth wondering whether a renewed interest in Hegelian ideas and similar European thought is not itself a consequence of the hatred of the 'metaphysical' that nearly destroyed political theory in the hands of the positivists.

What principally interests Riley is not simply whether or not Kojève takes a particular line. Had either of these been the main emphasis the piece, though good, would have fallen into a category we were not interested in representing. Riley's concern is to study Kojève's method of interpretation. It is how Kojève extracts what he does from Hegel, and how this 'reading', this interpretative method, works when applied to other thinkers that is the problem.

As such Riley is writing in a tradition that is relatively new in the political sciences, one represented in England, for example, by Dunn and Skinner. Its importance is clear. As long as we grant that classics of political theory, as tools to use as well as in their substance, will always be valuable, one cannot avoid the question of how to approach them. Riley demonstrates how far from being passive the action of 'reading' is, and how our understanding of a text is crucially dependent on the selective and analytic preconceptions we bring to the text. If it did no more, his critique of Kojève would be a valuable insight, and would further our understanding of an important element in the new Marxist canon.

The most valuable part of his essay is, however, to show what is by no means obvious, that the same interpretative mechanism cannot be relied on to work equally effectively on all texts. While no substantial injustice is done to Hegel, nor much violence to Kant, he convincingly demonstrates that Plato cannot be read with the same spectacles. This seems to have two rather vital consequences. First, that the author of a work in political theory himself determines to some extent what use can be made of his theory, and what preconceptions must be held by those who would usefully read him. While lip service might be paid to such a thesis automatically by anyone who has even the weakest notion of ideology, it is rare and valuable to have a proven example.

Secondly, Riley may be taken to argue an even more forceful point, for if one cannot use a Marxist framework to read Plato, can or   as a Marxist deal with the concerns Plato had? As Riley says, 'reading Kojève . . . forces one to rethink what counts . . . as an Hegelian, or Marxist, or Hegelo-Marxist view of anything'.

If Riley is right, and he seems to be, we are taught to be very much more cautious than we usually are in labelling *any* political thinker.

This concern for what we have called, vaguely enough, 'problems of ideology' now suffuses political theory, a result partly of the increased sophistication in the philosophy of science and social science that is one of the several strands in the re-emergence of political theory. The awareness that a crude fact/value distinction, forbidding 'normative' but allowing 'scientific' analysis is unduly simple spelt the end of the behavioural rule. An age where the philosophy of science is represented by writers like Kuhn and Toulmin, rather than Popper and Kaplan could not sustain that stranglehold.

This awareness that *no* ideas in political science are less than externally arguable has had several consequences. In terms of our contributions, two appear notably clearly. Peter Morriss' title here demonstrates one – the pervasive influence of an argument about the 'essentially contestable' nature of certain concepts in the political and social sciences. Not only does Morriss address himself directly to this argument, it is one met with, either directly or in thin disguise, in the articles by Gray, Miller, and Robertson. Indeed, two of our contributors, Gray and Macdonald, either have published or are about to publish separate critical contributions to the literature that has sprung up around the idea.

Allied to this, though more important by a long way, is the change that has come over mainstream (i.e., liberal-democratic) political theory with the publications of men like Barry, Rawls and Nozick. Though they are very different in detail and indeed sometimes openly hostile to each other, they are more alike on dimensions that concern us here, and more responsible collectively for the upsurge in creative political theory writing than one might at first see. Barry's *Political Argument*,[2] Rawls' *A Theory of Justice*[3] (and Barry's rejoinder, *The Liberal Theory of Justice*[4]) and Nozick's *Anarchy, State, and Utopia*[5] represent together a return to political theory in the grand manner. They are all attempts to do what the great men of the tradition did, to write constitutions, derive institutional designs, on the basis of presuppositions about man's basic nature and his, or their, values. Of course they are not value free, though they are equally obviously not *un*empirical. They reject both the idea that recommendatory normative analysis is taboo, and the notion that political philosophy can be no more than a handmaiden to other sciences.

Even given this there are some, Benjamin Barber in his contribution being most forthright, who think that the dead hand of analytic philosophy has not lifted far enough from political theory. It is not too difficult to identify the traditional positions from which these men start, at least as a first approximation; Barry is a utilitarian of some sort, Rawls leads from Rousseau, Nozick from Mill. They are users of traditions, creative writers of the architectonic political kind, and whether or not one accepts them, all political theorists today are indebted to their reopening of lost pathways. In our collection the relevance of the trio to Barber is obvious, given that he writes from the position of critic of Nozick.

Barber's piece is again, to a large extent, methodological. He is arguing, and with some success, that political *philosophy* is often (and in his example entirely) too apolitical. Nozick fails for him because Nozick is satisfied with what is 'philosophically true' even when the facts or behaviours of political life as we know it would often in practice invalidate some of these truths. The sharp sense of political reality that informs Barber's essay is shown, for example, by his argument that the task of political theory is misconceived if seen as that of justifying the existence of political institutions as against a non-political 'original position'. Instead, Barber argues, we must grant the political, and justify a particular but inevitable system of politics. Whether in the end this need discount

Nozick is both uncertain and irrelevant here. It certainly discounts, if accepted, a method of argument that takes an 'extra-social' definition of man and asks how much, why and where his liberty may be invaded. One is thrown instead towards questions of man's nature in civil society (clearly a quasi-empirical question) and questions about the way particular institutions, however justified in political logic, will apply in political practice.

This combination of theoretical rigour and behavioural observation is not new in political theory (it is exactly what Hobbes tried to do) but is new since the middle of this century. Notice how it is echoed in Miller's piece. David Miller is writing a piece of analytic political philosophy. He is trying to show the connection, perhaps even the causal connection, between two concepts, that of need and that of social justice. But instead of restricting himself to an almost grammatical analysis of how one word is covered by the extension of the other, his main argument is about the practical social consequences of basing social justice policies on grounds other than need. Miller not only provides logical grounds for believing that a man's need for X renders it unjust not to give him X, he provides us with a sharp insight into what we will do to that man if we give him X but explain our so doing on grounds, for example, of humanity. Miller's own justification for writing the article (though none is needed) is precisely that the actual policies in welfare states will depend on this justification. Only by digging into our views on human nature, particularly by taking a leaf out of Hegel and drawing the comparison between a society and a family, can he succeed in his argument. Yet this means not only that he moves much further than could be moved in the past (for it is unlikely that any connection between need and social justice could be established by purely logical steps, sticking to a strict view of analyticity) but that the move engages directly our empirical and normative beliefs about the nature of human deserts.

We may not agree with the analogy of family and society, but we are thinking about an existential relationship in considering the point, not about a formal one.

To take the point further, Gray's essay is a perfect example of how modern political philosophy differs from the old, in that he tackles a classic problem in liberal philosophy, but in so doing reviews a series of attempts all using old methods, in order to get himself to a solution, escaping the problems of the old by a new, empirical, substantive assumption.

It would be a gross mistake to think of Gray's piece, about the paradox of the happy slave, as being a purely intellectual exercise. Whatever its symbolic form, it is a treatment of a problem that could not be more relevant in an age where 'false consciousness' theories lie ready to seize any unwary liberal who dares suggest that a man's own ideas of his needs or interests must be superior to another's 'objective truth' about his position. And Gray's solution echoes not only this concern, but the methodology used by Miller, recommended by Barber, and exemplified by Barry, Rawls and Nozick.

Why cannot a free man will himself to be a slave? The problem is identical in substance to that raised, for example, by Marcuse in his analysis of false needs, it is a Rousseauian problem, it is the problem of alienation. Gray dismisses two different routes to the goal of demonstrating that the contented slave is not free. He dismisses any *a priori* interpretation of 'interests' that would make it impossible for the slave to know his interests less well than another. No liberal political theorist can do other. He rejects, too, the impoverished approach, so popular during the ailing days of the subject, making it logically, analytically impossible to conjoin the concepts 'slave' and 'free'.

He is right to do this because no logical approach, even if based on the pseudo empiricism of 'ordinary language philosophy' can prevent us uttering the phrase 'this man is a slave, has absolutely everything he wants, and cannot sensibly be held to be unfree'. We may desperately need to reject the truth of that sentence but analyticity will not convince.

If neither the false consciousness approach, nor the logical analyticity approach will do, Gray has naturally a major problem. His solution is inherently empirical, as was Miller's to the problem of need and justice. In this case Gray turns to a rich, even poetic notion of human capacity and nature. It is because of what an autonomous man would truly be like, what he would need to have as opportunity and capacity, that one cannot be autonomous and a slave. Naturally one cannot give any extensive account of an autonomous human nature; that, at least, is analytically true. So some may see Gray's solution as somehow incomplete, in that there is no list of those capacities or needs of the radically autonomous being which would be negated by slavery, however happy.

But this search for completion, for a deductive certainty in social theorising, is hopeless. Gray does make us see how any conception of human autonomy is incompatible, behaviourally or empirically, with any institution of slavery. But he does this without demanding the epistemologically privileged position required by the false-consciousness/alienation approach, by the deterministic Marxism that Laclau also gives up.

Turning now to the essays by Macdonald, Freeman, and Morriss, we retain to some extent the methodological theme, but it appears in the context of a more general change in political theorising. The effects of the behavioural revolution in political science were not all bad for political theory. As we pointed out earlier, there was often a strong commitment amongst the leading advocates of behavioural studies to what they called 'theory guided research'. While the actual notion of scientific activity they held may have been simplistic or inappropriate to political thinking, they did at least stress the need for explicit theoretical frameworks to identify the problems and data of empirical work. This marriage between substantive political research and rigorous general thought about politics gave birth to what has often been called 'Empirical Political Theory', a mixture of theoretical sociology, formal modelling, and other aspects of the more theoretically developed cognate social sciences.

Two of our essays, Freeman's critique of theories of revolution and Morriss' conceptualisation of 'power', are overtly of this genre. Michael Freeman writes critically of existing 'empirical', that is explanatory and predictive, theories of revolution out of a concern that political theory should indeed be such a discipline as can explain the causes and nature of political phenomena, and, where relevant and useful, have also a predictive function. His objection is not, as it is sometimes amongst more orthodox political theorists, that there should be attempts to create such theory at all. Rather, his concerns are two-fold. First, that any such theory should be sufficiently clear, rigorous and systematic to be, at least in principle, testable. Secondly, and perhaps most importantly, that political theory should not, in attempting to serve this 'scientific' cause, refrain from being normative and recommendatory.

He picks out, amongst the more influential of theorists of revolution in the behaviour mode, a common sin characteristic of so much of this sort of work. This is the tendency to define the subject concept in such a way as to facilitate the measurement and analysis of data. As he points out, rather than seriously examining the theoretical and historical nature of revolution in defining this explanandum, the theorists of revolution have tended to concatenate wholly different phenomena. Thus 'internal war', or revolts, crime, brigandage and so on have been lumped together into a subject, then putatively 'explained' by theories which have totally ignored the moral element in revolution.

The cause, though Freeman is too polite to say it this bluntly, is that Gurr and others working in the field could see how to measure riots, etc., but not how to measure that which they could not conceptualise, the actual phenomenon of revolution, in all its theoretical vitality. The result is not the creation of any understanding of revolution.

To repair this deficiency Freeman sets out his own definition of revolution, in a thorough examination not only of all that it might mean linguistically, but of what it has implied historically. In some ways his approach to the description of revolution is much like Laclau's to the definition of the antagonism between the state and democracy. Partly logical, partly historical, they both create an understanding of the problem to be solved by rejecting the merely contingent in our theoretical linkages. Freeman, for example, goes to some length to separate the elements of revolution that confuse the seizure of state power, the radical change in thought and ideology, the change in social behaviour. Whilst all of these play a part in the complex web of things that happen when a revolution occurs, none of them separately is the core of a revolution, and the linkages between them are not necessary or inevitable.

In much the same way Laclau is careful to distinguish between the way in which capitalism may be necessary for the full development of a trend in bureaucratic dominance, and the much more restricted and problematic sense in which bureaucratic domination may be said to be a necessary feature of capitalism per se. This careful work by theorists on the construction of what one may pardonably call 'ideal types' (though neither Freeman nor Laclau may accept the Weberian analogy, it is really quite fair) does indeed seem the only way that an empirical science of politics can develop. It should not be mistaken for the old 'handmaiden to the sciences' approach to political philosophy; they are not simply being critical of others' concepts, not only making logical distinctions the scientists may have had good reason to ignore. Rather they are building categories of understanding through which the political world may be viewed.

But here the normative element arises. There used to be, as we have commented before, an odd idea that value freedom should be sought at all costs. Freeman certainly does not attempt this, and would reject any such effort. The very notion of revolution, the complete overturn and destruction of a way of political life hated to the death by the insurgents, can hardly be studied without any concern for the values it involves. One can, and should, control and be aware of the values one carries, but to ignore them, or try to suppress them is likely only to render one's theory sterile.

Naturally, empirical theory cannot be only the creation of categories, although nothing more could be attempted in the compass of an essay here. It involves, ultimately, the collection and analysis of the data captured by the categories, and the formulation of linking hypotheses and their testing. As such it is a truly scientific, but equally theoretical enterprise. But described as such, it has only just begun to start in our discipline.

Peter Morriss, in his essay on the concept of power, is again principally concerned with empirical political theory. In some ways it comes closer than other contributions here to being in the mould of analytic political philosophy associated with the decline of the subject. For Morriss is concerned to analyse the concept because he feels the increasing belief that power is one of Lukes' 'essentially contestable concepts' is mistaken. The problems in the concepts arise from confusions 'layer upon layer of them; and, moreover, needless confusions'.

In his analysis though, Morriss shows himself to be clearly more interested in developing a concept that can be used in substantive research, and in the building of explanatory theories of political power, than in solving a purely philosophical conundrum. Furthermore his aim in tackling power here is to defeat the 'essentially contestable' thesis. This notion, although invented more than twenty years ago, has begun to play an increasing and pernicious role in much modern philosophically-oriented political theory. Not only is it, as Morriss says 'either a dereliction of duty or an admission of failure' to claim that disputes about a concept are inevitable. It is also to introduce through a back door an unwritten assumption about the presence and nature of ideological limitations in political discourse. Here Morriss' argument is invaluable, because his careful and rich analysis of this concept lays the ghost.

We can indeed hope to do empirical analysis, and create empirical theory about power, even though he admits 'power' has an evaluative or normative role in discourse. We can do this, furthermore, even though power refers, under analysis, to at least two fundamentally different notions, which Morriss refers to as 'influence concepts' and 'ability concepts'. He concentrates his attention mainly on the latter, suggesting the doing of research under the former to be both over difficult and theoretically obscure. The richness of his analysis cannot be described fairly here.

One should note again the two or three points of similarity between his and Freeman's approach to conceptual analysis and the other contributions here, which differentiate current thinking in political theory from the past. First, neither Freeman nor Morriss seeks for 'non-evaluative' conceptualisations, both accepting that moral questions must be asked and must be studied, even when a major aim is the creation of explanatory or descriptive theory. Secondly, they do not withdraw the analysis of concepts from the empirical domain, but instead concentrate on an understanding drawn from real examples, from an attempt to tackle actual political situations rather than linguistic paradigms. Finally they are aware of ideology, of interests, of the difficulty of approaching the design of concepts from a viewpoint that suggests the interests of researchers are irrelevant to their understanding of phenomena through concepts.

Macdonald's essay covers both methodological and ideological problems(though it is doubtful if he would accept that antinomy). His concern is more directly methodological because he discusses the direct effect of our information-collecting approach in society on our political choices. But it is equally an essay on ideological problems in the same sense as is Laclau's because of his emphasis on the ineluctable connection between moral choice and information, and especially information that is ordered over time.

The connections he draws are sometimes startling because we are unused to taking 'time' as a crucial dimension in political theory. However, if he is right in one of his central assertions, that normative statements are often disguised information statements (statements about consequences over future time), his essay is, additionally, a serious critique of both Rawls and Nozick. In fact his essay has two themes, connected, but perhaps easier to grasp if disaggregated. First, there is the argument that the necessary *empirical* component of political theory, the contribution of the social *sciences* to social philosophy, is not only problematic, but to be fruitful may force a revision of what we think of as the subject matter of the philosophical part of the enterprise. Crudely, he argues that information as relevant to political theory is information about choices, not about end states, and that these two sorts of information are neither logically nor factually interchangeable.

On the more purely methodological side, he points out here how little we are as yet able to handle, even technically, this sort of information. The technical problems are not perhaps exciting; the logical problems are. His example of 'experimental administration', say the English Educational Priority Areas, or the American Headstart programmes, is nicely concrete. How does one collect the information on the success of experimental systems with which to make political and theoretical choices about social engineering (the implicit goal of several papers here), when the analytic techniques available are static, but the programme dynamic, in intention and effect?

More generally, how does one decide between rival goals for the future in politics, when arrival at any of the putative goals may change one's values so as to change one's assessment of the relative desirability of the rival end points?

The second theme takes 'time' even more closely into account. (Time is crucial to the first theme as well, but mainly because information is defined partly in terms involving time.) The essence of this second theme is caught by his interesting criticism of Nozick's political plan: that its attempt to facilitate progress by facilitating experimentation breaks down when it is realised that transfer of experience information, especially over time between communes, is in no way provided for. Though disavowing the conservatism held to stem from the insight, Macdonald introduces here a Burkeian concern for identity of social institutions over time, as the necessary conditions of social progress.

The thrust of Macdonald's piece may be to make us shy away from any Popperian notion of social engineering. But if we shy away from it because we discover Popperian methodology to be less neutral than we thought, the creative, architectonic aspect of political theory seems all the more relevant, and as such is obviously timebound – note Macdonald's frequent reliance on the Aristotelian notion that the things we must learn in order to do something, we learn by doing it – and Aristotle was the founder of the idea that politics is architectonic. Is this what Macdonald is saying: the methodologies for ascertaining what we need to know in order to make certain world plans work are determined by those world plans? Does the general thesis of ideology reappear?

If the answer is Yes, it is only in keeping with the main thrust of all the essays in this book. They all seem to insist on, and justify, one premise: political choice, based on a creative perception of the nature of real political life, is not only the way to *do* political theory, but it *is* political theory, and as such is irremediably necessary to the world. One is reminded of the distinction Maurras, a political theorist after all, invented to describe and account for the sterility and *immobilisme* of the Third Republic, the most uncreative of all political systems which he said had made a total divorce between the political system, which he christened the *'Pays Légal'*, and the people, who lived in the *'Pays Réal'*. Our contributors are determined to live in the theoretically 'real' world.

Consider Miller: he requires us to solve an apparently conceptual, moral problem about the justifying premise of social justice by considering the impact on individuals of different justifications, and by thinking of political life through particular analogies, above all that of the family. He solves the problem by a choice of analogy, not by logic or by conceptual analysis. Consider Gray: he bases the interpretation of the satisfied slave, the man with no freedom and no wants, on an existential view of radical human autonomy. Consider Freeman: he requires, for the development of an *explanatory* theory of revolution, a historical and moral categorisation of rebellious activity, rather than an empirical concatenation of externally similar activities; he too imposes a political choice on the understanding of, and presumably the defence of, criticism of revolution. Consider Riley: he shows how the political choice of an analyst so constrains that analyst's reading that he is forced to make no sense at all of another thinker. Which, in reverse, shows how the prior *political* (and not epistemological, as it might usually have been seen) choice of the author, Plato or Kant in this case, makes it impossible to read him usefully and sensibly if you do not make that choice yourself. Trivial? Hardly. It is no truism at all to demonstrate that a Marxist cannot *understand* a Platonist without becoming one.

How different, after all, is Barber's argument? This rests on an ultimate rejection of the 'philosophically true', because of the absolute need to engage with the politically inevitable. Barber's piece may well have too much of a reformist intonation, but the central message is very clear — decisions made in the interpretation of political life, and in political choice, determine what can usefully be said and argued. That which cannot hold political water, the choice in Nozick to justify obedience to the state at all, rather than obedience to a particular state, cannot be valuable, whatever its logic.

Laclau ends up arguing the opposite of Barber here, because he argues for the study of the general contradiction between the general form of the state and the generalised conception of the democratic subject. But he, too, is stressing the priority of a *political* choice, the priority of a historical and contextual understanding of contradictions inherent in political life, which can neither be reduced to economic causes, nor dealt with by epistemological presuppositions. Truly, where Marxists fear to tread, only fools or the old style of political theorists rush in.

The last essay here, Robertson's attempt to reassert legal positivism against new arguments in jurisprudence, is a final affirmation of this position immanent in different ways in all the other essays. He claims, against Dworkin, that a legal positivism heavily indebted to Hart is the only form of legal philosophy valid inside a democratic state. In doing this he is rejecting any approach to natural rights theories about the politics/law interchange. Dworkin tries to argue that there is no judicial discretion in a legal system because judges operate by the balancing of principles to which there is always a right answer. Robertson counter-claims that principles like this cannot exist, that judicial discretion must apply, because we have only rules created by legislators who always leave fuzzy edges, and there exist *no* convenient non-political principles that can produce an answer to how a case should be decided independent of private political decisions.

When Dworkin develops, as a second line of defence, a theory of decision-making in hard cases that involves judges only in expressing the details of a political theory that arises from legal and institutional necessities, Robertson points out simply the impossibility of doing this without usurping legislative creativity.

In the legal system, as in any system, there is no way that concepts can be formed, no way that policies can be justified, no way the free can be identified, or the nature of democratic antagonisms outlined, short of a direct political choice of how to view the world. Legal positivism is true not because it does away with political intrusion by judges, but because it insists that their activity *is* political intrusion, that the simplest of statutory interpretations involves a creative grasp of political life, even if we would prefer only the parliament to do this.

In conclusion we can say only this: if our collection of essays does truly represent the rebirth of political theory, it does so for one reason, and the clue to that rebirth is contained there. Political theory can *never* be relegated to any subsidiary role.

Political understanding is not a handmaiden; political theory is not the neutral critical scholarship of working out what someone else meant (because that cannot be done independently of what the critic means anyway); political science does not operate with concepts that are empirically evident in a 'scientific' way; political policies cannot be justified without recourse to an empirical understanding of the nature of human autonomy, or human needs, or human self-respect; political data cannot be collected independently of the political system they are to be used within. *Political choice is supreme.*

Any editors must feel a certain hesitancy in saying what their contributors said. We do not, for a moment, suggest that this interpretation would necessarily be accepted by Gray, Miller, Morriss, or whomever. Certainly, it does not exhaust what they have to say. They had their own problems, which they have solved in their own lights. The role of the editorial introduction is to say what is possibly common to all of them, and what this represents for modern political theory. Clearly one could reject our interpretation and still value the separate contributions. Hopefully both the individual merits of the essays and the argument here of what they have in common will command some acceptance. Certainly the state of political theory today is healthy; certainly this health must depend on a rejection of the constraints of the past. Two things seem evident in the end: the health depends on allowing a great variety, and such variety is represented here: the health depends on the faith of political theorists that they have something of their own to say, and this surely all our contributions cry out.

NOTES

1 Peter Laslett, W.G. Runciman and Quentin Skinner, eds, *Philosophy, Politics and Society* (Blackwell, Oxford, 1972).
2 Brian Barry, *Political Argument* (Routledge and Kegan Paul, London, 1965).
3 John Rawls, *A Theory of Justice* (Oxford University Press, London, 1972).
4 Brian Barry, *The Liberal Theory of Justice* (Clarendon Press, Oxford, 1973).
5 Robert Nozick, *Anarchy, State and Utopia* (Blackwell, Oxford, 1974).

Deconstituting Politics: Robert Nozick and Philosophical Reductionism

BENJAMIN R. BARBER

Robert Nozick's influential book *Anarchy, State and Utopia* provides a great deal of new evidence for the view that contemporary Anglo-American philosophy is not an ideal vehicle for political thinking. Philosophers interested in justice, obligation, distribution and the state have moved vigorously to fill the conceptual vacuum left by the scientistic modesties and normative disclaimers of social science, but it is not clear that they have refuted Burke's belief that 'delusive geometrical accuracy in moral arguments [is] the most fallacious of all sophistry'. Nonetheless, Nozick's book is a serious, systematic, and often beguiling attempt to treat with fundamental political questions from a philosophical reductionist perspective. Its arguments, falling somewhere between the utilitarians' statist-egalitarian justifications and the anarchists' anti-statist-individualist counter-justifications, deserve serious and critical attention.

I

Anarchy, State and Utopia is an argument designed to show that it is possible to get beyond anarchism without violating anarchist premises; to reach minimal-statist conclusions starting with radical-individualist assumptions; in other words, to construct a defense of political legitimacy on wholly non-political grounds. This defence is deployed both against anarchists who believe that there is *no* legitimate form of the state consistent with radical individualism and personal autonomy, and against statists who believe that it is necessary to move beyond radical individualism to sustain any coherent theory of

political legitimacy. More is possible than the anarchists realise; less is possible than the statists wish, at least if philosophy
is to be the standard.

This dual strategy accounts for the differing intellectual
styles of Part I and Part II of *Anarchy, State and Utopia*. Part I
is a delicately balanced tower of accumulated deductions
anchored in a sub-terrestrial (i.e. invisible and thus unexamined) foundation of radical individualism. It is simply
taken for granted that men 'live separate existences' defined by
inviolable freedom and an absolute right to property; that 'no
moral balancing is possible' between these initially solitary
beings; and that, as a consequence, 'voluntary consent' is an
absolutely necessary prerequisite of each (every and any) step
taken towards political relations — towards exchange, justice,
the common pursuit of social goals, the compromising of
freedom for utilitarian ends, and so forth.[1] Traditional anarchist analysis despairs of taking a single legitimate step under
these conditions and thus, like Robert Paul Wolff in his *In
Defense of Anarchism*, generally concludes that anarchism is
'philosophically true'. Nozick's ingenuity is a good deal more
daring however, and permits him to make a journey to political minimalism that would leave less bold individualists
trembling. The trick is to make every step towards political
association hinge exclusively on *voluntary* exchanges that, if
they cross boundaries at all, do so only by permission or on the
basis of just compensation. Carefully executed, these tactics
neither violate rights nor resort to the rights-abdicating com-
promises of a social contract; yet they do eventuate logically in
an ultraminimal state. This stripped-down, proto-political
body does little more than guarantee the property rights of
those who contract (voluntarily) for its services; it becomes a
de facto state only in as much as it assumes the functions of a
private protective association dominant over a territory,
enforcing the rights of members against non-members, but
compensating (probably with services) non-members for
losses such enforcement might occasion (118). Anarchy is thus
surpassed — *aufgehoben* — without violating anarchism: the
absolute sacrosancity of individual autonomy. The Dominant
Protective Association which emerges as Nozick's minimal
state is not licensed by these arguments, but shown to be a

logically natural extension of hypothetical pre-statist conditions that require no licence.

If the style of Part I of *Anarchy, State and Utopia* is innovative and architectural, the style of Part II is more conservative and wary; it builds defensive trenches around the edifice
erected in Part I, suggesting that the edifice is the only building
capable of withstanding the stresses of weighty philosophical
criticism. 'So far from anarchy — to the borders of the
minimalist state — we may come, without compromising our
rights and freedom,' Nozick seems to say: 'but not one step
farther!' A dominant protective association is in fact 'the most
extensive state that can be justified . . . any state more extensive violates people's rights'. (149) Nozick's primary adversaries in defending his own careful voluntarism are utilitarians
and other proponents of 'end-state reasoning' who want to
make distribution and justice, and the state that enforces them,
dependent on some general pattern or principle imposed
impartially (and not necessarily with their consent) on all; who
insist, that is to say, on determining the justice and legitimacy
of political arrangements by reference to an ideal distribution
rather than actual (historical) distributions. John Rawls is
confronted as a prime target, perhaps because his modification
of Mean Utility might appear to acknowledge the lexical priority of liberty over equality and because hypothetical individual
consent (in the so-called original position) is the foundation of
the rules of justice. Nozick's argument is a simple one: 'No end
state principle or distributional patterned principle of justice
can be continuously realised without continuous interference
with other people's lives' (163); whatever the derivation of
Mean Utility, Justice as Fairness and other redistributive principles, their implementation necessarily bypasses voluntary
consent. They may originate in a kind of consent, but they
operate in violation of individual autonomy, and are thus
illegitimate. Taxation, for example, however just its objectives, is finally a form of forced labour, and stands in violation
of the paradigmatic natural right of self-ownership. Labour
may be sold but it may not be conscripted — no matter how
just the cause. The entitlement theory of justice (see below)
thus becomes a plateau above which no principle can justifiably rise (216–217), for it alone operates without violating

individual rights and without treating any single person as a means to some other person's ends. Indeed, entitlement theory does not treat with ideal patterns of human relations such as equality at all, since it can make 'no presumption in favour of equality, or any other overall end state or patterning' (233). Minimalism as defended in Part I thus defines the limits of Justice — not necessarily because we deserve what we are entitled to (the two are not synonymous in Nozick), and not necessarily because entitlements and voluntary transfers create end states that are just by some independent standard (they often are not, Nozick freely admits), but exclusively because theories that move beyond minimalism violate the principles of individual autonomy and self-ownership that Nozick believes any legitimate notion of justice must respect.

Part III of *Anarchy, State and Utopia* bears a striking resemblance to John Rawls' 'congruence' argument in *A Theory of Justice,* although Nozick does not seem to notice the kinship.[2] What he hopes for is 'the convergence of two independent lines of argument'. (333). He wants to show that certain rather glamorous exercises in utopia-building, if informed by the appropriate inclinations, may precipitate ideal political forms that turn out to be congruent with those produced more arduously by the much less glamorous exercises in deductive reasoning purveyed in Part I. Utopia turns out to be a model which, conforming to a perfect free market, 'is a framework for utopias ... the environment in which utopian experiments may be tried out' (312). This 'smorgasborg conception of utopia' permits consenting individuals to contract into (or out of) any particular utopia that suits them. No right can be violated because each sub-utopia depends on a set of voluntary exchanges the sanctity of which it is precisely the function of the greater utopian superstructure to guarantee. Undesirables with whom no one wishes to contract may have their feelings hurt but they will not have their rights infringed. Indigent lepers, for example, may find it difficult to contract into a sub-utopia providing medical services or welfare (their leprosy is not exactly a bargaining strength), but their autonomy will remain intact. Their malady is their own problem, however, for Nozick's utopia is, in effect, the Dominant Protective Association, and the utopias it facilitates

represent a pluralised group version of the radical individualism propounded in Part I. And, as we have seen, ideals such as
welfare, equality and community health entail the imposition
of patterned principles of redistribution that are beyond the
minimalist pale.

Nozick is, in any case, quite prepared to acknowledge that
the real purpose of the utopian argument is rhetorical. The
careful philosophical derivation of Part I, philosophically
compelling as it purports to be, is 'pale and unexciting . . .
hardly something to inspire one or to present a goal worth
fighting for' (xii). Thus, the congruence argument would seem
to hope to gild the grey on grey of philosophy with the silver on
gold of the liberal imagination. Nozick promises rather seduc-
tively that even redistributionists can find a home in his utopia
if the requisite contractees can be found: 'Though the
framework is libertarian and laissez-faire,' he notes, *'Individual communities within it need not be*, and perhaps no
community within it will choose to be so' (320, emphasis in
original). Part III is certainly not intended by Nozick to make
his argument, but it is clearly intended to make it palatable.

There are many objections that can be raised against this
elegant and often tasty schematic. Perhaps the most obvious
riposte is ideological: Nozick's logically coherent argument
has a great many politically incoherent consequences, with
which not even Nozick himself can feel very comfortable.
Nozick the citizen seems slightly disquieted by Nozick the
philosopher, whose commitment to following logic wherever
it may lead lands him, in his own words, in 'some bad company' (x) — viz., among those who 'take a similar position' but
arrive at it dogmatically and are 'narrow and rigid, and filled,
paradoxically, with resentment at other freer ways of being'. It
is not, however, the purpose of this essay to offer an ideological critique of *Anarchy, State and Utopia*. That critique seems
obvious enough; and has in any case been put with varying
degrees of passion by Sheldon Wolin, Brian Barry, David Spitz
and others.[3] I wish rather to join the more provocative question raised by Nozick's entire enterprise: the question, implicit
in the disjunction of Nozick's philosophical aspirations and
their political consequences, of whether philosophical analysis
of the kind practised by Nozick is fit for political theorizing or

relevant to political reality. My suspicion is that it is not. I hope to confirm this suspicion by examining two sets of premises in *Anarchy, State and Utopia*. The first set encompasses what I take to be the central working premises of Nozick's method: reductionism, residualism and what can be called the hypothesis of the rest position. The second set encompasses premises which underlie the operating concepts of the theory of the state generated by Nozick's method: in particular (as representative examples), the premises in which the crucial notions of freedom and entitlement are grounded. The deficiencies of the second set are, in effect, the deficiencies of the first — conceptually operationalised. If the arguments that follow can be believed, *Anarchy, State and Utopia* suffers as a work of political theory not because its impeccable logic can be faulted but because its impeccable logic is far too impeccable to be remotely political — because it uses apolitical concepts to move from apolitical premises to conclusions which are political in name only. The edifice Nozick constructs is indeed a utopia: an argument which stands, quite literally, nowhere and — like those haunted concrete bridges that can be found at abandoned highway projects — soars from mid-air chasm to mid-air chasm, as magnificent abstraction going from nowhere to nowhere, its dignity forever a prisoner of its uselessness.

II

The methodological premises of *Anarchy, State and Utopia* are undisguisedly reductionist: they assume that political understanding commences with pre-political or 'non-political' analysis. Politics is to be deconstituted in order to be understood and reconstituted; the point is to 'fully explain it in terms of the non-political', (6) a procedure which renders political ideas intelligible by assimilating them to philosophical categories untainted by politics. Nozick is hardly innovative in these methods, for deconstitution of the political has been the starting point for political thought in the entire contractarian tradition. Hobbes' resolutive-compositive method is an early and Rawls' original position a late example of the contractarian quest for political authority's pre-political foundations.

If the contractarian tradition has been dogged by anti-political tendencies from the start, Nozick welcomes these tendencies. He formulates what he takes to be the basic question of political theory in familiar contractarian terms: 'The fundamental question of political philosophy,' he writes, 'one that precedes questions about how the state should be organised, is whether there should be any state at all.' (4) The inertial frame of reference from which all movement is to be explained is the solitary individual hypothesised in pre-political stasis — presumably a creature sufficient unto itself, free (in Hobbes' image) to do whatever it has the power to do. Consequently, the only political question worth asking is the pre-political question 'why not anarchy?' (4)

Nozick is well aware of the importance of inertial frames of reference, since he sustains his own attack on redistributive egalitarianism by querying the self-evidence of its 'rest position . . . deviation from which may be caused only by moral forces . . . .' (233) What may be less obvious to him is that his own rest position is equally vulnerable. He has taken radical individualism — the autonomous person defined by natural rights and insulated by individuality from other autonomous persons — as his own rest position and has simply asserted that deviation from it requires justification.[4] Politics itself, a rather extravagant deviation by Nozick's standards, is thus put on the defensive: insupportable till proven otherwise.

Other inertial frames are obviously possible. Burke took political association and political gradualism for granted, and averred with no less assurance than Nozick that 'revolution *prima fronte* requires an apology'. The classical Hellenic experience, perceiving in sociability a natural human condition, tended to ask 'why not politics?' — placing the burden of advocacy and philosophical justification on those supporting 'idiocy' (individualism identified by its deviationist pejorative).

The inertial centre of gravity in the modern world has of course shifted from interdependence to independence, from polity to individual, from an equilibrium defined by citizenship to one defined by solitude (privacy). The burden of proof is now on the political association, not the individual; it appears as an aberration which, unless it can be rigorously justified (as liberals, constitutionalists and other generous minimalists affect to do), must be abolished (as anarchists think necessary). From this perspective, *all* political theory becomes minimalist theory — concessions made to politics which, however, are always limiting concessions, beyond which no deviation is permitted. The only viable query for this sort of political theory is how much (if any) deviation to permit — the burden of proof resting on those wishing to justify deviation in the first place. Individuals are taken for granted but society requires a warrant; private interests are given but public purposes must be demonstrated; personal and property rights are self-evident but public purposes in need of proof; hermits are free agents but citizens must carry a licence as well as a birth certificate (the social contract) and other *bona fides* without which their movement, their very existence, is suspect.

This sort of reductionism is conveniently absent-minded; it starts off with political constructs and then, in the name of rendering them systematically intelligible, reduces them to pre-political and non-political constructs; on the way, however, it forgets where it started, and thus insists that the philosophical abstractions (e.g. natural rights) it has artificially introduced for the sake of intelligibility are in fact wholly natural, a necessary rest position that is self-evident. By the same token, the political ideas that were originally to be explained by this method now become suspicious artifacts to be done away with unless they can be justified in terms of the non-political 'natural' categories to which they have been reduced. The *explanandum,* politics, disappears in the *explanans*, philosophy; but it never reappears in the mantle of intelligibility it supposedly was to acquire; instead, it is instructed to fight its way out, *if it can*, using only such weapons as philosophy deems legitimate. Philosophical anarchism (e.g. Robert Paul Wolff) suggests that politics will, under these conditions, never re-emerge at all. Nozick means to demonstrate that it can reappear, but only in the weak form of the Dominant Protective Association.

What starts then as reductionism in the contractarian style — resolution, then composition; deconstitution, then reconstitution — becomes, in Nozick a completely one-sided method. Reconstitution never takes place, for the components into which politics has been deconstitued turn out to be constitutionally un-reconstitutable! They will precipitate a radically circumscribed minimalism, but they will not precipitate anything like the politics from which they originally were extruded. *Anarchy, State and Utopia* is to be criticised not for its (conservative libertarian) politics but for the absence of a relevant politics altogether; not for its political inadequacies but for its inadequate conception of the political.

These problems appear not only in Nozick's method, but in the major concepts through which his argument is advanced. I want, therefore, before turning to the more general question of Nozick's apoliticity, to consider two of these concepts — freedom and entitlement — in the perspective of the above discussion.

III

Voluntary consent, in which Nozick's idea of freedom is embedded, is crucial to his argument, for it is the test of all political justification, the sole criterion by which public claims are legitimated, the absolute measure by which each step away from anarchy is to be gauged and approved. Only 'voluntary consent opens the borders [protecting individual from individual] for crossings', (58) Nozick posits; even in complex settings of social co-operation, seemingly mutualist interactions are to be reduced to 'a large number of bilateral exchanges' where it is possible to refer exclusively to consenting individuals (187). The general principle that emerges is a not altogether tongue in cheek paraphrase of Marx: 'From each according to what he chooses to do, to each according to what he makes for himself (perhaps with the contracted aid of others) and what others do for him and choose to give him of what they've been given previously . . . and haven't yet expended or transferred.' (160) Or, in Nozick's preferred epigram: 'From each as they choose, to each as they are chosen.' We do not distribute haircuts, or basket-ball tickets or spouses on the basis of an ideal pattern derived from need or desert. Why then, Nozick asks, should we treat differently with social and economic resources? If we cannot 'have' a pretty wife just because we 'need' one, why should we have a subsistence income just because we need one

— particularly if to get one requires that the freedom of others be violated?

The model of the free man deployed here is *homo economicus:* Hannah Arendt's *animal laborans* or Hobbes' natural man who is self-sufficient, unconflicted and hedonistic, a creature with clear interests rooted in unidirectional needs and calculable by instrumental reason. Reason, in this model, serves needs (Hume's '. . . is and ever ought to be the slave of the passions') and thus cannot enter into conflict with them (as it might do in, say, Rousseau or Kant). Nor can needs remain for long in conflict with one another, for ratiocination guarantees a clear vector resultant, however various and multi-directional the inputs.

Freedom, for *homo economicus*, is simply a matter of being unimpeded: able to move unobstructed in physical-mechanistic space. Nozick shares with the liberal tradition generally this physical-mechanistic rendering of human freedom,[5] although he is more consistently uncompromising about its infringement. Freedom construed in this manner depends on the integral particularity of the human actor: if inner needs are construed as being in conflict with one another, or with conscience, or with the dictates of reason, external human goals lose their objectivity, and the meaning of a free action becomes correspondingly indeterminate. Can we conceive of ourselves as 'free' when succumbing in the absence of external impediments to a passion of which we internally disapprove? Are we unfree when barred externally from temptations we despise or coerced into alternatives we prefer? (Rousseau's 'forced to be free'). The disintegral self characteristic of modern man finds it difficult to determine when it is free and when it is impeded, because it often cannot tell exactly who or what 'it' is.

Nozick is preoccupied with interference, but it escapes him entirely that men are frequently *self-interfering* — less enslaved by external obstacles than internal contradictions — and that self-interference, examined in the context of education, propaganda, advertising, and the manipulation of opinion, is a problem of major social and political import. In *Rameau's Nephew*, Diderot perceives that man 'has no greater opposite than himself'.[6] What are the conditions of freedom for a man who is his own worst impediment? Hobbes' war of all against

all has been converted by modernity into an interior battle —
'an unending struggle', in Ibsen's phrase, 'between the hostile
forces in the soul'. In this interior struggle, the conflict is not
that of man against man, but of desire against need, need
against conscience, conscience against custom, custom against
reason, and reason, come full circle, against desire; words like
'voluntary', and 'freedom', and 'consent' take on meanings in
these dark wars that Hobbes never dreamed of. Yet a political
theory that overlooks them cannot begin to grasp the nature of
modern politics. Its vision impaired by the blinders of physical
mechanism, it will be unable to entertain any but physical and
external notions of interference. It will be oblivious to the
possibility that law can act as an external enforcer of internal
obligations which, in the setting of democracy, will be able to
reconcile authority and autonomy (e.g. Rousseau's notion of
freedom as 'a law we prescribe to ourselves'); or that political
community may express human self-realisation in ways more
satisfying to our disposition towards freedom than libertarian
solitude.

When theory is emancipated from physical-mechanism, then,
voluntary consent ceases to function as a singular criterion of
political justification. It becomes merely one more example,
when it is implicated in practice, of the kind of controversy the
art of politics is designed to resolve. This may suggest a more
appropriate relationship between politics and philosophy than
is offered by Nozick: not one in which politics is defined by a set
of limits derived from pre-political standards posited by
philosophy, but one in which politics is itself the device by
which such limits and standards are deliberated and determined. Philosophy cannot legislate the meaning of critical concepts implicated in our common life; rather, the politics definitive of our common life establishes the meaning of the critical
normative ideas on which our mutuality hinges (e.g. freedom,
power, interference, consent). Politics thus achieves by necessity
what philosophy cannot achieve by abstract reasoning: the
elucidation of public standards that are not vulnerable to epistemological scepticism because, quite precisely, they claim only
to guide action, never to define truth, and are thus always
relative rather than absolute, concrete rather than abstract, and
determinative (action-oriented) rather than speculative (truth-
oriented).

This raises a second kind of difficulty for Nozick's notion of voluntary consent: its free market assumptions about the context within which political models are to be tested. Nozick appears to believe that the natural alternative to statist and other coercive models of human intercourse is a free market which operates under conditions of nearly perfect competition; that is to say, the liberty-securing utility of statist models is to be judged by a free market model which, however, (Nozick's residualism requires) is accepted not simply as a theoretical standard but as the actual condition that will prevail should statist alternatives prove philosophically unacceptable.

Libertarians, minimalists and anarchists have, of course, for a long time insisted that state coercion and individual freedom defined by simple market relations are the sole parameters — both conceptually and sociologically — of our political condition. They have argued, as a consequence, that our political choices are limited to points on a coercion/freedom (or public power/private rights) spectrum. 'Private' and 'power' are thus made into antonyms and, more importantly from the perspective of minimalism, both 'coercive' and 'public', and 'free' and 'private' are made into synonyms. Armed with this neat thesaurus, it is not hard for Nozick to construct a powerful grammar of minimalism: 'public' means 'coercive', and freedom therefore requires maximum privacy. Yet there do seem to be alternative grammars. Many of the contractarians with whom Nozick makes cause repudiate these anarchist polarities and instead dichotomize public-power-deployed-for-public-purposes and private-power-deployed-for-private-purposes, a construction that renders freedom and privacy as antonyms rather than synonyms, and one that suspects that private (i.e. illegitimate) coercion can be as insidious to rights, perhaps more insidious to rights, than public (legitimate) coercion. The chief objective of this kind of theory is the legitimation rather than the limitation of public power.

Nozick will not acknowledge the threatening potency of coercion in the private sector, however, for the free market model admits no such beast into private relations. Thanks not to an invisible hand, but to a disappearing club, Nozick is wholly innocent of problems of power. He does not have to read good will and natural harmony into natural market relations because he has read violence, deceit, corruption and terror out of them. He can count on the integrity of voluntary consent because he has discounted influence, blackmail, enticement, titillation and the many other carrots by which men attenuate its vitality and corrupt the autonomy on which it depends.

Nozick's problem is evident in an illustration he has chosen himself: a state wishing to compel social co-operation prohibits emigration, thereby buying mutuality at the (to Nozick unacceptable) price of liberty, so to speak (173). Yet take the more provocative counter-illustration of 'voluntary emigration' by middle Americans fleeing inner city jungles. Here 'consenting' individuals presumably freely contract to move from locale to locale in a series of private, bilateral exchanges. But as urban sociologists will quickly point out, neither those who emigrate nor those who stay are acting with very much knowledge, foresight or liberty. Both tend to be victims of social forces they cannot control and may not comprehend, and not interfering with their movement may contribute less to their freedom than would public (political) discussion of the causes of urban blight and a public programme that would neither coerce those who wanted to stay into going (e.g. the middle class) nor coerce those who wanted to go into staying (e.g. the poor) — the one because they are victims of fear, the other because they are victims of poverty.

In short, politics is devoted to the legitimation of power and influence not because legitimised public power seems preferable to natural liberty, but because it seems preferable to illegitimate private power — which is natural liberty's nefarious twin, because, in other words, if men cannot be free in political communities they probably cannot be free at all. Nozick may well convince us that, in the abstract, a state ought never to use some men as means to the welfare of others ('. . . no moral balancing can [i.e. ought to!?] take place among us' 33), but if we are also convinced that men will use one another in any event, often in private ways that are explicitly arbitrary and unjust; or persuaded that the interdependence of the human condition makes such usage inevitable; then we may well want to override abstract principle and opt for a coercive state that (at least) uses men as justly and fairly as possible. Likewise, although it seems quite likely that 'no end-state principle or distributional principle of justice can be continuously realised without continuous interference in other people's lives', (163) it is not at all clear what moral we are to draw from this lugubrious lesson. Not, at least, if it turns out that our lives are being continuously interfered with anyway, even in the absence of end-state principles. The attraction of patterned principles of distribution is not that they are non-interfering, but that they appear to be less unjustly and illegitimately interfering than non-redistributionist alternatives — which are not only interfering but arbitrary, subjective and non-adjudicable as well. The logical antonym of legitimate interference may, as Nozick the philosopher claims, be non-interference, but its political antonym, as Nozick the citizen no doubt has experienced, is *illegitimate* interference. By the same token, the opposite of moral balancing is not no-balancing-at-all, but *immoral* balancing. We are always juggling with other men's fates, whether intentionally or not; for our lives are always entwined with the lives of others in an ecology no less precariously balanced than nature's. This may not, it is true, be self-evident to the philosopher; but it is the starting place for all *political* theory.

IV

It may now be apparent that Nozick's argument about freedom and free market relations leads directly to his argument about entitlement and distributive justice. For the key to Nozick's conviciton that free market exchange is the only justifiable form of political interaction *inter homines* is his belief in the natural credibility of entitlement as a basis for a rights-respecting theory of justice. In entitlement theory, Nozick finds an escape from moral balancing into a world that establishes rights of property without acknowledging either clubs or carrots.

As in the case of voluntary consent, entitlement conceals an unexamined premise and an unexamined context of political consequences. Nozick is attracted to it as a generic concept, but it is hard to discern whether he takes it to have a concrete form of which he particularly approves. There are salubrious references to the 'classical liberal's notion of self-ownership', (172) and to a Lockean limit on rights of accumulation (178); yet

Nozick remains strangely diffident in specifying *which* entitlement theory he wishes us to adopt. Thus: 'Whether or not Locke's particular theory of appropriation can be spelled out so as to handle various difficulties, I assume that any adequate theory of justice in acquisition will contain a provision similar to the weaker of the ones we have attributed to Locke.' (178) It might be thought that whether this or some other concrete theory of entitlement could 'handle various difficulties' would be of greater moment to Nozick, since the objections often offered to appropriation theories resting on entitlement have queried precisely their subjectivity and partiality — their refusal to conform or to even acknowledge objective criteria by which their mutual contradictions might be adjudicated. Nor is it very reassuring to find Nozick referring readers back to redistributionist principles when confronting problems of conflicting entitlements.[7]

The number of entitlement theories that are in fact available to proponents of a theory of justice based on just acquisition rather than just distribution is much greater than Nozick would seem to suggest. Robert Filmer's *Patriarcha* provides an alternative account of entitlement that bears little resemblance to Nozick's Lockean derivative, and so of course do the less fastidious theories of medieval kingship Filmer hoped to prop up. Theories of acquisition based on divine right and/or heredity are in turn rivalled by theories of acquisition based on conquest. In more recent centuries, religion, caste and race have also entered into discussions of just entitlement. The only thing these myriad forms share is their common lack of single, rational, non-arbitrary principle of distribution. The very absence of end-state principles that to Nozick is their virtue, disqualifies them as rational political theory.

The fact that most entitlement theories manifest themselves politically in élitist and authoritarian forms is not an accident: it is a feature of the inherently subjective internal structure of the entitlement argument which, as Nozick acknowledges, begins with the premise that what we are entitled to and what we morally deserve are two different things. Nozick is hardly an authoritarian; but in place of the arbitrary power of an entitled political élite, he has in effect posited the equally arbitrary power of a natural élite — namely, those contestants who turn out to be winners in the social darwinist sweepstakes that masquerade as a free marketplace.

Redistributionist theories are but a response to these sorts of embarrassments. Rawls' original position, for example, is his attempt to create a hypothetical environment from which the subjective and partial views of individuals and groups definitive of entitlement theory are barred. The result is a relatively objective setting for an impartial debate about the principles of justice. What we required from Nozick, if he means us to take entitlement theory seriously, is a demonstration that appropriation rooted in self-ownership establishes a title more tenable — not than redistributionist alternatives — but than titles based on conquest, or scripture or royal lineage. What are we to say when confronting a king, a conqueror, a hereditary land-holder and a tenant farmer, each of whom points to a single track of land and exclaims in unison with the others, 'This hectare is mine by all rights! My title to it rests on a long, historically vindicated tradition of Imperial Dominion/right by conquest-primogeniture/right of usage!'? The Holy Roman Empire of the German Nation came to a bad end, in part because it could offer no satisfactory answer to this query. Nozick's philosophical question is 'Why not anarchy?' but the more practical political question ought to be 'Why not give America back to the Indians?', who, by Lockean standards, would seem to be its only legitimately titled proprietors? Stated in less historical terms, what we require, along with Nozick's theory itself, are the criteria by which the theory can be evaluated; and we require, also, that these criteria be morally relevant and not arbitrary.

The problem is that under the guise of entitlement all kinds of fraudulent claims may be advanced. Delegitimising principles of public redistribution in theory does not eliminate arbitrary private principles of redistribution in practice. In the free market it is not right but power that prevails, and in the absence of public counter-coercion, there is nothing to prevent private coercion from running amok. Thus, titled or not, the Indians lost their land because Europeans stole it from them by force — finding new bases for their title afterwards. The prevailing theory of entitlement generally turns out to be the theory most conducive to prevailing power, justice being on the side of the holdings of the strongest. The virtue of redistributionist theories

is that they are grounded in ideas of impartiality and disinteres-
tedness that give them some protection against the subjugation
to raw power and interest to which all political theories are
vulnerable. Entitlement theories have no such protection; when
Nozick warns us of the 'great ingenuity with which people
dream up principles to rationalise their emotions', (240) he is in
fact identifying the chief weakness of entitlement theory itself.

None of these difficulties strikes at the heart of Nozick's
position, however; for his notion of justice depends not only on
just acquisition, but on just *transfer* (by voluntary, bilateral
exchange). And ultimately he is in a position to say: 'Distribute
goods as you will — distribute them on the basis of total
equality if you will: nonetheless, legitimate transfers accomplished through voluntary exchanges among consenting adults
will quickly result in inequality; and there is not a thing respec-
tors of freedom can do about it, other than regret it.' This
powerful riposte brings us back to the central charge of the
essay: that Nozick's philosophical rendering of crucial political
questions distorts the character of politics and puts relevant
political answers completely beyond our reach.

V

The argument that a proper regard for free transfer will always
necessitate the compromising of equality (even where equality is
the starting point) — that principles of patterned distribution
will thus have to be *continuously* interfering with freedom to be
effective — is presented in the form of an (initially) devastating
example. Nozick postulates that in a society where income is
equally distributed, a number of basketball fans agree to pay 25
cents extra each time they watch Wilt Chamberlain play, and
that his team's owners simultaneously contract with Chamberlain to permit him to pocket the surcharge. A series of wholly
voluntary exchanges between Chamberlain and his fans and
Chamberlain and his employers results in a loss of equality. Yet
unless we forbid 'capitalist acts among consenting adults', violating the basic freedom on which contracts depend, there is
nothing we can do or ought to do. Justly transferred holdings
come to be redistributed in a fashion that, because it is
inegalitarian, we may want to disapprove, but because it is the

consequence of autonomously reached bilateral agreements, we are in fact compelled (if we wish to follow rational principles) to tolerate. Redistributionists who wish to preserve a pattern of equality will be forced to intervene not once, but again and again; freedom will not simply be compromised, it will be eradicated.

Compelling as this argument is, it confirms only the apoliticity of Nozick's reasoning. For at the political level, the Chamberlain example proves quite the opposite of what Nozick intends: namely, that private acts often have public consequences which we may neither anticipate nor intend. This is precisely why political acts cannot be deconstituted into private acts without losing their salient character. Our intent in paying a surcharge is to see Chamberlain play; but it is not (necessarily) to guarantee that he earns $250,000 a year (would we refuse to watch him if he played for free?); and it is certainly not to create a society with radical income differentials or to set a precedent for some general distributional principle. Nor, presumably, do we intend in paying a surcharge to redistribute the power associated with wealth in ways that may attenuate not only our own future ability to affect the market, but also the ability of persons who were not party to our bilateral agreements with Chamberlain yet who stand to suffer as a result of his enhanced power. Chamberlain with $250,000 a year is a Chamberlain capable of affecting society in ways that may compromise the freedom or security or power of those who have never even heard of the National Basketball Association.

A publicly responsible electorate might not wish to forbid capitalist acts among consenting adults *per se*, but it would insist on monitoring the public consequences of such private acts, even in the limited context of basketball. That is, it would necessarily concern itself with traffic snarls leading to the stadium where Chamberlain played (which, *note bene*, would involve non-Chamberlain fans), with health and safety precautions within the arena (it could hardly permit three million fans to contract bilaterally with Chamberlain to watch him play on the same night in an arena seating five thousand), with Chamberlain's own possible use of his new wealth to coerce/cajole fans into signing new, more expensive contracts, with problems of equity among Chamberlain and his fellow players, and so forth. Public intervention in these areas might lead to public interdiction — perhaps even of the original agreement between Chamberlain and the fans. Nor would the fans necessarily object. For — and this is the fatal weakness of Nozick reductionism — fans are also citizens, and what they intend as private fans cannot and will not predetermine what they intend as public citizens. They make contracts with Chamberlain as private persons, but they may well remedy the public inequities of these (and all other) private contracts when they act as citizens to enact public laws of progressive taxation, or antitrust laws, or public safety standards. They will thereby *intentionally* undo in public what they may have *inadvertently* done in private — e.g. strip Chamberlain of (say) seventy five percent of his income, insist that his team-mates share in the balance, restrict the number of such contracts that can be made, and so on. Nor is there any contradiction here: that we are willing to pay a 25 cent surcharge as private persons does not entail that we are willing to tolerate economic inegalitarianism, or monopoly or exploitation as public citizens. If only one of us had entered into a contract, there would have been no *public* problem: but since (say) 100,000 signed contracts, a public issue is created. Once there is a public, there is a public problem. Enter politics!

Nozick's reductionist illusion is to think that because acts are private they are without public consequences; but we are a public by virtue of our plurality, and we are thus constrained to substitute legitimate public standards for arbitrary private ones. After all, John D. Rockefeller contracted freely and bilaterally with scores of smaller companies to buy them out; the gargantuan monopoly he created, however, was hardly a private affair. Indeed, it offered a greater threat to the free market than the government which tried without much success to break it up. Nozick's market does not finally protect freedom against public power; it protects private power against public legitimacy. Nozick believes that he is propounding a logically coherent argument in defence of pure individual freedom. And so he is; and, in philosophical terms, with considerable success. But a logically coherent argument by philosophical standards is not yet a political argument at all. Philosophical argument offers abstract alternatives; if none seems defensible, none is accepted;

we simply return to point zero. Political argument begins with concrete givens; if abstract alternatives prove indefensible we do not return to point zero; we are left rather with the givens. The relevant political question therefore becomes: is a particular alternative *more* tolerable/acceptable/legitimate than the given to which it is a response? If so, regardless of its status as measured by abstract and absolute philosophical criteria, it is the preferable alternative.

Rousseau, contractarian that he seemed in part to be, nevertheless understood that the aim of political thought was not to justify deviations from our (hypothetical) natural isolation, but to legitimate the (concrete, given) ties which inevitably bind us together: 'Man is born free; and everywhere he is in chains. . . . How did this change come about? I do not know. What can make it legitimate? That question I think I can answer.' Thus opens the *Social Contract*. To the philosopher, what cannot be justified, cannot be. If reality defied the prohibition, all the worse for reality. But the political theorist knows that power seeks no other warrant for existence than its own success, and that the political task is not to wish it away, but to make it legitimate. Our choice (alas!) is not between political bondage and natural freedom but between political bondage and political freedom — between slavery and citizenship. We can be arbitrarily and heteronomously dependent or rationally and (within limits) autonomously dependent. Political relations, *esse inter homines,* defy the abstract choice preferred by philosophers between absolute coercion and total non-interference. They can only be more or less justly coercive, more or less legitimately interfering, more or less rationally dependent.

Political theory may derive sustenance from hypothetical history, but it always confronts real history as a given; which is to say, it begins with the subjugated dependent rather than the free hermit — with historical men already the victims of illegitimate coercion, blind force and arbitrary power. The significant political question is thus always how to render coercion less illegitimate, force less blind, power less arbitrary.

Robert Nozick would appear to want to say, with Howard Roark in Ayn Rand's *The Fountainhead:* 'I came here to say that I do not recognise anyone's right to one minute of my life.

Nor to any part of my energy. Nor to any achievement of mine. No matter who makes the claim, how large their number or how great their need. I wished to come here and say that I am a man who does not exist for others.'[8] The trouble is, our wishes notwithstanding, we *do* by virtue of our plurality and our dependency exist for one another, and it is this reality from which politics emerges. In Philip Slater's words in *Earthwalk,* 'The notion that people begin as separate individuals, who then march out and connect themselves with others, is one of the most dazzling bits of self-mystification in the history of the species.' Because we do not in fact march out and connect ourselves to others, but are born in Siamese bondage to our fellow men, we do not as political creatures have the philosopher's luxury of justifying the hypothetical steps by which such a journey might have been made, had it been made. We can only seek ways to legitimate the connections with which our condition has at once cursed us (slavery) and blessed us (civil community). Churchill's ironic comment on democracy (the worst form of government in the world except all the other forms) in fact is a bitter tribute to the reality political theory must confront. Not best or nothing; only better or worse. These are the only choices in a world when men interfere, coerce, interdict, infringe, use, hurt and oppress ineluctably — in or out of regimes, with or without legitimate cause — because dependence is intrinsic to the human condition. Political thought aspires even at its least amibitious (non-minimalist liberal thought, e.g. Locke) to minimise the costs of dependency by maximising the legitimacy of its forms. It has also aspired to more ambitious goals: in its republican form it has tried to transform common weakness into social equality, common dependency into social mutuality, common exploitation into social co-operation, and common fear into social security by developing modes of legitimate political exchange grounded in citizenship, community, democracy, fraternity and civic freedom. This more ambitious Rousseauian tradition has made its objective *public seeing:* illuminating with a public light what to individuals living in private caves remain invisible. It is not only Plato who understands politics as a form of perception, although his imagery of the Cave is particularly revealing of its epistemological features. There is also a tradition of public thinking in liberalism, perhaps most clearly evident in Kant. If politics is public seeing, it is simply beyond the purview of reductionists; they confine themselves to exploring the Cave — the world of private perception — and, quite naturally, insist there is nothing there of the political to be found.

Some critics have worried about certain political implications of Nozick's philosophical exercises; but Nozick is not politically conservative, or politically reactionary or politically libertarian; he is politically irrelevant. Not recognising the public meaning of public, he does not really have a political theory at all. As a rhetorical model, *Anarchy, State and Utopia* may seem to endorse some rather strange political practices. However, Nozick correctly maintains that his book is not a 'political tract' (xii), that his arguments are 'fascinating in their own right', and that his principal guide is logic and not reality. The state is confronted by him as an engrossing idea which, however, to the degree it cannot be philosophically justified, can be safely ignored. Neither choice nor action is at stake, only inference and ideation. Nozick plays games ingeniously, but playing games and playing politics are distinctive projects that can be confused only at considerable risk.

To be unable to think politically in a major book about the state is in fact no small mischief in times as politically desperate as our own. Our present condition remains pierced by the forbodings of Yeats' *Second Coming*:

> Somewhere in the sands of the desert
> A shape with lion body and the head of a man,
> A gaze blank and pitiless as the sun,
> Is moving its slow thighs . . .

Yet if Robert Nozick were to be asked

> . . . what rough beast
> Its hour come round at last
> Slouches towards Bethlehem to be born?

it would appear that he might feel constrained to reply, 'The sphinx is a beast of dubious rational origin; besides, I can conceive of no philosophical justification that would permit a statue to move'.

Nonetheless, it moves. And if it has not yet found its way across the Charles, it has been seen all too recently gaping from across the Potomac at a nation whose troubles seem quite beyond the ken, let alone the ministrations, of philosophical reductionism.

(This article was originally published in the *Journal of Politics* and is reprinted here by kind permission of the Editor.)

NOTES

1 All page citations in the text are from Robert Nozick, *Anarchy, State and Utopia* (Basic Books, New York, 1974).
2 See J. Rawls, *A Theory of Justice* (Harvard University Press, Cambridge, 1971) especially chapter 87, 'Remarks on justification'. Rawls notes there, supporting a strategy Nozick clearly shares, 'Justification is a matter of the mutual support of many considerations, of everything fitting together into one coherent view.' p. 579.
3 See S. Wolin, 'Review of Nozick', *New York Times,* 11 May 1975; B. Barry, 'Review of Nozick', *Political Theory* III, 3, August 1975; and D. Spitz, 'Justice for Sale', *Dissent*, Autumn 1975.
4 That his argument amounts to mere assertion can be seen from the following, which is the sole defence for reductionism offered in *Anarchy, State and Utopia*: 'The possible ways of understanding the political realm are as follows: (1) to fully explain it in terms of the non-political; (2) to view it as emerging from the non-political but irreducible to it . . .; (3) to view it as a completely autonomous realm. Since only the first promises full understanding of the whole political realm, it stands as the most desirable theoretical alternative, to be abandoned only if known to be impossible', p. 6.
5 I have tried to elucidate the limits of physical-mechanism as a basis for models of freedom in my *Superman and Common Men: Freedom, Anarchy and the Revolution* (Praeger Publishers, New York, 1971), Chapter 2.
6 Cited by L. Trilling, *Sincerity and Authenticity* (Harvard University Press, Cambridge, 1971) p. 30. The modern novel is, of course, filled with self-conflicted characters; Joseph Heller's Bob Slocum, for example, who asks in *Something Happened:* 'I wonder what kind of person would come out if I ever did release all my inhibitions at once, what kind of being is bottled up inside me now. Would I like him? I hope not. There's more than just one of me, probably . . . I hope I never live to see the real me come out. He might say and do things that would embarrass me and plunge him into serious trouble, and I hope I am dead and buried by the time he does', p. 248.

7 In a note, Nozick offers this startling concession to the redistributionists:
'If the principle of rectification of violations of the first two principles yields
more than one description of holdings, then some choice must be made as to
which of these is to be realised. Perhaps the sort of considerations about
distributive justice and equality that I argue against play a legitimate role in
this subsidiary choice,' p. 153. But questions of conflict are hardly
'subsidiary', as my argument above shows.

8 A. Rand, *The Fountainhead* (New American Library Edition, nd), p. 686. I
am grateful to Ben Zingman for suggesting the relationship between this
passage and Nozick's individualism.

A Preface to Revolutionary Theory
MICHAEL FREEMAN

THERE is something puzzling about the place which the theory of revolution currently has in political science. Everyone would agree that 'revolution' was one of the great themes of classical political theory. But, in the early years of the 'behavioural' movement, the subject received little attention. The leading concepts of the time were those of 'stability', 'equilibrium' and 'consensus', and the central problem was that of the maintenance of democracy. Gradually, 'revolution' crept back into the discipline, though often in strange disguises, such as 'collective behaviour', 'internal war' and 'civil strife'. In 1962 James Davies published a widely-discussed article under the title 'Toward a Theory of Revolution'. In 1970 Ted Robert Gurr produced a much-acclaimed book, *Why Men Rebel*. In the 1975 Greenstein-Polsby *Handbook of Political Science* the subject is recognised under the rubric of 'Revolutions and Collective Violence'.[1]

This rubric exhibits very clearly what is puzzling about the status of the theory of revolution. Why is 'revolution' coupled with 'collective violence' as a single subject of political science? After all, most collective violence has nothing whatever to do with revolution, and much of it is not even political (e.g. organised violent crime). Is there some good scientific reason why 'revolution' lacks sufficient integrity or importance to deserve a rubric of its own in such an authoritative handbook of the discipline?

If this rubric suggests some uncertainty about the suitability of 'revolution' as a subject of scientific theory, then it accurately expresses the unease which permeates the recent literature. 'Revolution' has been back in the discipline for some time, but its theoretical development has been disappointing. One judicious reviewer has summed up a widespread conclusion as follows: 'Unfortunately, the main feature that may be noted about much of the theoretical analysis of revolutions is its thinness and triviality . . . [T]he theories tend to leave the reader with the fairly disappointed feeling that perhaps the whole exercise of reading and examining the theory was not worth the effort.'[2] I shall offer an explanation of this state of affairs and thereby indicate how we may escape from our present impasse. I shall do this by means of a critique of that particular tendency in the theory of revolution which has promised most because it has been the most methodologically self-conscious and which has yet created the problems which we must now solve. This involves a re-consideration of what a theory of revolution entails and what we may reasonably expect from such a theory.

In 1961 Harry Eckstein, on behalf of the Center of International Studies of Princeton University, convened a symposium of distinguished social scientists, who were asked to write papers 'on the application of contemporary social theories to the study of internal wars'.[3] These papers provided the basis of a well-known book, *Internal War*, edited by Eckstein and published in 1964. The contributors included Talcott Parsons, Karl Deutsch, William Kornhauser, Lucian Pye, Gabriel Almond, Sidney Verba and S.M. Lipset.

Notwithstanding the eminence of these participants, Eckstein admitted, in his introduction to the book, that the purpose of the symposium had been misconceived. It had been a mistake to ask social theorists to apply their theoretical equipment directly to the subject of internal war. Before theoretical study was possible, it was necessary to 'reflect on how the subject could be shaped for theoretical processing'.[4] Certain specific preliminary operations had to be carried out, at least in tentative form.[5] The first of these operations was *delimitation*. 'To carry on theoretical study, one must first have a subject to study. The task of delimitation is, in a nutshell, to state unambiguously what that subject is.'[6]

The criteria for the satisfactory delimitation of a subject are derived from the definition of theory. Eckstein defined theories as 'testable (that is, falsifiable) generalisations stating relations

among concrete phenomena or, more broadly, abstract forms
approximated in concrete experience'.[7] Phenomena must be so
delimited that valid generalisations can be made about them.[8]

In the delimitation of theoretical subjects, two problems
arise. The first is to find a homogeneous set of cases. The second
is not to set the requirement of homogeneity so high that no two
empirical instances can be considered alike. 'While, to be sure, a
statement about two or three cases is certainly a generalisation
in the dictionary sense, a generalisation in the methodological
sense must usually be based on more; it ought to cover a number
of cases large enough for certain rigorous testing procedures
like statistical analysis to be used.'

Revolution, Eckstein declared, was 'one of the classic themes
of social thought'.[9] However, the subject of his book was internal war. Why the change of subject? In an article 'On the
Etiology of Internal War', published in 1965, Eckstein defined
'internal war', explicitly distinguished it from 'revolution', and
offered a justification for the definition and the distinction. 'The
term "internal war" denotes any resort to violence within a
political order to change its constitution, rulers, or policies.' Its
relationship to revolution is that of genus to species.

Eckstein offered three justifications for the delimitation of
'internal war': a) that all cases of internal war had common
features; b) that internal war combined different types of violence; c) that very limited results had been obtained from historical studies of revolutions.[10]

These justifications are extremely weak. The first two fail to
distinguish internal war and revolution, for revolutions also
have common features and combine different types of violence.
However, the weakness of argument in Eckstein's objection to
the comparative history of revolution is the most interesting.

He makes the following objections to such studies: they deal
with 'the so-called Great Revolutions of history'; they ignore
'the vast spectrum of coups, putsches, uprisings, riots, and so
forth'; and they draw mammoth inferences from very few
cases.[11]

Eckstein makes no attempt to substantiate these charges nor
to draw out sympathetically whatever merits these works may
possess. But, even if the charges are true, several points must be
made in reply. First, certain revolutions may be *properly* called

Great Revolutions: we must ask what such a claim could mean. Second, the comparative history of revolution is not required to consider the vast spectrum of coups and so forth, since they are not revolutions. Third, it is not bad scientific method to draw mammoth inferences from very few cases if the inferences consist of, or lead to powerful and testable generalisation.

The second of Eckstein's pre-theoretical operations he calls *problemation*. To theorise, it is necessary to have problems to solve. The first step in problemation is raising questions. 'Undoubtedly questions are matters of arbitrary interest; methodological precepts can contribute little to raising them. The ability to put them is a gift, a matter of being imaginative enough to see unresolved issues in empirical experience.'[12] Eckstein suggests that questions about internal war can best be arranged in relation to the phases through which every internal war must pass. These phases are a) pre-revolutionary conditions; b) courses; c) outcomes; and d) longer-run consequences.[13] Clearly, revolution can be 'problemated' in exactly the same way.

No questions about internal war, Eckstein states, have been more thoroughly neglected by social scientists than those raised by their long-run consequences. 'Despite the protracted normative argument between pro-revolutionaries and anti-revolutionaries initiated by Paine and Burke, almost nothing careful and systematic has been written about the long-run social effects of internal wars. . . . But in regard to etiology, to 'causes', we are absolutely inundated with print.'[14] Yet Eckstein, in his 1965 article, concerns himself with etiology. One may reasonably conclude that, if the long-run consequences of internal wars raise important theoretical questions thoroughly neglected by social scientists, they constitute an obvious subject for the imaginative social scientist to take up.

Theoretical questions must concern phenomena that occur frequently enough to permit, as answers, testable generalisations.[15] One further step in problemation is noteworthy. 'It consists of determining what problem must be solved if a question is to be answered. One must always try to discover what is really puzzling about a question, to analyse it to the point where its crucial elements are revealed.' He gives, as an example of this process, 'Weber's famous question about the origins of modern capitalism in the West'.[16]

This is an interesting example, for one would not have thought that Weber was particularly concerned, in his study of the origins of capitalism, with phenomena that occur frequently enough to permit testable generalisations nor to delimit his subject so as to include 'a number of cases large enough for certain rigorous testing procedures like statistical analysis to be used'. Consider his opening statement: 'A product of modern European civilisation, studying any problem of universal history, is bound to ask himself to what combination of circumstances the fact should be attributed that in Western civilisation, and in Western civilisation only, cultural phenomena have appeared which (as we like to think) lie in a line of development having *universal* significance and value.'[17]

Among the cultural phenomena that have appeared in Western civilisation and which (as we like to think) have universal significance is not only the spirit of capitalism but also the spirit of revolution. Weber's notion of particular phenomena having universal significance suggests what might be meant by a Great Revolution.

We can now judge whether Eckstein succeeded in showing that 'internal war' was a superior theoretical subject to 'revolution'. His own discussion of 'problemation' suggests that he did not. The phases of internal war turn out to be the same as the phases of revolution. The long-run effects of internal wars are important because of their relevance to the protracted normative argument between pro-revolutionaries and anti-revolutionaries. Weber's 'problemation' of capitalism points us back to Great Revolutions. Nothing supports Eckstein's preference for 'internal war' except his insistence on having 'a number of cases large enough for certain rigorous testing procedures like statistical analysis to be used'. But this insistence is not derived from his 'problemation' but from his definition of theories as testable generalisations.

Eckstein's etiology of 'internal war' was, on his own admission, sketchy,[18] but was developed and refined by Ted Robert Gurr. Despite the title of his book, *Why Men Rebel,* Gurr's subject is not 'rebellion' but 'political violence'. He defines 'political violence' as 'all collective attacks within a political community against the political regime, its actors —

including competing political groups as well as incumbents — or its policies. The concept represents a set of events, a common property of which is the actual or threatened use of violence, but the explanation is not limited to that porperty.'[19]

Gurr says that the concept of political violence subsumes revolution, 'defined as fundamental sociopolitical change accomplished through violence'.[20] The relationship between 'political violence' and 'revolution' appears to be clear: genus to species again. But the apparent clarity is misleading. For Gurr's definition of 'political violence' makes no reference to change, while 'revolution' is defined as 'fundamental sociopolitical change'. Thus 'revolution' is a very special kind of 'political violence', a fact to which Gurr is perfectly insensitive.

How does Gurr justify his delimitation of 'political violence'? It has common properties; it has great social impact; it is frequent.[21]

Despite an appeal to statistical evidence of homogeneity, Gurr, like Eckstein, fails completely to show that the common properties of political violence make it a superior theoretical subject to revolution. Indeed, Gurr writes: 'The properties and processes that distinguish a riot from a revolution are substantively and theoretically interesting, and are examined at length in this study [not true — MF], but at a general level of analysis they seem to be differences of degree, not kind.'[22] But, since he defined revolution as fundamental sociopolitical change, his contention that the difference between a riot and a revolution is one of degree, not kind, is false.

Gurr claims that there has been a convergence of recent case, comparative, and theoretical studies, which formulate similar propositions about various kinds of political violence.[23] Like Eckstein, Gurr is suggesting that he can develop a set of theoretical generalisations in which those about revolution would be a sub-set of a larger set about a more general class of phenomena. Does he fulfil this promise?

'Political violence' is classified by Gurr into three main types: turmoil, conspiracy and internal war. Internal war includes revolution, but also guerilla and civil wars. So, 'revolution' is now a sub-type of one type ('internal war') of 'political violence'. It is also distinguished from guerilla and civil wars. Gurr does not explain these puzzling distinctions.

Gurr seeks to discover, not why political violence occurs, but the determinants of the extent and forms of violence.[24] He gives two reasons for 'problemating' thus. Firstly, the extent and forms of violence are relevant to the effects of violence on the political system. Secondly, the magnitude of political violence is ethically important.[25] Both these reasons would justify a considerably greater interest in revolution than Gurr shows. And, even though Gurr appeals to the effect of political violence in order to justify his focus on its extent and forms, he, like Eckstein, makes no attempt to theorise its effects.[26]

We have seen that Gurr offered three reasons for delimiting the subject of 'political violence': its common properties, its social impact, and its frequency. We have seen, too, that the first two reasons do not justify a preference for 'political violence' over 'revolution'. Gurr, like Eckstein, must rest the case for the delimitation of his subject on its frequency. His conception of 'theory' is much like Eckstein's: 'an interrelated set of general, falsifiable hypotheses that specify causal or concomitant relationships between independent and dependent variables'.[27] Hypotheses that specify systematic relations between variables 'are subject to scientific assessment only if substantial numbers of cases are examined'.[28]

Gurr develops a large number of hypotheses about the extent and forms of violence. There are seven about the 'determinants of internal war' but none about the revolution.[29]

'Revolution,' Eckstein had written, 'is one of the classic themes of social thought.'[30] We have seen that Eckstein and Gurr, in their attempt to introduce methodological rigour into this area, have made the subject of 'revolution' disappear. The only plausible argument that either has had for not theorising about revolution is that a theory of revolution can be derived from a more general theory, either of internal war or of political violence. This argument, however, founders on two sharp rocks. Firstly, neither author shows how this derivation could be made. Secondly, the claim itself violates one of Eckstein's methodological principles. For, if 'problemation' is a necessary pre-theoretical exercise, we cannot know what the relationships between theories of revolution, internal war and political violence are or ought to be before we have formulated our problems. Neither Eckstein nor Gurr examines the problems raised by the classic theorists of revolution and therefore their claim to have superseded the classic methodologies is unjustified. They assume that the problems of the literature they criticise were the same as their own. This assumption they do not analyse and is in fact false.

The classic theorists of revolution, from Burke to Arendt, derived their conception of revolution and its problems from theories of man, society, government and history. Eckstein and Gurr, by contrast, derive theirs from a naive and mechanical empiricist methodology. This inadequate methodology leads to three major failures in their theory.

Firstly, their definition of 'theory' in terms of testable generalisations leads both authors to require of their subject-delimitation 'a number of cases large enough for certain rigorous testing procedures like statistical analysis to be used'. This, in turn, leads them to seek more general subjects, while the problems posed by revolution are not only forgotten but can no longer be solved. Thus, the conception of 'theory', which is taken for granted and pre-methodological, shapes the problems to be solved. Eckstein and Gurr do not just happen to problemate badly; their bad problemation is induced by an *a priori* epistemological commitment.

Secondly, the same conception of theory leads them to reject the theoretical analysis of Great Revolutions without any serious consideration of what such analysis has yielded in the past or might yield in the future. Once again, epistemological dogma obstructs the search for significant problems.

Thirdly, both Eckstein and Gurr nervously mention the importance of the social consequences of revolution and their moral significance, but neither can theorise on either subject. They cannot theorise the consequences of revolution because these consequences are not readily susceptible to statistical analysis. They cannot theorise the ethics of revolution because their brand of empiricism cannot generate theory of this kind.

I hope to have established that conceptions of 'theory' are not innocuous and shape both the problems that are posed and the solutions that are offered. Adequate theorisation requires that delimitation and problemation precede not only substantive theory but commitment to a particular conception of theory. We must know exactly what we want to discover about exactly what before we can know the form the discovery can take. This does not mean that any answer to any question is a theory. Eckstein was right to say that theory entails generality. But to commit ourselves *a priori* to particular testing techniques is disastrously restrictive.

Attempts to show that 'revolution' is an unsuitable subject for theory have failed. Theories of internal war and political violence may be possible and desirable. One day, a general theory of revolution may be derivable from a still more general and powerful theory. That day is not in sight. Until it is, the case for attempting a theory of revolution seems compelling.

But what is to be done? Where does the theory of revolution begin?

If one thing is certain about revolutions, it is that they do occur, have occurred and probably will occur. If another thing is certain about them, it is that they are important. Yet neither of these things is certain.

This last claim seems perverse. There could not possibly have been (it may be protested) so much discussion of revolution since, say, 1789 if there had not been revolutions and if they had not been important. But this intuition yields under analysis. A revolution appears to have begun in France in 1789. But in what did it consist? In the abolition of the monarchy? Then it did not occur in 1789. In the triumph of the bourgeoisie? Then it neither began nor ended in 1789. In the modernisation of France? Then the distinction between revolution and evolution dissolves.

The intuition that a revolution began in France in 1789 dies hard. But it is not easy to say precisely what made the events of that year revolutionary. And, if it is intuitively obvious that certain long-term social changes have been important, it is not nearly so obvious why such short-term events as those of 1789 should be so regarded, however sensational they may have been. There are coups d'état and there is long-term social change. What are revolutions if they are neither?

The term 'revolution' is used in various ways in ordinary political discourse. 'Join the Revolution!', cries the revolutionary, meaning 'Join this movement which aims to effectuate a revolution'. 'The Russian Revolution took place in 1917', an historian might say, meaning 'The Bolshevik faction seized state power in 1917 and proceeded to change Russian society'. 'The Revolution has only just begun', a revolutionary leader might say on attaining power, meaning 'The struggle for, and attainment of, state power are only means to the end of Revolution, which consists in the radical restructuring of society'.

There are three meanings of 'revolution' here: a) *the revolutionary struggle* — the organised attempt to effectuate a revolution; b) *the revolutionary seizure of state power* — the seizure of state power in order to effectuate a revolution; and c) *the revolution* — the radical restructuring of society.

Ordinary usage is too imprecise for rigorous analysis. Contrary to ordinary usage, therefore, I confine the term 'revolution' to the third set of phenomena. I do this for two reasons. Firstly, I thereby associate 'revolution' with 'radical social change', which is conceptually proper. Secondly, we foreclose fewer issues by definition if we make it an empirical, not a logical question as to whether a revolutionary struggle or a revolutionary seizure of state power is a necessary condition for a radical restructuring of society.

There are, therefore, logically, the following types of revolution:

1 Revolution following both revolutionary struggle and revolutionary seizure of power: the most familiar case.

2 Revolution with neither revolutionary struggle nor revolutionary seizure of state power. There are two subtypes.
  (a) The state initiates the revolution.
  (b) Revolution is the unintended outcome of a set of reformist changes.

3 Revolution after revolutionary struggle without revolutionary seizure of state power: the ideal anarchist revolution.

4 Revolution after revolutionary seizure of state power without revolutionary struggle: the uncontested revolution.

The phrase 'radical restructuring of society' does not distinguish between revolutionary and evolutionary change. There are two grounds on which they can be distinguished. Revolutionary change is purposive, planned with a radical set of goals in mind; evolutionary change, on the other hand, is either wholly unplanned or consists only of planned piecemeal reforms with no overall plan for radical change. Also, the term 'revolution' suggests a greater urgency and speed of change than does 'evolution'.

It is hard to decide whether speed of change should be included in the definition of 'revolution'. Hastiness is one of the chief faults with which critics of revolutionaries charge them. Many crimes are alleged to follow from this fault: mistakes, injustices, chaos, violence, repression. We should be reluctant to include in the definition any controversial property with the result that normative disputes are loaded from the outset. If revolutions have properties which observers find admirable or deplorable, these properties should be established by empirical inquiry, not by stipulative definition. Revolutionaries in power often say that revolutions are slow, hard and long labours. Historians often note that, in this, the revolutionaries are factually correct.

Nonetheless, if we are to sustain a distinction between revolution and radical reform, then some sense of urgency must be retained in the meaning of 'revolution'. Revolutionaries seek some radical changes without delay, even if they are patient about their long-term objectives. Too much should not be expected from definitions. There is no sharp discontinuity between a revolution and radical programme of reform. It will suffice, for the present, to define 'revolution' as an urgent, planned, radical change in the structure of society with a view to an ultimate, overall structural change.

This definition of 'revolution' excludes what many, including Eckstein and Gurr, have included: violence, illegality and popular participation. Thus, I hold it to be a mistake to stipulate by definition that revolution is a type of political violence or internal war. Why?

Some persons have advocated a 'non-violent revolution'. If revolutions are violent by definition, these persons advocate what is impossible by definition. But, if there are objections to 'non-violent revolution', they surely depend upon some empirical laws of politics and not upon a semantic or conceptual claim. If we define 'revolution' without reference to violence, we are free to investigate the nature and strength of these laws.

The empiricist methodology of Eckstein and Gurr leads them to make two mistakes concerning the relationship between revolution and violence. Firstly, they ignore the possibility of non-violent revolution because such revolutions are rare or (so far) unknown. This makes them uninteresting for empirical theory, but not for normative theory. Secondly, by making revolutions violent by definition, they load the normative arguments, for violence is not ethically neutral.

'Popular participation' is commonly included in the definition of 'revolution', usually for persuasive effect: either to legitimate revolutions ('democratic' by definition) or to discredit coups d'état (not revolutions by definition). I shall say that a revolution may be carried out as a consequence of a coup (seizure of state power by a small élite) or of a popular revolutionary struggle. It is an empirical question what the consequences of these different types of revolutionary seizure of state power are. We therefore ruthlessly excise from the definition any democratic prejudice that popular revolutions have more beneficial consequences than élitist revolutions, while not, of course, inserting the opposite prejudice.

I should also like to emphasise that revolutions are not necessarily illegal by definition. Even the revolutionary 'seizure' ('attainment' would be a less tendentious word) of state power need not be illegal. Lawfully elected governments may initiate revolutions.

Thus, coups may be revolutionary or non-revolutionary. Revolutions may be legal and constitutional or they may not be. To insist on this is to depart from prevalent conceptualisations of revolution, but such a departure is necessary to rid ourselves of various misleading prejudices. The question as to whether revolutions are lawful or unlawful, democratic or undemocratic, is not to be settled by definition.

The concept of 'restructuring' entails an old structure and a new one. 'Revolution' is the passage from one to the other. A revolution may, therefore, involve five phases:

1 the old regime;
2 the revolutionary struggle;
3 the revolutionary attainment of state power;
4 the revolutionary transformation of society;
5 the new order.

Only phases 1, 4 and 5 are necessary by definition, but phases 2 and 3 are empirically common. The phases may not be empirically distinct. The revolutionary struggle, for example, may continue during the period of revolutionary transformation. And, although the definition of 'revolution' requires that there be a radical break between the old regime and the new, there may be various specific causal links between the two.

I shall call these five phases *the revolutionary process*. It must be remembered that the term 'revolution' is confined to phase 4 only. Earlier, I argued that the only ground on which Eckstein's concept of 'internal war' could plausibly seem superior to that of 'revolution' was that it was more general. I sought to show that this ground was illusory. We can now see that 'internal war' is *narrower* than 'the revolutionary process', for, by confining itself to the 'resort to violence', it is limited to one form of the phase of revolutionary struggle. 'Revolution', as I define it, is not a type of 'internal war', but one of its possible 'longer-run consequences', about which Eckstein has been unable to theorise. It is hard to theorise about 'longer-run consequences' because this concept is so indeterminate. Is the concept of 'revolution' as radical social change less indeterminate or determinate enough?

We face a fundamental problem here. In order to render the concept of 'revolution' more precise, we have, it seems, to perform two operations: to define 'social structure', and to define 'radical change' in social structure. The fundamental problem is that these two operations seem to require a general theory of society before we can construct even a definition of revolution. No satisfactory theory of this kind exists. It is therefore not possible to derive a satisfactory definition of 'revolution' from such a source.

We may, however, suggest a conception of society which will meet our needs, at least provisionally. Let us consider a society to be a collective (i.e. co-operative and/or coercive) enterprise which determines a) what is valuable; b) the mode of production of valued things (which may be material or non-material); and c) the mode of their distribution. A revolution or radical social change occurs when there is a *substantial* change in at least one of these three variables. The clearest case of revolution is, of course, when there is a change in all three. It may well be that, empirically, a substantial change in any one will always be accompanied by a substantial change in the other two.

It may seem plausible to conceptualise revolutions as being merely redistributive. They may be thought of as redistributions of political, economic and cultural benefits and costs. But, if redistribution (of such things as powers and rights as well as of wealth) is a leading feature of revolutions, it is not the only one. A revolution may change what people want distributed as well as the pattern of distribution, and it may change, not only what is produced, but how much, as well as what products are distributed and how.

The term 'substantial' change leaves a considerable degree of vagueness in the definition of 'revolution' and makes societies susceptible of degrees of revolution: the more substantial the change, the more revolutionary the new regime. It is neither possible nor desirable to remove this vagueness. A society is not either revolutionary or non-revolutionary; it is more revolutionary or less revolutionary.

Since substantial redistributions constitute revolutions, the conceptual distinction I made between revolutionary seizures of state power and revolutions breaks down: a change in control of the state power and revolutions breaks down: a change in control of the state constituting a substantial redistribution of power. This awkward fact cannot be denied. Revolutionary seizures are *partial* revolutions. Phases 3 and 4 of the revolutionary process are not completely distinct, even conceptually. But the relation between them is clear and the distinction between them is important. Seizure of the state is not a (conceptually) necessary condition of a revolution. Nor does a thoroughgoing revolution necessarily follow seizure of the state. Thus, seizure of the state is a very special, and limited, kind of revolution. Whether we call it a limited revolution or a non-revolutionary coup is a mere semantic issue, for the conceptual position is clear.

It has been my intention to construct a concept of revolution which is, as far as possible, value-neutral. I do not wish to rule out normative theories of revolution — my intention is the opposite — but I do wish to rule out normatively loaded definitions. Thus, revolutions are not definitionally good or evil, 'progressive' or 'reactionary', liberating or tyrannical. 'Counter-revolution' is not the logical opposite of 'revolution', but a type of revolution whose special characteristic is that the social order it overturns is itself a revolutionary one. This neutral conception of revolution departs from most classic usages and is like that aspired to, but not achieved, by empiricist theorists.

The task of a theory of revolution is to develop a system of general concepts and propositions which will solve the problems raised by revolutions. In order to theorise about revolution, we must determine what problems it raises. In order to do this systematically, we must determine the best method for identifying the problems raised by revolution.

Although Eckstein treated the issue of 'problemation' with some care, he was uncertain about its method. At one point, he suggested that methodological precepts could contribute little to the identification of problems. The process was arbitrary or, if not arbitrary, a matter of imagination. However, he did point to three sources of problems: a) 'unresolved issues in empirical experience'; b) 'unresolved issues in the literature'; c) 'existing paradigms'.[31]

All three of these categories are unsatisfactory, either in themselves or in the way they are treated by Eckstein. Firstly, issues do not arise directly from 'experience'. To become an *issue*, an 'experience' must be interpreted as problematic. Thus, violence may be directly experienced, but to interpret violence as problematic is a theoretical operation.

'The literature' also does not yield problems as directly as Eckstein suggests. Among authors he cites are Burke, Paine, Brinton and Arendt. Yet he is not able to use their works as sources of problems. One reason why this is so is that he is insensitive to the difficulty of drawing problems from different 'paradigms' and treating them as if they belonged to the same one. It is not accidental that a theorist committed to a falsificationist version of empiricism should be unable to tackle the problems raised by the paradigms of Burke and Paine.

If the problems of revolution are to be subjected to systematic theoretical analysis, it is not enough to pull them randomly from 'experience' or 'the literature', though neither of these sources should be rejected as useless. The problems must be stated in terms of a single, coherent 'paradigm'. This prescription, though a necessary warning against incoherent electicism, raises many difficulties. There is no one paradigm for the study of revolution. Different paradigms produce different problems. To decide which paradigm to adopt, we need a set of meta-paradigmatic criteria for the evaluation of paradigms.

This seems daunting. However, there is one meta-paradigmatic criterion of evaluation which should be non-controversial: scope. If paradigm A solves all the problems solved by paradigm B and at least one more, A is superior to B. The difficulty, in practice, is that A and B are likely to solve different, and only partially overlapping problems. Some may well object that talk of 'paradigms' is too 'scientistic', extending a dubious concept from the natural sciences dubiously to the social, or that, be the last point as it may, the 'paradigms' of the social sciences have proved so unsuccessful, particularly in the theory of revolution, that 'paradigm' is a methodological concept of very dubious value.

If there is no existing paradigm of revolution sufficiently successful to command our allegiance, and if all problems about revolution are paradigm-dependent, how can we find problems, the solution of which will constitute an adequate theory of revolution? Problems do arise from experience, the existing literature and existing paradigms, but, if their solution is to constitute a coherent theory, they must be re-formulated in terms of a coherent set of concepts. At this point problemation is linked to delimitation, for the concepts with which the subject is conceptualised must be the basis for those with which its problems are posed and solved. The aim of such an operation is to produce a theory superior in scope to those now available. The best way to achieve this is to criticise the one-sidedness of the prevalent paradigms.

The most obvious form of one-sidedness is scientism. Eckstein, the empiricist, referred to 'the protracted normative argument between pro-revolutionaries and anti-revolutionaries', related this normative argument to scientific problems about the long-run consequences of internal wars, and deplored the neglect of these problems by social scientists. We have seen that he not only neglected them himself, but neglected to consider how, in principle, social scientists could contribute to normative argument.

The scientistic answer to this problem is that normative disputes can be treated scientifically as conflicting ideologies. Thus, from the standpoint of a scientific paradigm, whether empiricist or Marxist, pro-revolutionary and anti-revolutionary paradigms, such as those of Burke and Paine, are ideological phenomena, of which a scientific account can be given.

This move entails transferring normative theories of revolution from the philosophical level — at which they are accepted as possessing a legitimate autonomy — to the scientific level — at which they are legitimate only as objects of science. This move itself needs to be justified. The justification entails the demonstration that the autonomy of normative theory is illusory. There are well-known attempts to provide this demonstration — by Marxists and logical positivists, for example — but there are grounds for believing that these attempts have not been successful. One is that there have recently been powerful counter-attempts to demonstrate the legitimacy of normative theory, most outstandingly by John Rawls.[32] Another is that both empiricists and Marxists persist in raising normative problems, albeit uneasily or surreptitiously.

I conclude, therefore, that there are two types of theory of revolution, the normative and the scientific; that neither can be reduced to the other; but that the two are interrelated. The most general problem of the theory of revolution is to integrate the two.

I have argued that the empiricist scientific theory of revolution is inadequate, partly because it raises normative questions it cannot formulate, still less answer. We should seek out the most important normative problems raised by revolution before formulating the scientific ones because, while it is not scientifically improper to allow ethical problems to guide scientific theorising, it may, as we have seen, be ethically unsatisfactory to theorise scientifically without regard to ethical problems.

The most general ethical question that can be asked about revolution is this: 'Are revolutions good or evil?'. This can be shown to be a badly posed question on two grounds. The first is that it presupposes that all revolutions must be one or the other, a position that no serious normative theorist would wish to hold. The second is that, since we have defined 'revolution' in terms of a radical change in values, it is extremely implausible that all radical changes in values should be good or all should be evil.

There are two questions into which the general ethical question can be refined: a) Are revolutions *usually* good or evil?; and b) Under what conditions are revolutions good or evil?

The first of these questions does bite in a way that the most general ethical question does not, for important theorists have held either that revolutions are usually good or that they are usually evil: this is the 'protracted normative argument' to which Eckstein referred. Why this should be so can be seen from my definition of 'revolution', for revolutionaries seek to change values radically and urgently while conservatives regard radical changes in values and urgent social change to be usually undesirable.

The second question bites, too, for many theorists have sought to specify the conditions under which revolutions are justified. A common solution is to say that revolution is justified if, and only if, it transforms a 'tyranny' into a 'free' society.

The terms 'tyranny' and 'freedom' have quite different meanings in different paradigms. It is, therefore, never a straightforward empirical question whether a particular revolution has passed this test. A normative theory of revolution, to be adequate, must specify the meaning of these terms in such a way that particular revolutions may be assessed: that is, 'tyranny' and 'freedom' must be empirically investigable.

I cannot here demonstrate the superiority of any particular normative theory over its rivals: such a demonstration may even be impossible in principle. But I am proposing that normative theories of revolution have the form of comparing the new order with the old with reference to positively or negatively valued observable properties. Thus, the general normative question — Do revolutions tend to produce better social orders than the ones they overthrow? — raises the empirical problem of comparing old and new orders in terms of the relevant properties. What properties are relevant is a paradigm-dependent question. Normative theories are not, however, necessarily self-confirming. They may indicate the relevant properties, predict empirical findings, yet be falsified by empirical investigation. Normative paradigms of revolution may therefore be falsifiable.

Thus, we do not need to limit ourselves to the vague notion

that the 'long-run consequences' of revolution are somehow 'ethically important', for, with the use of a particular normative theory, we can generate definite hypotheses about the consequences of revolution. For example, Karl Popper has argued that one particular feature of revolutions — the radicalness of its aims — presupposes a level of social knowledge, the inevitable lack of which will lead to a repressive new order.

Theories of revolution are theories about revolutions. Revolutions are made by revolutionaries with the aid of ideas about revolutions. Theories of revolution differ in the views they take of the ideas of revolutionaries. Are such ideas ideologies to be explained or theories which explain? Do they have causes and consequences and may we make ethical judgements about them?

Revolutionary ideas are always prescriptive and they always prescribe revolution. This gives rise to two important problems. Since the aim of revolution is a new social order, what happens to ideas prescribing revolution in the process of establishing the new order? Can revolutionary ideas be transformed into ideas supportive of order or must they be suppressed for order to obtain? And, since revolution emerges from an old order, how does such an order beget revolutionary ideas? Conservatives are typically uncomfortable with the latter question; revolutionaries with the former. Because both are committed to a form of social order, both have difficulty in giving an adequate account of the relation between social order and revolutionary ideas. The problems are both empirical and normative, of understanding the causes and consequences of revolutionary ideas and of judging their beneficial or harmful qualities.

Revolutionary ideas are both ideologies and normative theories. As ideologies, they are to be explained by features of the old regime. As theories, they prescribe and their prescriptions are to be evaluated by normative theory. The relationship between these two statuses of revolutionary ideas raises deep philosophical problems, for the belief that ideas may be explained by their causes may be incompatible with the belief that their holders may be praised or blamed for their merits or shortcomings.

The normative theories of pro-revolutionaries and anti-revolutionaries typically differ in the views they take both of the consequences of revolutionary ideas and of their causal weight. Anti-revolutionaries hold that revolutionary ideas are a) utopian, i.e. incapable of being fulfilled, and b) dangerous, i.e. tending to do more harm than good. Pro-revolutionaries do not merely deny these claims, but attribute the 'problems' of revolution to causes other than the ideas of the revolutionaries.

It is clear that here a normative dispute turns on issues that are empirical and meta-empirical. Do revolutionary ideas have these consequences or do they not? If certain revolutionary ideas are constantly followed by certain (undesirable) phenomena, are these phenomena the effect of the ideas or of other causes?

One difficulty in solving the problems raised by disputes between anti-revolutionaries and pro-revolutionaries is that their different paradigms will generate different descriptions of the new order. The 'tyranny' of the anti-revolutionary may be the 'democratic dictatorship' of the pro-revolutionary. The 'anarchy' of the former may be the 'problems of revolutionary transition' of the latter. One person's 'freedom' may be another person's 'repression'.

But let us assume for the moment that we have solved this problem. All agree that the new order is characterised by P. The problem is: why P? The anti-revolutionary says that P (which he deplores) is the result of the revolutionary theory/ideology. The pro-revolutionary, who also deplores P, says that it is caused by factors beyond the control of the revolutionaries. How is this common type of dispute to be solved?

Any P may be explained by either its past or its present. Its past consists of the old regime, the revolutionary struggle, the revolutionary seizure of state power, and the revolution. Its present consists of internal and external forces. Any of these may explain P.

Empirical possibilities are immense so that I can only give examples.

1 *The old regime* The old regime is governed by a policy of 'divide and rule'. The rulers foster hostility between different sections of the population. The revolutionary rulers inherit these hostile groups. They must suppress the internecine strife by force. The practices of the old regime explain those of the new.

2 *The revolutionary struggle* An unpopular old regime generates a revolutionary alliance of groups whose ideas are mutually incompatible except for their common hostility to the regime. The new order can only be maintained by the control of conflict between these groups. A feature of the new order is explained by a feature of the revolutionary struggle.

3 *The revolutionary seizure of state power* The revolutionary state may be faced with domestic enemies, foreign enemies, ills of the old regime to cure and goals of its own to attain. The character of the new order may be shaped by the form of state necessary or chosen to deal with these problems.

4 *The revolution* The character of the new order may be explained by that of the revolution. For example, whether the chief goal of the revolution is redistribution or general increase of wealth, this feature of the revolution will shape the revolutionary regime.

5 *Internal problems* a revolutionary regime may face internal problems in no way caused by its ideology, e.g. crop failure. They may explain its practices.

6 *External problems* The practices of revolutionary regimes may be affected by foreign enemies or competitors.

Certain general features of revolutionary regimes may be explicable by general laws of society. For example, we may be able to explain the failure of a revolution with egalitarian goals by reference to laws specifying the necessity of some inequalities. If putative universal laws of this kind are too controversial to be persuasive, laws of lesser generality may be thought more plausible: e.g. that certain levels of inequality are necessary in poor countries wishing to develop their economies very rapidly.

We have seen that general normative questions about revolution lead to questions about the qualities of revolutionary regimes. Normative questions about these qualities lead to questions about the explanation of their existence. In these explanations, the problem of the causal weight of revolutionary ideas arises. The problem of the causal weight of revolutionary ideas is related to that of the moral responsibility of revolutionaries: a theory which specifies that revolutionary ideas constitute an important cause of undesirable properties of revolutionary regimes will tend to condemn revolutionaries. But, whatever solution we propose to the problems concerning the consequences or quality of revolutionary ideas, the problems themselves lead to questions about the origins of such ideas.

If revolutionary ideas have causes, they must come from the old order. Revolutionary ideologies/theories are putative solutions to problems posed by the old order. Those problems of the old order perceived as such by revolutionaries cause their theories to come into being. This formulation leaves two questions unanswered. What makes a phenomenon of the old order into a 'problem'? What leads some persons to believe that problems of the old order require revolutionary solutions?

A social phenomenon becomes a problem when it frustrates a desire or violates a value of an individual or group. Problems may arise from biology (e.g. the desire to eat), psychology (e.g. the desire for companionship), or society (e.g. the desire for justice). Insofar as a problem is created by the social violation of a socially-produced value, it constitutes a contradiction in the old order. All societies contain contradictions.

A problem, or set of problems, leads to revolutionary struggle if the following conditions are met: a) it is perceived to be intolerable; b) it is perceived to be insoluble through reform; c) it is perceived to be soluble through revolution; d) the conditions of revolutionary organisation exist. These conditions are met by revolutionary theorists/ideologists and political leaders. An intolerable problem is not a sufficient condition of revolutionary struggle, for it may lead to either fatalism or reformism. The revolutionary theorist/ideologist is a necessary condition, therefore, of revolutionary struggle, for s/he is necessary to the fulfilment of condition c.

To say that we have passed from the old order to the phase of revolutionary struggle is to say that the old order has produced the idea that its problems can be solved only by an urgent, radical change in the content, mode of production or mode of distribution of values. To say that the revolutionary struggle has been successful, in the sense that the revolutionaries have seized state power, is to indicate that the initiation of the revolution is at hand. A revolution is an ambitious and complex project. Its goals are not likely to be mutually compatible nor compatible with its situation. Thus, from the revolutionary point of view, revolutions always have 'problems'; from the anti-revolutionary point of view, they usually fail. Empirical analysis can show why revolutionaries adopt the goals they do and why they meet the problems/failures that they do. Normative analysis must take such empirical study into account, as well as assessing the seriousness of the problems and the possibility of alternative solutions.

I have proposed that fruitless talk about empirical theories of long-run consequences be replaced by the problem of identifying what is really puzzling about revolutionary regimes and seeking explanations of those features. This task is of the first scientific and ethical importance. It leads us to certain key questions. How far do revolutionary ideologies explain the relevant features of the new regimes? How far should we explain them as more or less rational responses to problems they face, problems which may or may not exist independently of ideology, may or may not be inherited from the old regime or from the revolutionary struggle? How far is the character of revolutionary rule conditioned by the particular problem of counter-revolution, domestic and/or foreign? How far are cause and consequence linked by the fact that the character of the new order is shaped by its need to solve problems, the failure of the old regime to solve which precipitated the revolution?

The proposed model of the revolutionary process has been analytical and abstract. This process has been conceived as a radical change from one form of society to another. A new, and necessary, dimension is introduced if we conceive of it as a *development*. We are here at the conjuncture of the theory of revolution and the theory of modernisation. My definition of revolution was formulated so that these two theories might be smoothly joined. A revolution is not merely a redistribution of valued things nor a change in values, but may be a change in the mode (including the efficiency) with which they are produced. Thus, we can define 'modernisation' as an improved capacity to produce valued things. It may be, of course, that changes in values and distribution are necessary conditions of modernisation, but that is an empirical question.

We are now in a position to analyse a problem raised by the experience of revolution. In the modern period (since 1789), it has been empirically typical that revolutions have had the aims of increasing production of more than one valued thing (e.g. wealth and freedom), of redistributing more than one (e.g. wealth and power) and of changing values. Intense normative disputes have taken place as to whether revolutions have failed to achieve these aims and, if so, whether the failure was an inevitable consequence of the revolutionary enterprise. We can see that such disputes require, for their resolution, agreement on the meaning of the key concepts — which, since they are paradigm-dependent, may be extremely difficult — and empirical analysis of the revolutionary regimes. But we can also see, not only that any two aims may be incompatible, but that, in particular, 'productive' and 'redistributive' values may be. The establishment of laws governing the relationship of these two kinds of values is an important scientific problem for the theory of revolution, not least because of its relevance to normative puzzles.

Revolutions inherit and produce severe social problems. Where revolution is effectuated through the seizure of state power, it tends to strengthen the state in order to solve these problems. These problems may be internal to the revolutionary process as such: e.g. the control of conflict. They may pertain to the aim of revolutionary modernisation: e.g. the mobilisation of resources. They may also pertain to the external relations of the revolutionary state. The state may have enemies; it may make enemies. Revolutions tend to send ripples at least, if not waves of panic and opportunism, through the international system. All such problems tend to explain what has been commonly observed, and sometimes deplored, about modern revolutionary states: their strongly centralised character.

'Revolution' is related to 'modernisation' as follows. 'Modernisation' — the improved capacity to produced valued things — may cause revolutions. Revolutions whose aims give priority to modernisation are modernising revolutions. All revolutions, whether modernising or not, constitute a process from old to new order. Each phase of this process may be affected by internal or external forces. External forces may, for example, support or undermine the old regime; support or oppose the revolutionary struggle; and affect the character of the new regime, in particular its success in modernising society.

The process of a modernising revolution will be affected by two other general factors. The first is the degree of modernisation of the old regime: we may conjecture that the less modern the old regime, the more authoritarian the new. The second is the place of the revolution in the world-history of modernisation: the later the revolution, the more authoritarian the regime, and the less successful the modernisation, *ceteris paribus*.

The concepts of 'revolution' and 'modernisation' both have 'before' and 'after' components: old and new regimes, pre-modern and modern societies. These two sets of components do not fit neatly together, however: as the first hypothesis in the preceding paragraph indicates, a modernising revolution may take place in a relatively modern old regime.

A modern society is, typically, industrial, and a pre-modern society agricultural. In a pre-modern society, the basic relations of production depend upon the ownership and/or control of land. These relations of production hold between two classes which I shall call, following Barrington Moore, lord and peasant. Lord and peasant are subject to the state. These three components of the social structure are bound together by a traditionalistic culture.

Within this society a new class may emerge, which is bourgeois in two interrelated senses: a) it arises in the towns rather than the country; and b) it is relatively free from the traditionalistic culture. 'Modernisation' means an increase in power but it also pre-supposes power in the modernisers. Peasants, the least powerful class in pre-modern societies, are the least likely to initiate modernisation. This process may, therefore, be set in motion by lords, state or bourgeoisie, or by external forces, acting alone or as stimulants to domestic classes.

Modernisation means an increase in power and is likely to lead either to new distributions of power or to new ways of exercising it (or both). It will also undermine the culture which legitimated the old order. The modernisation of economic production will create a further class, the proletariat, and the modernisation of culture another, the intelligentsia. The intelligentsia are not defined by their relationship to the means of economic production but as the producers of ideas. The intelligentsia will articulate the strains between the traditional and the modern culture.

There are three main general causes of revolution associated with modernisation. Firstly, traditional dominant groups, lords and/or state may resist pressures from modernising forces, e.g. bourgeoisie and/or 'progressive' intellectuals. Secondly, external intervention may produce a modernising revolution with or without a nationalist counter-revolution or frustrate indigenous modernising forces. Thirdly, subordinate classes, peasants and/or proletarians, may become revolutionary as they see themselves as victims rather than beneficiaries of modernisation.

Barrington Moore has suggested that modernisation by the state leads to fascism, by the bourgeoisie to liberal democracy, by peasants, intellectuals and proletarians to state socialism. In the terms of my model, his argument is that the structure of the old regime determines the way in which the society will modernise, which will in turn determine the political form of the new regime.

This thesis has been criticised severely and in great detail on both theoretical and empirical grounds. The following hypotheses, based on my model, may not be vulnerable to these criticisms. The necessary conditions for a liberal-democratic revolution are: a) that it be led by the bourgeoisie or a bourgeois-aristocratic alliance; *and* b) that it come early in the world-history of modernisation; *or* c) that it be carried out with the aid of a foreign power which meets the first two conditions. If no combination of state, lords and bourgeoisie is able to modernise effectively, then a communist revolution based on an alliance of intellectuals, peasants and proletarians is likely, with an authoritarian socialist outcome. The occurrence or outcome of a modernising revolution may be controlled by external forces. These may be strong enough to prevent a revolution occurring, even though the internal conditions are ripe; to initiate a successful counter-revolution; or to divert a revolution from the direction in which the internal forces would otherwise take it. The combination of external and internal forces may produce outcomes intended by no-one.

A revolution is a radical change in values, but it is not a total change. Elements of the old regime will persist in the new. When revolution involves seizure of state power, there is likely to be radical political change. If the conditions for modernisation are favourable, radical economic change is likely. Political and economic change will entail some cultural change. But culture governs the private sphere and may resist change. Cultural revolutions are logically possible; cultural obstacles to revolution empirically more common. Traditional or old-regime cultures (these are not synonymous) may affect the new regime in two ways. The new regime may incorporate elements of the old culture in order the more easily to mobilise the people for revolutionary objectives. Or, the new regime may suppress manifestations of traditional culture which have a counter-revolutionary tendency.

Eckstein noted that the empirical theory of revolution was almost exclusively concerned with etiology. This holds true of the literature today.[33] Implicit in this literature is the following scientistic argument: revolutions should be studied scientifically — what is it to study something scientifically? — it is to explain it — the scientific theory of revolution should therefore explain why they happen, give their etiology. I have sought to show that this approach has confused revolutionary struggle with revolutions, with extremely restricting consequences for the theory of revolution, and prevented itself from posing a large number of important questions about revolutionary regimes. These problems are not a whit less scientific and meet much better Eckstein's prescription that we look for what is really puzzling about our subject.

I have also criticised the empirical theory of revolution for committing itself to a particular conception of 'theory', entailing particular testing techniques, before deciding what problems the theory was to solve. This commitment also led to an excessive emphasis on etiology, to an inability to distinguish qualitatively between revolutions, and to ignore the classic and normative problems of revolution.

I have accepted Eckstein's prescription that delimitation and problemation precede theorisation, and sought to show, not only that an emphasis on etiology alone is not enough, but that the choice of 'internal war' or 'political violence' as dependent variables in place of 'revolution' narrowed rather than broadened the scope of the theory. I conceptualised 'revolution' as a process, constituting an episode in history and situated in an international system. These last two dimensions, absent from the empirical theory, show how revolutions differ in importance, i.e. in their impact historically and internationally.

I claim that this model of revolution is not only a richer source of both scientific and normative problems, but enables us to integrate the two systematically. Normative disputes cannot be solved directly by scientific inquiry, but some scientific models are more relevant to classic disputes than others: my model has been formulated with these disputes in mind.

Notwithstanding my criticisms of the empirical theory of revolution, my alternative method for theorising about revolution rests upon certain empiricist assumptions: 'fact' and 'value' are treated as analytically separable, though intimately associated within any given paradigm; I assume that theory consists of generalisations that are empirically testable, even falsifiable. I am, of course, aware that I have been skating cheerfully on thin epistemological ice. It is proper to raise epistemological questions about political theory, but there must come a time when the epistemology has to stop. Mine has been a critique of the empirical theory of revolution from within. I have tried to show that, accepting the basic empiricist assumptions I have just mentioned, this type of theory is capable of much richer development than it has enjoyed in more than a decade and a half of endeavour.

NOTES

1 J.C. Davies, 'Toward a theory of revolution', in *American Sociological Review*, 27 (February 1962), pp. 5–19; T.R. Gurr, *Why Men Rebel* (Princeton University Press, 1970); C. Tilly, 'Revolutions and Collective Violence', in *Handbook of Political Science*, eds. F.I. Greenstein and N.W. Polsby, (Addison-Wesley, Reading, Mass., 1975), Vol. 3, pp. 483–555.

2 A.S. Cohan, *Theories of Revolution: An Introduction* (Nelson, London, 1975), p. 211.

3 H. Eckstein, ed., *Internal War: Problems and Approaches* (Collier-Macmillan, London, 1964), p. 4.
4 *Ibid.* p. 7.
5 *Ibid.*
6 *Ibid.* p. 8.
7 *Ibid.* pp. 8–9 (footnote).
8 *Ibid.* pp. 8–10.
9 *Ibid.* p. 1.
10 H. Eckstein, 'On the Etiology of Internal Wars', in *History and Theory,* IV (1965), pp. 133–4.
11 *Ibid.*
12 Eckstein, *Internal War, op. cit.* pp. 23–4.
13 *Ibid.* pp. 24–8.
14 *Ibid.* p. 28; 'Etiology', *op. cit.* p. 136.
15 Ecklestein, *Internal War, op. cit.* pp. 29–30.
16 *Ibid.* p. 31.
17 M. Weber, *The Protestant Ethic and the Spirit of Capitalism,* trans. Talcott Parsons (George Allen and Unwin, London, 1930) p. 30 (emphasis Weber's).
18 Eckstein 'Etiology', *op. cit.* p. 160.
19 Gurr, *op. cit.* pp. 3–4.
20 *Ibid.* p. 4.
21 *Ibid.* pp. 4–5
22 *Ibid.* p. 5.
23 *Ibid.*
24 *Ibid.* p. 8.
25 *Ibid.*
26 *Ibid.* p. 12.
27 *Ibid.* pp. ix, 16–7.
28 *Ibid.* p. 21.
29 *Ibid.* p. 366.
30 See Eckstein's claim quoted above on p. 49.
31 Eckstein, *Internal War, op. cit.* pp. 23–8.
32 J. Rawls, *A Theory of Justice* (Oxford University Press, London, 1972).
33 Recent exceptions are S.N. Eisenstadt, *Revolution and the Transformation of Societies* (The Free Press, New York, 1978) and T. Skocpol, *States and Social Revolutions* (Cambridge University Press, Cambridge, 1979).

Freedom, Slavery and Contentment[1]
JOHN GRAY

IN the introduction to the revised version of his lecture 'Two Concepts of Liberty', Sir Isaiah Berlin[2] seeks to correct what he judges to be an error in his original account. He suggests that his first definition of negative freedom as the absence of the interference of other agents in the area in which a man wishes to act has damaging and paradoxical implications. For, though it captures as a paradigm case of negative unfreedom the case of the imprisoned man who is prevented by the deliberate interferences of others from doing as he wishes, it makes the measure of a man's freedom relative to the nature of his desires. Indeed, it is an acknowledged feature of Berlin's original conception that, since we cannot know in advance of empirical research what it is that a man wants, negative freedom is consistent with any social circumstance. This is to say that attributions of negative freedom can (logically) tell us nothing informative about the alternatives actually available to anyone except insofar as they contain references to the state of mind or feeling of the agent, or presuppose the truth of some general propositions about human wants. Since the degree of a man's negative freedom is the extent to which his desires are frustrated by the interferences of others, he may always increase his freedom by trimming his desires. As he recognises, Berlin's original account has the consequence (a consequence he regards as paradoxical and damaging in the case of 'positive' conceptions of freedom) that it precludes our characterising as unfree a wholly-contented slave.

His recognition of this error in his original account leads Berlin to modify his conception of social freedom. This, he says, entails not simply the absence of frustration (which may be obtained by killing desires), but the absence of obstacles to possible choices and activities, absence of obstructions on roads along which a man can decide to walk. Such freedom ultimately depends not on whether I wish to walk at all, or how far, but on how many doors are open, upon their relative importance in my life . . . . The extent of my social or political freedom consists in the absence of obstacles not merely to my actual, but to my potential choices, to my acting in this or that way if I choose to do so. Similarly, absence of such freedom is due to the closing of such doors or failure to open them, as a result, intended or unintended, of alterable human practices, of the operation of human agencies . . . .[3]

Berlin is joined in this view by J.P. Day.[4] He argues that whether a man wants to do something is irrelevant to whether or not he is free to do it. He goes on to suggest that it was through confusing being free with feeling free that Epictetus was misled into the paradoxical view that freedom is achieved through the removal of desires rather than through the securing of opportunities for action in which they may be satisfied. The teaching of Epictetus, Day concludes, though it 'probably provides the best anodyne available to despairing slaves, . . . has nothing to say to those who hope to become, or to remain, freemen'.

According to such writers as Day and (with important reservations) Berlin, being free to do something is not to be identified with doing what one wants to do, or with feeling free to do it, and it presupposes neither of these things. Nor should being free to do something be equated with having the ability to do it. The logical relation of freedom to ability, unlike that of freedom to desire or to will, is that the former presupposes the latter: a man must be able to do something before he can be free or unfree to do it. Lastly, according to this view, the answer to the question whether a man is free to do something does not depend in any way on answers to such questions as whether it would be right for him to do it, or whether it is in his real interests that he do it. On the contrary, it is insisted that questions of the morality or the prudence of a man doing something cannot sensibly be raised unless he is free to do it. On this view, answering the question whether a man is free to do something does not involve making an evaluative judgment of any sort. The question is an empirical question, though sometimes, perhaps, a peculiarly difficult one, to which there is always a single right answer. Accordingly, to say of a man that he is a free man is not to appraise the value of his way of life; it is not to say, for example, that his way of life is worthy of respect, or that it expresses his nature as a man better than any other could. It is to say, in the first instance, that he possesses certain legal rights, centrally important among which is the negative right not to be treated as a chattel. Now, since a slave is precisely one who lacks these basic rights, themselves partially constitutive of social freedom, it follows inexorably that a slave, however contented, cannot be free. Epictetus' notion of the contented slave who may be freer than his master is thus simply incoherent, or else a misleading metaphor.

This argument, which henceforth I shall call the *definist* argument, is certainly swift, and it looks pretty conclusive. Is it the end of the matter?

A *counter-argument*. In a recent paper,[5] G.W. Smith tries to show, not just that the definist argument is not as conclusive as it seems, but that it is impossible to guarantee logically the falsity of the claim that an avowedly contented slave is socially free. Taking as his departure-point the view that the measure of an agent's social freedom is the extent of the range of options open to him, Smith considers (only to reject) several proposals about how this range can be delimited so as to ensure that the contented slave's options are indeed foreclosed.

In summary, Smith considers first the most obvious move of defining the range of options counterfactually: the contented slave is unfree because, if (contrary to fact) he were to try to do what the law (or his master) forbids, he would be frustrated. Such a counterfactual construal of the agent's options may be interpreted more or less strongly, but neither way yields a satisfactory account of how the happy slave's options are restricted. If the counterfactual definition is applied weakly, so that it covers only wants the slave could actually conceive, and which we can't be sure he won't conceive, then it will give the desired result in the case of many living slaves, but it breaks down in the case of those slaves who live and die contented with their lot, since we cannot here say that their condition of servitude was ever an obstacle to their doing something they wanted to do. Nor can the desired result be obtained by strengthening the counterfactual definition so that it comprehends wants the slave never conceived, and perhaps never could have conceived. Admittedly, such a strongly counterfactual definition will yield the conclusion that a lifelong contented slave *may* be described as socially unfree, but nothing so far *compels* us so to describe him. True enough, imputing appropriate counterfactual wants will yield the required conclusion, but imputing different wants will produce just as easily the contrary description. A wholly *formal* approach of this kind is unsatisfactory, according to Smith, since, while it permits us to describe the contented slave as socially unfree, it allows us also to describe the contented free man in the same way.

Smith goes on to consider D.D. Raphael's attempt to remedy the defects of a purely formal account of social freedom by specifying the hypothetical desires in respect of which the contented slave is judged unfree. These are specified as, not just desires he might conceive, but as desires conceived in special and privileged circumstances, namely, circumstances where he has experienced both slavery and emancipation. As it had been expounded so far, Smith suggests, Raphael's account fails to serve its purpose. There is nothing unintelligible in the supposition that an emancipated slave might positively prefer to return to slavery, and, having done so, might live and die without ever regretting his decision. In such a case, Raphael's account cannot resist the counter-intuitive implication that the slave is socially free. As Smith makes clear, however, there is more than this to Raphael's account: it involves an appeal to 'a norm of human nature in which the desire for self-fulfillment *would* be restrained by conditions of slavery', where this norm is understood to designate 'the natural character of an average human being in normal circumstances'. But just how is the norm of human nature related to the idea of social freedom?

Smith suggests three ways in which such a norm might be invoked to answer questions about social freedom, none of which (he says) guarantees the social unfreedom of a contented slave. First, the norm might be construed *inductively* as incapsulating *evidence* about the dispositions of average human beings, upon which are based *predictions* about the preferences a slave may be expected to display once he has had the chance to make an informed choice between slavery and emancipation.

Once again, this will not defeat the claim that a contented slave is socially free wherever, knowing both conditions, he displays a positive preference for slavery over emancipation. Secondly, the norm of human nature may be construed as *constitutive* of the concept of social freedom. Here social freedom is characterised as the absence of obstacles to a specific range of actions identified by reference to the characteristic desires of the normal man: the hypothetical desires relevant to judgments about the social freedom of a contented slave are those of a normal, self-fulfilled individual, regardless of whether the slave is, or could ever become, such an individual. Like the purely formal approach examined earlier, this approach is strongly counterfactual, but, as Smith observes, it aims to avoid the arbitrariness of that approach by regulating the counterfactual imputation of wants by reference to the material content of the norm of human nature. The difficulty is to find a decision-procedure for norms of human nature which excludes such judgments as those embodied in the Stoic view that the wise slave is freer than his master.

Smith rejects the most-obvious procedure in which what is treated as decisive is the choice of individuals who have been adequately acquainted with the various kinds of experience endorsed by the competing norms. This, he says, requires what is logically impossible. For, whereas the constitutive view of the rule of a norm of human nature in making judgments about social freedom expresses the conviction that the agent's own preferences are to be overridden if they fail to conform to the norm, the content of the norm cannot itself be explicated solely by reference to agents' preferences if it is to be invoked to sanction discounting such preferences. Moreover, Smith emphasises, the independence of agents' preferences without which the norm of human nature cannot perform this function of supporting the overriding of preferences renders it necessarily non-empirical in character.

There is a third view, however, expounded by Raphael. Here social freedom presupposes, not merely the availability of alternative courses of action, but the ability to choose between them: a degree of rational choice-making competence, or *autonomy*, is taken to be one of the logically-necessary conditions of social freedom. The norm of human nature is connected non-contingently with the concept of social freedom, then, in that it supplies us with *criteria for the identification of autonomy*. Thus Winston Smith in Orwell's *1984* is said by Raphael to be 'dehumanized' and (when he comes to love Big Brother) to lack the natural competence of a rational chooser. Equally, if a slave (having experienced both) were to prefer slavery to emancipation, Raphael would say that the slave's preference revealed a psychological disability, doubtless attributable to his social conditioning, as a result of which he is incapacitated for autonomous choice. In this version of the definist argument, where the norm of human nature is taken as furnishing criteria for the identification of autonomy, the problem of the contented slave appears to be dissolved. For it is the preference expressed by the slave in the crucial situation of choice between emancipation and slavery that determines whether or not he is autonomous. Since autonomy is one of the logically-necessary conditions of social freedom, those who prefer slavery demonstrate their heteronomy and so cannot (logically) be free in the slavery to which they return.

As Smith goes on to argue, however, the appearance that the problem has been dissolved may once again be deceptive. The solution works only if we are ready to identify autonomy by reference to *what the agent chooses* rather than by reference to *how he makes his choices.* The force of Raphael's conception of autonomy is that slavery cannot be a possible object of autonomous choice: but this conception has all the difficulties which Raphael himself acknowledges, of Idealist conceptions of the 'real will'. Nor does Smith find inherently plausible the idea that a decision to return to slavery is bound to be less than fully autonomous: for an agent might surely have good reasons for making such a choice — reasons entirely appropriate as grounds of action to an autonomous agent. In any case, an approach which identifies autonomy by reference to the ends an agent adopts is generally uncongenial to liberal thought, which is reluctant to identify freedom of choice with choosing what is right.

Smith comments that there is here a dilemma for liberals, which he characterises as a tug-of-war between reason and freedom. If the ultimate principles of morals and politics are matters of reason, and it is possible to determine whether an agent is autonomous by reference to the ends he adopts and the choices he makes, then it follows that one can't disagree persistently and fundamentally with others about such issues without coming eventually to challenge their status as autonomous agents, or to doubt one's own. If, on the other hand, liberals reject the idea that autonomy involves finding rational answers to basic moral and political questions, then they acknowledge that social freedom is an *essentially contestable concept*[6] — that is to say, a concept whose subject matter is such that it is inherently liable to intractable and rationally-unsettlable dispute about its proper applications. If they do this, however, then they must accept that a slave might autonomously choose to return to slavery, and they must swallow the paradox that a contented slave enjoys social freedom. In the one case, a (highly implausible) conception of autonomy resists the counter-intuitive conclusion only by definitional fiat; in the other, a less-demanding conception of autonomy, conjoined with the view that there is no way rationally to settle disputes between exponents of rival conceptions of social freedom, leads directly to the absurd result. As Smith puts it:

An examination of the idea of social freedom applied at its limits, as it were, to the problem of the perfectly contented slave, thus implies that Berlin's stricture about it being necessary to distinguish the Stoic sense of freedom from the concept of social freedom is totally without force. If the principle of distinction is taken to be conformity with liberal political values, they *ought* not to be distinguished; and if the point of it is the description each produces of the contented slave, they cannot be distinguished.[7]

Either way, the conclusion stands: no way exists whereby the contented slave can be shown to be unfree.

What are we to make of Smith's argument? Certainly it is both ingenious and provocative. Exploiting a plausible-looking understanding of social freedom as a conjunct of two things, a range of legal rights securing certain important opportunities to act and a measure of rational choice-making competence (autonomy) assuring that a span of alternatives is subjectively available to him, Smith claims that the fact that the slave lacks these rights cannot be shown to diminish his options, and argues that no way exists (which is not arbitrary and question-begging) of defining autonomy which guarantees its incompatibility with slavery. Yet, for all its ingenuity, it's hard to resist the intuition that Smith's argument fails to give the conception of social freedom which is its departure-point — freedom as the non-restriction of options — a fair run for its money. After all, since he lacks the legal rights of a free man, a slave will be liable to punishment in areas where a free man has immunity, and his status will deprive him of certain powers — such as the power to transmit property — which a free man has even if he never uses them: aren't these genuine restrictions of the slave's options? Again, isn't it a little cavalier to repudiate without further ado as dubiously definist and unacceptably stipulative the claim that there is a conceptual connection between autonomy and the idea of a free man? Might not a conception of human nature be elaborated and given rational support which licenses such a conception? The difficulty, of course, is that it is not clear if the intuitions which these objections express can be cashed out in arguments more persuasive than Smith's. More specifically, is there an account of freedom as the non-restriction of options that is less vulnerable to Smith's objections than the views he canvasses?

Freedom as the non-restriction of options

In a well-known paper,[8] S. I. Benn and W. L. Weinstein reject the conception of freedom as the absence of impediments or constraints and develop the most forceful argument we have so far for the account of freedom as the non-restriction of options. Claiming that it is apposite to discuss whether a man is free to do something only if it is a possible object of reasonable choice, they declare programmatically that: 'Our conception of freedom is bounded by our notions of what might be worthwhile doing. . . . Incomprehension, not hostility, is the first obstacle to toleration.'[9] According to Benn and Weinstein, then, the concept of freedom in moral and political contexts has uses which are typically normative rather than merely descriptive: to refer to freedom in these contexts is to invoke a principle, to identify a range of considerations salient to policy in the circumstances under discussion. More particularly, they claim that 'whenever we say of a person that he is free from X, or free of X . . . it is some condition contrary to that person's supposed interest'.[10] In this they follow Spinoza, who says that 'children, though they are coerced, are not slaves', because 'they obey orders given in their own interests'. If, then, judgments about social freedom are evaluative judgments informed by a view of human interests, we need to be clear about the concept of having an interest if we are to be clear about the relation between slavery and social freedom. A brief glance at the literature on interests in politics,[11] however, confirms that once again we are in search of a decision-procedure for norms of human nature.

Speaking generally, elucidations of the concept of having an interest tend to span a range of conceptions extending from a behaviouralist extreme to one which is only vestigially behavioural in denotation. The term 'interests' has been used, at one extreme, for example, to denote the expressed preferences of an individual or a group; but in this, straightforwardly want-regarding, use it is impossible for an agent to be mistaken about his interests, since these are (definitionally) constituted by whatever it is that his preferences show he wants. This understanding of what it is to have an interest, then, while it identifies a legitimate use of the term 'interest' doesn't capture much of the sense of talk about interests, in which it is often proper to say that, if they are based on misinformation, faulty reasoning, or an inadequate grasp of the available alternatives, satisfying an agent's expressed preferences may not be 'in his interests'. Also, this first understanding makes it impossible to say that a man has interests of which he is ignorant, and it commits us to saying that, whenever a man changes his mind about what it is that is in his interests, it is the interests that have changed. In disallowing statements to the effect that a man made a mistake in identifying his interests, this conception is clearly of no assistance in showing that a condition of slavery, because it is prejudicial to a man's interests, must be restrictive of his freedom; for it leaves no way in which a man's own preference-judgments may be overriden by others as part of a policy designed to protect his interests.

In order to remedy these limitations, a second understanding of interests is often proposed: in this conception, expressions referring to interests are used in the evaluation of policies and institutions, for example, with a view to assessing how far they maximise the agent's opportunities to obtain whatever it may be that he wants. This second understanding is an improvement on the first, since it allows us to say that a man is mistaken about his interests, or that he has interests of which he is unaware, but it has been objected that it is still inadequate in that it does not permit us to say of an agent who is not somehow radically cognitively deficient that changing the character of his wants is a condition of promoting his interests; and this is something we must say if we are to be able to object to voluntary servitude on the ground that it permits an agent to injure his interests even when he never regrets his choice.

A third understanding of interests has accordingly been proposed, according to which promoting someone's interests is synonymous with maximising the fulfilment of his needs, or of his opportunities for need-fulfilment. Now, admittedly, we do speak about policies being designed to further men's understanding of their own needs, and about institutions (such as educational institutions) being constructed so as to enable men to discover that they have needs of which they would otherwise be unaware. It is not clear to me, however, that such policies must or can be justified by considerations to do with the protection or promotion of human interests. After all, even if a man may be said to have an interest in satisfying his needs, that cannot be his only interest, since he will also, presumably, have an interest in satisfying his mere wants. Promoting someone's interests cannot be synonymous with maximising the fulfilment of his needs. Nor is it obvious to me that anything of value is achieved by linking interests to needs. For, in the first place, in considering the proposal that there is an internal link between the notion of interests and needs, we must beware of an ambiguity which often haunts talk about needs, and which damages many accounts of the concept.[12] Sometimes 'need' is used as a noun denoting inclinations whose thwarting results in felt frustration. Used in this fashion, however, the notion of having a need fails to elucidate that of having an interest in the desired way. For, whereas there is nothing incoherent in the supposition that it might be in the interest of an agent, none of whose inclinations are suppressed or thwarted, to develop capacities and form need-patterns that would make possible for him a way of life he would value highly once he had experienced it, but which he would never seek out if none of his needs (so understood) were ever frustrated, this is a supposition the first understanding of needs does not allow us to entertain. Sometimes 'need' is elucidated as a verb whose uses make a reference to 'those conditions instrumental to the attainment of one's full development as a person'.[13] As Connolly (to whom I owe this understanding) makes clear, in this account, need-statements will always be triadic: a person will need something in order to do, be, or become something. The trouble with this account, however, when considered in the context of an elucidation of what it is to have an interest, is that it is altogether formal — a feature of similar accounts which has led some writers (e.g. Barry) to stigmatise the notion of a need as so irremediably porous as to be almost useless in political thought. Further, if the notion of interests is so closely tied to the notion of a need, 'interests' must be similarly stigmatised.

A fourth understanding of interests (elaborated by Connolly) seeks to salvage the notion from hopeless indeterminacy by making it once again want-regarding. In this account, a man has an interest in whatever it is that he would choose, having experienced the results of a relevant range of appropriate policies. The concept of having an interest remains tied logically to the choices an agent makes (as shown in his behaviour), but the choices he makes once he has experienced the full range of genuine and relevant alternatives is privileged over the other. The wants which are extensionally equivalent with his interests are, then, the counterfactual wants he will have if he has a clear awareness of the full range of alternatives, based on an experience of their consequences. It will be objected at this point, no doubt, that all of Smith's arguments may be invoked with undiminished force against this fourth understanding of interests. The trouble with the *choice criterion* of interests, whose affinities with Mill's *preference criterion* of the higher pleasures will be obvious, is that it will yield a result that defeats the counter-intuitive view about slavery and social freedom only on very dubious assumptions about the uniformity of human nature. Have we any more reason to suppose that everyone will prefer emancipation to slavery than we have to think that all who have tried both will plump for chess in preference to soap operas? We will have this assurance, the objection might be developed to contend, only if we make the preference for emancipation over slavery a criterion for the identification of the privileged choice conditions in which a man's (true or real) interests are revealed. But isn't this, as Smith has argued, just another definist manoeuvre? Hitherto, we found ourselves in a position where the emptily-formal character of notion — that of having a need — could be obviated only by attaching to it a substantive view of human nature — of human potentialities and human flourishing, which, in its very nature, is bound to be disputable. At that point, we found, arbitrariness appeared to have crept back in: the inherently controversial aspect of conceptions of interests cashed out in terms of needs deprived us of any rational assurance that well-founded judgments about social freedom, however informed by considerations to do with human interests, will always be such that they make social freedom and the condition of slavery mutually exclusive. Now, with respect to the concept of autonomy, we have an emptily-formal concept, a notion liable to yield a diversity of rival conceptions, a choice between which can be made only by invoking a substantive conception of human nature — which is bound to have an inherently disputable character.

The argument appears to have run full circle. Turning to Benn and Weinstein for an account of freedom as the non-restriction of options, we found that questions of social freedom arise only in respect of possible objects of reasonable choice, where the standards of reasonableness derive (at least partly) from norms about human interests. Surveying accounts of what it is to have an interest, we found the conception of interests most intuitively germane to the question of slavery and social freedom is cashed out in terms of a view of autonomy that looks suspiciously question-begging. Further, since there is a range of conceptions of autonomy, resting on different views of human nature and specifying different and incompatible accounts of the autonomous man's preferences, nothing has been said so far that decisively counts against the Stoic view, with its unacceptably problematic consequences. If the concept of autonomy is thus an essentially contestable concept, then the idea of a free man, the concept of social freedom and the definition of liberalism, will be similarly contestable. Different views of human nature, arising no doubt from rival moral and political commitments, will specify different and perhaps incommensurable views of the conditions and nature of autonomous choice, and, so, at several removes, of the nature of social freedom. It will be seen that the source of the unacceptably permissive implication of Smith's argument is the essentially questionable character of views of human nature itself. A presupposition of Smith's argument, however, is that judgements about social freedom are not in fact (what some writers assert they are) solely judgments about what is the case. If they are factual rather than evaluative judgments, and refer primarily to the objective circumstances of action, then the purely formal argument which Smith dismisses will be seen to be unexceptionably (because inevitably) definist. Let us consider, then, whether a definist argument cannot be rehabilitated.

The definist argument re-stated

Crudely, the definist position is that, for a man to be free to do something, it must be true of him that he is not obstructed in doing it by the intervention of other agents. Differing definist positions are yielded by different views of what can count as obstruction, but all definist views express the necessary truth that, if social freedom involves a range of rights to act, and if the condition of slavery comprehends the absence of these rights, then a slave cannot enjoy social freedom. Again, the definist position presupposes that the question, *whether or not* the agent under consideration possesses the rights of a free man, is an empirical question. To answer the question, whether a man is a free man or a slave, does not on this account commit us to any evaluative judgment about that man or his deeds. Nor is the question about a man's status as a slave or a free man one which requires reference to his psychological condition: it is a question about his social (and legal) circumstances, *simpliciter*. It is impossible, on this view, for there to be unsettlable disputes about a man's status, once the relevant facts are known.

Writers in this tradition differ among themselves as to what may constitute a preventing (liberty-limiting) condition. The great majority, of whom Oppenheim[14] may be taken as a typical but unusually fair-minded and lucid example, contend that being free to perform an act entails, not only that it has not been rendered physically impossible by the intervention of another, but that other agents have not rendered ineligible the relevant alternatives to it. Being free to act, then, on this view, involves the absence, not just of force, but also of coercion (which comprehends, among other things, the threat of force). More recently, however, a number of writers[15] have sought to undermine this widely-accepted, commonsensical view, according to which being free to act implies the non-punishability of the act as well as the absence of forcible restraint with respect to it. I shall consider briefly the arguments of the boldest and most ingenious of these recent writers so that I can then examine their cogency as supports of the definist view.

In his recent paper, Steiner acknowledges that it is a well-supported conclusion of the literature on the subject that the distinction between interventions that are threats and interventions that are offers presupposes a standard of normalcy specifying the expected and morally-required course of events which it is the point of the intervention to alter. In the received view, it may be said that refusing an offer doesn't diminish my welfare, whereas threats make a worsening of my condition a consequence of non-compliance. Offers expand options, but threats restrict them: for, while option X would be open to me in the ordinary way, only option X plus a penalty will be available to me once it is covered by a threat. It is in virtue of their relation to this standard of normalcy that threats, but not offers, are generally thought to be restrictive of liberty. Now, as Steiner observes, it is necessarily true that, since the non-compliance condition of an offer is the norm itself, complying with an offer makes one better off than does complying with a threat, but it is not true that offers are always more resistible than threats. Speaking generally, threats and offers affect an agent's practical deliberations by changing the desirability of doing an action relative to that of not doing it. From the agent's standpoint the force of the intervention depends, not on its distance from the norm, but on the difference in desirability between the two sets of consequences it generates. It is true both of threats and offers that compliance will leave the agent better off than he would otherwise have been (given the intervention), and nothing here hinges on the intervention's relation to a standard of normalcy. Since it is by appeal to this standard that threats are distinguished from offers, and no other way has been shown to exist in which these interventions affect the practical deliberations of the agent, Steiner concludes that negative libertarians have given us no reason for supposing that threats, but not offers, can be restrictive of liberty.

What is the relevance of Steiner's argument to the question of slavery and social freedom? Firstly, in restricting discourse about social freedom to circumstances where one man's acting in a certain way is rendered *physically impossible* by the intervention of another, it licenses the inference (as Steiner makes clear) that freedom is the personal possession of physical objects. Why is this so? Steiner's case against the orthodox version of negative libertarianism is that no good reason can be given within such a perspective for treating threats as restrictive of liberty and that, accordingly, a consistent negative libertarian will allow only physical force to be restrictive of social freedom. If the only preventing condition which can affect a man's liberty is one that renders certain actions physically impossible to him, then, Steiner reasons, to be free to do something is simply to have the 'physical components' of that action at one's disposal — to have unimpeded motion in the area of physical space occupied in the action and unobstructed control over the particular material objects disposed of in the action. But, Steiner continues, the relation between an agent and a portion of physical space which he occupies, and between an agent and a material object of which he disposes, is commonly called *possession*. Thus, he says:

Statements about the freedom of an individual to do a particular action are therefore construable as claims about the agential location of possession of the particular physical component of that action. The statement that 'X is free to do A' entails that none of the physical components of doing A is possessed by an agent other than X. The statement that 'X is unfree to do A' entails that at least one of the physical components of doing A is possessed by an agent other than X.[16]

Steiner's argument, then, proceeds by way of a criticism of the conventional conception of negative liberty to the proposal that such liberty be identified with the control of material things.

Secondly, since on this view (as on others) freedom (that is to say, possession) is a triadic relation obtaining between an agent, an object, and all other agents, so that any agent's augmentation of freedom entails a corresponding diminution of the freedom of another, it follows (according to Steiner) that aggregate individual freedom is not a variable magnitude.[17] Thirdly, and as a consequence of the second point, liberalism is best characterised, not as a political philosophy in which liberty is assigned lexicographical priority over other political goods, but rather as that doctrine which requires that freedom be distributed equally among men. The legal condition of slavery is excluded by liberalism, then, because its defining feature, the possession by one man of property rights in another, is inconsistent with the central, equal-freedom principle of liberalism.

Does Steiner's reconstructed negative libertarianism permit a restatement of the definist argument less vulnerable than Berlin's to Smith's strictures? I think not. For, in the first place, it is not altogether clear on Steiner's account how we are to make comparative judgments regarding aggregate individual freedom, and it is, accordingly, a matter of legitimate and perhaps unsettlable disagreement whether the equal-freedom principle is satisfied in any particular case. The inherently controversial aspect of judgments about freedom, its magnitudes and distribution, arises from the circumstance that the subject matter of discourse about freedom is actions rather than behaviour, and actions (unlike behaviour) are conventionally (and often normatively) constituted entities. This is indicated obliquely in Steiner's remark that '. . . to act is, *among other things*, to occupy particular portions of physical space and to dispose of particular material objects, including, in the first instance, parts of one's own body'.[18] The problem concealed by the phrase I have emphasised is that an action bears no determinate relation to the behaviours in which it may be performed and, therefore, no one-one identity relation. Steiner's equivocation between action and behaviour is shown in his discussion of an incarcerated individual who, while prevented from performing an indefinitely long list of actions, is, according to Steiner, 'not prevented from jumping up and down, nor from singing *Waltzing Matilda*, nor from twiddling his thumbs in a clockwise direction, nor from twiddling his thumbs in a counter-clockwise direction, and so on'.[19]

If the subject matter of freedom is action rather than

behaviour, then it will be seen that the disputable character of judgments about freedom has its source in the fact that *we have no principle of counting for free actions which is not also a principle of evaluation of their worth or significance*. Nor will this appear particularly surprising when we reflect that some of the centrally-important areas of controversy about freedom have been historical disputes about whether certain classes of individuals should be enabled by law to perform certain actions (e.g. to marry) whose performance had hitherto been restricted to some dominant group. Any judgment comparing the overall freedom of an agent, a group, or a whole society with that of another, or at another time, cannot avoid being an evaluative judgment about the relative value of the actions it comprehends. Interestingly, this is clearly recognised by Berlin, when in a crucially-important footnote he acknowledges the evaluative character of judgments about freedom, saying:

The extent of my freedom seems to depend on (a) how many possibilities are open to me (though the method of counting these can never be more than impressionistic. Possibilities of action are not discrete entities like apples, which can be exhaustively enumerated); (b) how easy or difficult each of these possibilities is to actualise; (c) how important in my plan of life, given my character and circumstances, these possibilities are when compared with each other; (d) how far they are closed and opened by deliberate human acts; (e) what value not merely the agent, but the general sentiment of the society in which he lives, puts on the various possibilities.

Berlin continues:

All these magnitudes must be 'integrated', and a conclusion, necessarily never very precise, or indisputable, drawn from this process. It may well be that there are many incommensurable kinds and degrees of freedom, and that they cannot be drawn up on any single scale of magnitude . . . Total patterns of life must be compared directly as wholes, though the method by which we make the comparison, and the truth of the conclusions, are difficult or impossible to demonstrate. But the vagueness of the concepts, and the multiplicity of the criteria involved, is an attribute of the subject-matter itself, not of our imperfect method of measurement, or incapacity for precise thought.

A similar, though more restricted, point is made by Hart, when in an important argument, he says of Rawls that:

He admits that different opinions about the value of the conflicting liberties will affect the way in which different persons view this conflict (between them). Nonetheless, he insists that to arrive at a just resolution of the conflict we must try to find the point at which the danger to liberty from the marginal loss in control over those holding political power just balances the security of liberty gained by the greater use of constitutional devices. I cannot myself understand, however, how such weighing or striking of a balance is conceivable if the only appeal is, as Rawls says, to 'a greater liberty'.[21]

It must not be thought that Steiner's argument, in denying that individual freedom is a variable magnitude, escapes the problems created by the indeterminacy of the expression 'a greater liberty'. For, Steiner's principle of the conservation of freedom notwithstanding, these problems break out in any judgment concerning the distribution of freedom. No scientific, value-free artificial language can be construed in which egalitarianism — whether about freedom, or about any other good — can become a descriptive notion.[22] This crucially implies, further, that, since slavery may be and has been a matter of degree, there may be deep disagreements — and disagreements having an ineradicable evaluative dimension — about whether or not the restrictive institutions in which a man lives are such as to render him a slave.

The difficulties inherent in making judgments about degrees of slavery are well illustrated by the case of the Mamelukes,[23] slaves who succeeded in establishing dynasties of their own, both in India and in Egypt, and who preserved their power under Ottoman rule by the expedient of securing for their sons — who as Muslims were free-born — the rights and privileges hitherto enjoyed only by slaves such as themselves. Examples such as that of the Mamelukes display the difficulties which will often be found when attempts are made to apply the concept of slavery to concrete historical groups. They confirm that the definist argument — even when restated ingeniously by such as Steiner — begs important questions, which no consideration of slavery and freedom can afford to ignore. Indeed, inasmuch as Steiner's reconstructed negative libertarianism cannot account for, and support, the well-founded comparative judgments about social freedom which we continually make, it must be rejected as providing an account of the concept of freedom which collapses into incoherence. Despite his clear awareness that comparative judgments present a difficulty for his account, Steiner offers no plausible account of their status, having recourse to the oblique and unsatisfactory claim that, though actions are not themselves countable, yet there may be some common element in situations where discourse about freedom is appropriate which allows for some measure of quantifiability. My contention is that this common element will be found to be precisely that which the definist position as restated by Steiner excludes, namely, a range of evaluative judgments tied to a conception of a worthwhile human life. The conclusion is inescapable that the definist position can be made consistent only by the heroic move of claiming that comparative judgments about social freedom are, despite appearances, impossible. Such a move has the consequence, however, of rendering rational discussion of degrees of slavery in their relation to social freedom equally impossible. The upshot of these reflections is that, far from any convincing testament of the definist position emerging in Steiner's account, we find there is good reason for supposing the definist standpoint to be ultimately self-defeating.

A *naturalist solution*

The hinges on which Smith's argument swings are two: first, the claim — which I endorse — that the formal notions of freedom and autonomy cannot by themselves guarantee an incompatibility with slavery; and second, the contention that the views of human nature which inform these bare notions and render them substantive are essentially contestable. It is this latter, second claim which I propose to question as a preliminary to elaborating my own naturalistic resolution of the problem of slavery and freedom. I wish to point out to start with that there is a deep gulf between the view (surely an uncontroversial one) that conceptions of human nature have always an inherently questionable, corrigible, disputable aspect, and the claim — which I take it is the one made by those who contend that the concepts of moral and political thought are all of them essentially contestable — that no considerations can ever be found which so inform our assessment of the merits of rival conceptions of human nature that one view of human nature stands out as clearly rationally preferable. Smith's argument, as I can see it, requires that the second of these claims be endorsed. My contention, on the contrary, is that the problem of the contented slave can be resolved by supplementing the bare notion of autonomy with an account of human nature that is bound to have a disputable character, but which is in no way beyond criticism or rational support.

That uses of the notion of autonomy in moral and political contexts always endorse some account of human nature suggests that we will be wise if we consider what it is for *a man* — rather than a dolphin, say — to be autonomous. This involves recognising that there are certain activities and involvements which are constitutive of human social life. Without such complex reactive attitudes as resentment and gratitude, without such involvements as friendship and rivalry, there would be nothing that we can recognise as a human society. I suggest that the capacity for sustaining complex emotional relationships, to harbour long-range projects and to resent their frustration, be accounted among the *symptoms*[24] of autonomy in a man. I suggest that, confronted with a man who cared nothing for natural beauty, parental affection or sexual love, who sought no satisfactions in the life of the mind, in the development of his bodily powers or in religious devotion, we would be disinclined to qualify him as autonomous; and the source of our disinclination is not any logical property of the bare formal notion of autonomy, but rather our invocation of the concept of a human life. A man's life, we may say, has characteristic phases and aspects; these define what may be called the *necessary form* of a human life. Our doubt that a cocaine addict, who says he cares for nothing but the euphoria produced by his drug, may be accounted autonomous, can, I believe, be explained satisfactorily only by invoking the concept of a happy human life. When we judge that a man cannot enjoy great happiness even if the narcotic euphoria be prolonged indefinitely, such a judgment — like many judgments of importance in ethics — must be supported by appeal to an idea of the kind of happy life that only an autonomous man can have. Such considerations deriving from the notion of a happy human life frame *boundary conditions* within which the concept of autonomy is at home: they furnish criteria for the application of that concept in social contexts. I contend, then, that the concept of a human life enters into any judgment we make about the autonomy of human beings; and considerations deriving from the concept of a human life support our disinclination to account some behaviours — such as that of the cocaine addict — features of the life of an autonomous man. It is by invoking those considerations, I suggest, that we override the avowals of the slave that he is content with his lot, and dismiss the claim that there could be a 'truly contented' slave.

It is those aspects of a human life, helping to define its necessary shape, that inform our judgments when we distinguish an imposition of a cost upon a man's activities from a restriction of his options, which we appeal to when we individuate options and aggregate them so as to produce some view of a man's overall freedom. The slave's options are restricted in that, regardless of his own preferences, his status deprives him of the opportunities he would need if he were to have a chance to flourish as a man. There will, no doubt, be hard cases, where we are unable to make confident comparative judgments about agents' chances of flourishing in diverse conditions of restraint and restriction of options; but, contra Smith, the fact that concepts such as that of a human life are open-textured does not mean that they are quite bereft of any criteria of proper application. It is to some such distinction between concepts whose applications are inherently disputable and concepts that are so deeply contestable in character that any wager on an eventual convergence in their uses would be unreasonable that Stuart Hampshire may be presumed to invoke when, in his book, *Thought and Action*, having asserted that 'there are some concepts that are permanently and essentially subject to question and dispute and are recognised to be at all times questionable',[25] and having included among these concepts the concepts of mind and action, he goes on to support a definite metaphysical view of the nature of mind and action. Nor can it reasonably be thought to be a powerful objection to my account that no complete and fully determinate list can ever be given of the symptoms of a happy life. As Strawson observes in the context of an important argument for the constitutive role of the reactive attitudes of resentment and gratitude in moral personality and moral community:

The central commonplace that I want to insist on is the very great importance that we attach to the attitudes and intentions towards us of other human beings, and the great extent to which our personal feelings and reactions depend upon, or involve, our beliefs about these attitudes and intentions. I can give no simple description of the field of phenomena at the centre of which stands this commonplace truth, for the field is too complex. Much imaginative literature is devoted to exploring its complexities; and we have a large vocabulary for the purpose.[26]

The point that our inability to settle in advance all reasonable disputes about what are the indispensable defining features of human social life does not undermine the enterprise of elucidating the concept of a human life has been made forcefully by Peter Winch in the context of a criticism of some traditional approaches to the metaphysics of human nature:

... if one recognised the possibility of being mistaken in one's initial belief that one had understood what was being said, or that one had shown it to be unintelligible, one can equally, after discussion, recognise that one may have over-estimated the difficulties which have emerged in its course. But that does *not* mean that one's views are subject to the test of some ultimate criterion, the criterion of what does and what does not belong to human nature. It means only that new difficulties, and perhaps new ways of meeting the difficulties, are always lurking below the horizon, and that discussion continues. Sometimes, if one is lucky, the discussion clarifies or extends one's conception of what is possible for human beings. But it is no use saying that this is contingent on what *is* or *is not* possible, for human beings; for our only way of arriving at a view about this is by continuing to try to deal with the difficulties that arise in the course of discussion.[27]

The upshot of the work of Strawson, Hampshire, Winch, and others influenced to varying degrees and in different ways by the philosophy of the later Wittgenstein is that certain practices and reactive attitudes are so foundational in our thought that any approach to moral and political dilemmas which neglects their relevance is bound soon to run into conceptual difficulties. Plainly, the account of man and society elaborated by writers in this tradition breaks with the notion of necessity as consisting simply in analyticity which was propagated by some of the positivists of the Vienna Circle. Their claim is that, in the area of social practices and reactive attitudes with which we are concerned, the distinctions between natural and conceptual necessity and between *a priori* and synthetic truths no longer have force or utility. The links that hold between moral, political and (in general) practical concepts germane to these areas must be regarded as internal or criterial, but this is not to say that such concepts are altogether mutually constitutive. It would be wrong to suppose, accordingly, that, in working out these in respect of the problem of the lot of the contented slave by the research programme intimated in this philosophical tradition, I have accorded to the relations between autonomy and happiness (for example) any character of vicious circularity. Some degree of circularity is inevitable (and virtuous) whenever an internal link is postulated between concepts, but it is no part of my argument that autonomy and happiness are concepts identical in meaning or equivalent in extension.

One illustration of the fact that my argument in no way commits me to the (surely unacceptable) view that statements about autonomy and happiness are intertranslatable may be found by noting the point that nothing I have said entails that a choice of slavery must be heteronomous. Like Smith, I find no difficulty in the proposition that an autonomous agent might freely choose to forfeit his autonomy and thereby to relinquish some of his prospects of happiness, but I see no necessity in the claim that what a free man chooses when he does this must be conceived as freedom. We can imagine easily enough, after all, reasons that might move an autonomous man to prefer slavery, and we need not suppose any of them to make reference to his concern for his own freedom. My claim, then, is not the implausible one, canvassed by Smith, that a free man could not (logically) display a preference for slavery; but the claim that a man who acts successfully upon such a preference at once ceases to be a free man and forecloses some of his chances of happiness. Nor is it true that my account commits me to the Socratic paradox that an agent cannot freely choose what is bad. For, while it claims as a necessary truth that a free act, and an option, must contain or presuppose some good or positive value, the resultant on-balance of a free act is not thereby precluded from being a bad state of affairs. It seems clear, in fact, that some such account as mine is intimated by the prohibition of voluntary servitude endorsed by most writers in the liberal tradition, which (as J.S. Mill's discussion of the question[28] makes particularly clear) has its source in a concern that men should not relinquish their own freedom, an action which Smith's account has the disadvantage of rendering logically impossible in the contexts with which we are here concerned.

While my argument is not vulnerable to such objections, I do not want to deny that areas of difficulty remain in my account — difficulties which perhaps infect all that has so far been written on these issues. It might be admitted, for example, that freedom and happiness are concepts criterially connected in the way I claim, and yet denied that anything substantive follows from this connection for theoretical and practical dilemmas in morals and politics. For, while freedom and happiness may well be linked together in any moral outlook, there could yet turn out to be an irreducible diversity of moral practices, each conceiving freedom and happiness differently. In that case, human flourishing would stand for nothing definite, and could not usefully be invoked to settle the question of the social status of the happy slave. More radically, it could be objected that the distinction between essential corrigibility and essential contestability which I have put to work in my account has no application in the areas of thought and practice with which we have been concerned. It might be urged against my account, indeed, that in supposing any elucidation of the concept of a human life to be available which is neutral as between rival metaphysical accounts of human nature, it is failing to take seriously the limitations of conceptual analysis identified by those who emphasise the essential contestability of being moral and political concepts. Accordingly, it cannot be denied that if, as Smith and others have suggested, metaphysical views of human nature occupy a logical space of deep contestability, then, like the solutions of the problem of the contented slave that Smith criticises, my own solution is saved from being emptily formal, definist and question-begging only at the cost of being inherently and radically contestable. If this last objection to my account can be made out, no way remains whereby we can resist the paradoxical and disturbing implications of Smith's arguments.

NOTES

1 Several people have helped me with this paper. For comments, stimulus and insight, I wish particularly to thank Sir Isaiah Berlin, Nick Bunnin, Bill Connolly, Philippa Foot, R.M. Hare, Martin Hollis, Michael Lockwood, Michael Freeman, Felix Oppenheim, Derek Parfitt, Ann Raphael, Geoff Smith, and Hillel Steiner.

2 I. Berlin, *Four Essays on Liberty* (Oxford, 1969) pp. xxxviii-xl.

3 Berlin, *op. cit.*

4 'On liberty and the real will', in *Philosophy*, Vol. 45, 1979, pp. 177–92.

5 'Slavery, contentment and social freedom', in *Philosophical Quarterly*, vol. 27, 1977, pp. 236–48.

6 The term is used first by Gallie in his 1956 *Aristotelian Society* paper on 'Essentially contested concepts'.

7 Smith, *Philosophical Quarterly*, 1977.

8 S. I. Benn and W.L. Weinstein, 'Being free to act and being a free man', in *Mind*, vol. 80, 1971, pp. 194–211.

9 Benn and Weinstein, *op. cit.*

10 Benn and Weinstein, *op. cit.*

11 I am particularly indebted to W.E. Connolly's treatment of the concept of interests in his *Terms of Political Discourse*.

12 Connolly is clearly aware of this damaging equivocation, which he discusses on pp. 59–62 (*op. cit.*).

13 Connolly, *op. cit.*

14 See F. Oppenheim's *Dimensions of Freedom*.

15 Such as W.A. Parent, *American Philosophical Quarterly*, vol. 11, 1974, pp. 149–67; and H. Steiner, *Proceedings of the Aristotelian Society*, vol. 75, 1974–5, pp. 33–50.

16 Steiner, *op. cit.* p. 48.

17 Steiner, *op. cit.* pp. 48–9.

18 Steiner, *op. cit.* p. 47.

19 Steiner, *op. cit.* p. 45.

20 Berlin, *op. cit.* p. 130.

21 H.L.A. Hart, 'Rawls on liberty and its priority', in *Reading Rawls*, ed. N. Daniels, p. 241.

22 I am indebted to Felix Oppenheim's paper, ' "Facts" and "Values" in Politics: are they separable?', in *Political Theory*, 1973, for my understanding of a descriptive approach to these questions.

23 I am grateful to Nick Bunnin for drawing my attention to this example. The information derives from the *Encyclopaedia Britannica* (1974) Vol. 2, p. 399 *et seq.*

24 I use 'symptom' here in the sense in which Wittgenstein intended in his discussion of 'criterion'. On this see R. Albritton, 'On Wittgenstein's use of the term "criterion", in *Journal of Philosophy*, (1959) Vol. 56, pp. 845–57.

25 *Thought and Action*, p. 230.

26 *Freedom and Resentment*, p. 5.

27 *Ethics and Action*, p. 88.

28 See *On Liberty*, Chapter 5, 'Applications'.

Democratic Antagonisms and the Capitalist State[1]
ERNESTO LACLAU

IT has become usual, in the course of the last ten years, to lament the absence of a Marxist political theory. This lack has been attributed to the variety of factors. Norberto Bobbio,[2] for instance, ascribes it to the Marxist classics having concentrated their attention almost exclusively on the problem of the seizure of power — neglecting, as a result, the distinct bourgeois forms of law and the State — and to the identification of Communism with the withering-away of the State. Umberto Cerroni[3] finds an explanation in the economism and pragmatism which characterised the thought of the Second and Third Internationals. Nicos Poulantzas[4] imputes it to the twofold circumstance of the epistemological break which occurred in Marx's thought — thus rendering obsolete the predominantly political writings of his youth — and the incomplete character of his later works, which thoroughly analysed only the economic instance of the capitalist mode of production. Lastly, Danilo Zolo[5] refers to an historical tradition which has 'added together (in the Marxist theory of the State), as a single body, doctrinal elements of markedly heterogeneous origins'. Whatever explanation one might accept, the lack of a coherent and mature Marxist theory of the State is widely documented and acknowledged. So how, then, might this problem be overcome? Is it simply an *ommission*, easily remedied through the development of a theory which is already implicit in the Marxist analysis of capitalism? Attempts to accomplish this, however, have led to theoretical constructs so diverse, and so incompatible with each other, that we have to abandon the illusion that the rescue of the political theory 'implicit' in Marx's works is a straightforward and obvious task. Where, then, does the difficulty lie? Is it that the historical experience of the working-class movement, with all its errors and deviations — such as revisionism and Stalinism — has thrown up 'epistemological obstacles' standing in the way of a proper understanding of Marx's thought? Or is it a question of a wrongly-formulated problem — is it that the *type* of double implication which has been sought between Marxist economic theory and political theory cannot, by definition, exist?

Before taking up these questions, it is worth recording briefly the new kinds of problems facing socialist political practice in the latter half of the twentieth century, problems which have constituted a powerful challenge to the Western Marxist tradition, strongly rooted in an economistic and class-based perspective. On the one hand, the increasing penetration of the State into economic life has heightened the importance of the political with respect to the actual mechanisms for the reproduction of the system. This has broken up the narrow economistic perspective which construed the level of politics, and especially the State, as simply the superstructure of a process whose fundamental explanation was to be sought in the internal logic of the accumulation of capital. On the other hand, this same increasing bureaucratisation has brought about a politicisation of social antagonisms, with the resulting emergence of new political subjects — national, racial and sexual minorities, students, women, and so on — which have tended to occupy a central place on the historical scene, and which, nevertheless, it is difficult to characterise through a purely class-based analysis. The same is true of the liberation movements in the periphery of the capitalist world, whose national and popular forms of struggle stubbornly resist any characterisation in terms of a pure class analysis.

Still, class reductionism is so deeply rooted in our habits of thought that it has ended up by affecting those very currents which have laid down some of the bases necessary to overcome it: it is significant that, after fifteen years of Althusserianism, and the consequent insistence that every class contradiction is always overdetermined, we should hardly have advanced one step further in the elaboration of theories concerning the various non-class antagonisms which, under capitalism, can intervene in a process of overdetermination.

It is clear that a Marxist theory of the capitalist State is inseparable from a correct understanding of the specificity of the political antagonisms which constitute the texture of present-day capitalist societies. In this article, we propose to set out some starting-points for the analysis of the relations that exist between capitalist development and the multiplication of the democratic antagonisms to which we have previously referred. This, in turn, will shed light on the first problem: the difficulties whic have impeded the formulation of an adequate Marxist political theory.

I

Let us begin to look at the problem by considering one theoretical current which has postulated a double implication between Marxist political and economic theories, and an essential unity between a sizeable part of the works of the young Marx and those of his maturity; I refer to the Della Volpean school.[6] Cerroni, a prominent member of this school, has held that

It is time to requalify the place that the critique of the State holds in Marx's thought and consequently to specify that his scientific communism is born out of two fundamental instances: the socialisation of the means of production, and the socialisation of power or the withering away-supersession of the State. These two instances can be formulated in another way as instances of a radical theoretical and historical critique of both political economy, on the one hand, and politics (and law) on the other.[7]

The two instances, according to Cerroni, are unbalanced in Marx's work: the critique of politics is central to the preoccupations of his youth, and subsequently reappeared in his analysis of the Paris Commune and in the *Critique of the Gotha Programme*; whereas the writings of the mature Marx are almost exclusively dedicated to the critique of political economy. However, there can be no doubt, for Cerroni, that Marx saw a double implication between (capitalist) civil society and the representative State. The overcoming of extra-economic coercion under capitalism represented the consummation of the political liberation of civil society. But, at the same time, political society freed itself from any social conditioning. One fundamental consequence flows from this:

The political emancipation of civil society is thus the recognition of sovereignty of the individual before the community and the recognition of sovereignty of the State before the citizen. Political emancipation opens the door simultaneously for authoritarianism of private property and of the State bureaucracy, for an authoritarianism absolutely unheard of in history. But it is an authoritarianism mined internally by two contradictions: by the contradiction between private property (capital) and wage labour, and by the contradiciton between sovereignty delegated to the political élite and the formal recognition of the equal political capacity of all. The analysis of the first contradiction is known: Marx has dedicated the major part of his life to it. But the analysis of the second one remained hardly as a rough outline.[8]

This means that a) the central aspect of the *specifically political* Marxist theory should be constituted by the analysis of the contradiction which arises between the principle of equality and the delegation of sovereignty, the source of political alienation; and b) this is a contradiction specific to capitalism, since only in capitalism is coercive political power separated from economic power and confronting an atomised society.

In this sense, Cerroni has identified as one of the great merits of Lenin his having hit upon the contradiction which runs through modern democracy; its two souls, one egalitarian and the other élitist. In contrast to the Marxism of the Second International, which conceived of political democracy as a simple sham to disguise the imposition of class domination, Lenin's experience in Russia — the fact that his revolution had to be *at the same time* both democratic and socialist — led him to recognise, as the first to do so since the young Marx, the contradictory nature of bourgeois democracy. Hence his assertion that while the democratic republic is the best possible covering for capitalism, there comes a point where bourgeois democracy goes beyond the framework of capitalism, making it possible for the proletariat to subtract from the hegemony of the bourgeoisie and win a majority of the people to the side of socialism. This possibility is inscribed in the dual soul of modern democracy, which constitutes its fundamental contradiction:

. . . the soul which is liberal, guarantistic, representative, proprietary, élitist, which is the true and real soul, the historical soul of the modern bourgeois republic, and the soul which is Rousseauian, revolutionary, populistic-plebeian, which hovers in the skies of Utopia so long as it is not taken over by a social force entirely antagonistic towards the bourgeoisie, and until this new social force dares to turn this antagonistic utopian soul of democracy into an effective lever for the overthrow of the proprietary-capitalistic structures, effected through the consensus of the proletariat and the working people.[9]

It is not strange that the Della Volpean school should look on Rousseau as a precursor of socialism. Because if the essential contradiction of *capitalism,* on the political level, is that which is implicit in the opposition between the principle of equality and the principle of representation, and if overcoming this contradiction depends on direct democracy and the suppression of the State, Rousseau must then be considered a critic of capitalism. Moreover, Colletti goes so far as to affirm[10] that, in the realm of political theory, Marx and Lenin have added nothing to Rousseau except for their analysis of the economic basis of the withering-away of the State.

The result of this dual contradiction of capitalism, according to Cerroni, is that socialism and democracy mutually require each other. 'Political democracy tends towards socialism, and socialism towards political democracy.'[11] The very development of capitalism has led to a situation where the defence of democratic-parliamentary institutions is increasingly linked to the anti-capitalist struggle and to a strategy for socialism. This is the case of the way that the increasing intervention of the State in various spheres of private life multiplies the bureaucratism which is inherent to the specifically political contradiction of capitalism, and extends it to areas from which State activity had been absent in the phase of liberal capitalism. The result is twofold: firstly, the institutions of formal democracy appear less and less tied-in with capitalism, and secondly, increasingly broad sectors are thrown by this process into the struggle for democracy, that is, into the anti-capitalist struggle. In this way there arises a polarisation in Western societies, around the struggle for the socialisation of power. However, since socialism implies both the socialisation of power and the socialisation of the means of production, the working class — whose interests favour economic socialisation — still has an important role to play;

its protagonism consists of hegemonising an historical bloc towards which the forces involved in an anti-capitalist and democratic struggle will gravitate.

I have detailed Cerroni's analyses at some length, both because I would coincide with his political conclusions and with a good deal of his analysis, and also because they represent one of the more serious attempts to give coherence, in terms of double implication, to the political theory of the young Marx and the economic theories of the mature Marx. I believe, however, that Cerroni has fallen short of his goal, because he has not managed to prove one particular point which is vital for his thesis: i.e. that the political contradiction whose resolution involves the socialisation of power, is exclusive to capitalism. Let us identify the conditions for its proof. The first is that the political contradiction of capitalism could not logically be conceived of without referring at the same time to its economic contradiction (otherwise, there would be no double implication). The second is that the implication must in fact be double, and not operate in only one direction; because if the implied contradiction does not in turn imply that which has implied it, then the first contradiction would simply be an abstract moment of the second (the concept of capitalism, for example, implies the concept of the market, but the inverse does not hold true — since the market exists in modes of production other than capitalism, and is not, therefore, an exclusively capitalist institution). The third condition of proof is that capitalism must be the precondition for the emergence of the contradiction, and not merely the condition of its unfolding (that is, the concept of capitalism would have to be the *logical precondition* for the said contradiction to reach full development).

Are these conditions met by Cerroni's idea concerning the mutual implication between the representative State and capitalism, and between democracy and socialism? We suggest that they are not. Let us analyse the assertion that 'political democracy tends towards socialism, and socialism towards political democracy'. If by this we are to understand that there exists a relationship of double implication between socialism and democracy — the latter being taken to mean the socialisation of power — then the proposition is a tautology, given that, according to Cerroni, the socialisation of power is one of the defining characteristics of socialism. If, on the other hand, what is being stated is that in the present phase of Western capitalism, *representative* democracy and socialism tend increasingly to imply each other, then this is a point where we can in fact coincide; but in any case, this calls for the analysis of a specific conjuncture, and it cannot be determined at the abstract level of capitalism as such. There is, however, a third possibility: that of arguing, as does Cerroni, that capitalism, by giving rise to the separation between the economic level and the political level, is the *source* of the contradiction between the democratic principle of equality and the bureaucratic principle of representation. We must, therefore, pose the question as to whether it is certain that the democracy/bureaucracy contradiction is a capitalist contradiction (please note the exact sense of the question: it does not ask whether it is present in capitalism, but whether it is intrinsically capitalist).

It is certainly the case that the capitalist mode of production is founded upon a separation between political power and economic power which did not exist in earlier modes of production. It is also certain that the capitalist juridical order gives rise to the possibility of a contradiction between the juridical principle of equality and the principle of representation. And, lastly, it is certain that in mature capitalism there is a growing tendency towards the bureaucratisation of power and the intervention of bureaucratic power into civil society. But is this sufficient evidence to assert that the principle of bureaucracy represents an essentially capitalist element? If we consider all of the features which the phenomenon of bureaucracy has assumed in the contemporary world — its complexity, its close relation to the increasing division of labour, etc. — we might be tempted to conclude that it is. But strictly speaking, we would have falsely construed the problem. Because we would have taken it for granted that it is the *totality* of the features of bureaucracy which enters into contradiction with the democratic principle. If, on the contrary, we were to discover that it is only *one* of the theoretical determinations of the concept of bureaucracy which contradicts the principle of democracy, then a twofold alternative is presented: either this particular determination is specific to capitalism, in which case Cerroni's point of view would still be valid, or else the said determination is not specific to capitalism, in which case it would not be possible to derive from capitalism as such the *emergence* of the contradiction, even when it might be accepted that only capitalism creates the historical conditions for its full development.

Let us look at the point in some detail. Why should there be a contradiction between 'the delegation of sovereignty to a political élite', and 'formal recognition of the equality and the political rights of each individual'? The contradiction is not inherent in the concept of representation as such, since it does not follow logically that any kind of representation leads necessarily to the bureaucratisation of power. The only thing which can be affirmed is that the principle of representation opens up the *possibility* of the bureaucratisation of power. But one must avoid confusing the possibility of such a development with the development itself. Could it, then, be said that the contradiction consists of the actual separation between political power and civil society? But in such a case, there would be no contradiction; we are dealing, simply, with a form of organisation of society which would only be contradictory if either a) it can be demonstrated that there exists a contradiction between these two concepts — but there is nothing in the concept of civil society which is contradictory towards the concept of political power; or b) some anthropological assumption is introduced — such as the notion that the essence of Man is Freedom; but this is the kind of approach which Cerroni, rightly, rejects. So if we must accept that the representative State does not give rise to the contradiction of democracy versus bureaucracy, but only to its possibility, then we must also conclude as a result that the emergence of the contradiction does not take place at the level of the juridical system, but rather, outside it; it is the contradiction between the real, extra-juridical phenomenon of bureaucracy, and the juridical postulate of citizenship. This becomes yet more clear if we consider that Marx's analyses in his *Critique of Hegel's Philosophy of Law* concerning the principle of representation — which are the analyses upon which Cerroni, ultimately, bases his case — do not locate the contradiction at the level of the mere analysis of juridical forms, but instead outside of them. As Zolo states,

The oppositional couple of 'political State' and 'real State' thus expresses, in the theoretical-political syntax of the young Marx, the fundamental theoretical contradiction between the (constitutional) form and the (popular) content of the modern representative State, establishing, as opposed to Hegel, a meta-juridical notion of 'the people' which is not open to formalisation, an original totality and an inalienable sovereignty. . . .[12]

Yet a contradiction in which only one of the poles is juridical may be a political contradiction, but obviously it cannot be a juridical contradiction. Several consequences flow from this conclusion.

If the original approach consisted of affirming that capitalism generated political, and not solely economic contradictions, this was because the social atomisation peculiar to capitalism required, as a necessary political form, the representative State, and because the democracy/bureaucracy contradiction was inherent to this State. The capitalist character of the State determined the capitalist character of the contradiction. If we have now established that the political contradiction operates *outside* the juridical forms of the State, that it is a contradiciton *between* the actual existence of the bureaucracy and the juridical system, then it follows that the capitalist character imputed to the contradiction must be suspended.

In this way we have mapped out our task in a twofold sense: (a) we have determined the location of the political contradiction which we have to analyse; and (b) we have determined which feature of the bureaucracy we must isolate in order to determine the character, capitalist or otherwise, of the political contradiction: namely, that which makes bureaucracy contradictory to the juridical principle of citizenship. That is, we have to separate out from the phenomenon of modern bureaucracy all that we know about it — its rationalising character, its connection with the increasing division of labour, etc. — and then concentrate our attention on that feature which causes it to contradict citizenship. The answer here is clear: bureaucracy contradicts the notions of equality and political participation, which are implicit in the idea of citizenship, in that it monopolises political power and imposes its decisions coercively upon the rest of the community. But if the sole content of this contradiction is given by the fact that it constitutes bureaucracy as a coercive institution, then we are not dealing with a contradiction which logically and necessarily implies capitalism, but instead with a contradiction which postulates as one of its poles, purely and simply, the general form of the State, understood as the general principle of domination.[13] Thus we arrive at a decisive point in our consideration of the Della Volpean theory of the State, since this theory is based to a large extent on the assertion that there does not exist a general form of the State, and that every *political* contradiction present in capitalism has to be a contradiction inherent to the representative bourgeois State and not to the State and law in general. Della Volpe, following his method of the 'determinate abstraction', rejects as indeterminate and ahistoric any proposition concerning the State in general, and in particular the attempts by Engels to construct a genetics of the State form, based on the principle of the class struggle. This is also the error which Cerroni finds in Lenin, when the latter, in his youthful polemic with Peter Struve, sustained that what characterises the State is not the organisation of order, but rather the concentration of power in the hands of a special category of persons. Cerroni asserts:

> ... Here, the differentiating characteristic of State force is that of being a force *separate* from society (from production and its trades): therefore a *socially caused force,* a separate coercive power, which is postulated by the atomisation and the disaggregation of society. But in fact Lenin uses this intuition only to reaffirm, with Engels, that such a separation is characteristic of *all* historical types of State. And also, like Engels, he does not realise that there are types of political organisation in which coercive power is not separated from economic power (from property), nor that the modern separation involves not only 'special detachments' of armed men, but also the entire body politic, and likewise the representative State, which, through political representation (the delegation of power through elections) *separates itself from and unites itself to* the world of 'productive activity' ...[14]

Here, however, Cerroni's interpretation is clearly erroneous. It is simply not certain that Lenin's 'intuition' — supposing that we do accept such a term for his simple and elementary affirmation — implies the supposition of the atomisation and disaggregation which is peculiar to capitalist society. Lenin simply affirmed that it was wrong to identify the State with the organisation of order in a society, given that in order for there to be a State, coercive power has to be concentrated in a certain fraction of the society. And for this to happen, consequently, it is not necessary that there be a separation between political power and economic power. It is clear that for Lenin, the abolition of the State under communism does not consist solely of the abolition of the specifically socialist State which superseded the bourgeois State, but rather of the abolition of the general State form. This point illustrates one of the methodological and epistemological limitations of the Della Volpean school, whose insistence on the need to eliminate 'indeterminate abstractions' from Marxist discourse leads it to confuse the concretisation of the abstract which is characteristic of metaphysical thought — and which, as such, ought to be avoided — with the theoretical construction of the object, which demands a respect for the levels of abstraction appropriate to the various stages of analysis, and the consequent assignation of the various determinations of the said object to each of these levels. The result has been an empiricist approach, which assigns exclusively to the most concrete level of the object, the totality of its theoretical determinations. It is thus that the mere *presence* of some contradictions in capitalism has been considered sufficient evidence to impute to them a capitalist characterisation. The position of Engels and Lenin seems, then, to be more justified than that of Della Volpe and Cerroni.

By this I do not, of course, mean that I am adhering *tout court* to the Engelsian conception of the State. This conception seems to be wrapped-up in a positivist and evolutionist theorisation with which I am far from coinciding. And it is indeed true that Engels hypostasised in his analysis numerous 'indeterminate abstractions'. However, his very preoccupation with establishing a genetics of the *State* form made him sensitive to a number of phenomena which are absent from Marx's analyses, and especially from those of the mature Marx. In another essay,[15] I have made reference, for example, to one of Engels' texts from *The Peasant Wars in Germany*, which is perhaps one of the rare moments of the Marxist tradition in which the theme of the general form of the State emerges clearly. In fact, in his endeavour to account for the rise of a communist ideology in the Munzer rebellion, Engels is obliged not only to leave class analysis to one side, but indeed to make this exclusion the actual explanatory principle of the emergence of such an ideology. It is precisely the marginal character of the rural masses who followed Munzer, marginal even with respect to the dominant relations of production, which explains how the negation of the State is not centred on the negation of a specific class State, but on the State form as such: that is, the general principle of domination. Engels is quite explicit about this:

. . . they had neither privileges nor property: they not even had the kind of property the peasant or the petty burgher had, weighed down as it was with burdensome taxes. They were unpropertied and rightless in every respect; their living conditions never even brought them into direct contact with the existing institutions, which ignored them completely . . . *This explains why the plebeian opposition even then could not stop at fighting feudalism and the privileged burghers . . ., why, an absolutely propertyless faction, it questioned the institutions, views and conceptions common to all societies based on class antagonisms' . . ..*[16] (my italics)

As we see, the general form of the State can, in certain cases, constitute a determinate abstraction. Engels' conception contains, however, apart from this exceptional insight, two drawbacks. The first is that the notion of the general form of the State, understood as the principle of coercion in general, demands a break with a merely institutionalist conception of the State, based on a distinction between the public and the private — a break which Engels at no time makes. The second is that the marginality, and indeed the exceptional character, of the Munzerite rebels would seem to exclude, for Engels, the possibility that social agents constituted as a class could engage the State in the kind of non-class antagonism which we have just described. Consequently, if we wish to maintain the coherence of our approach, and to assert that the general form of the State is — not only in marginal cases, but in every historical situation — a determinate abstraction, we will have to show that social agents constituted as classes also take part in a kind of antagonism different from that which arises between classes, and one of whose poles is the State as the abstract principle of domination. We shall return to this point presently.

However, there is one basic objection which could be put to us: that up until this point, we have proved that the State pole of the democracy/bureaucracy contradiction does not have to presuppose the capitalist State, but that so far we have accepted the other pole of the contradiction in its capitalist form (accepting, for the time being, that the juridical form of the citizen is an inherently bourgeois category). And this objection would, of course, be valid, for if it is demonstrated that the democratic pole of the contradiction, the juridical form of the citizen *as it arises from law under capitalism*, is essential for the emergence of the contradiction — then one must draw the conclusion that this type of contradiction could only emerge in a capitalist State. Our distinction between the general form of domination and the specific form of the capitalist state would thus be bereft of all relevance. If, on the other hand, we were to apply to the case of democracy the same method which we have used in that of bureaucracy, and we were to discover that that which enters into contradiction with the bureaucratic principle is not the set of features which constitute citizenship as such in bourgeois legality, but is instead a simple general form, one which is present within that legality but which cannot be reduced to it, we would have proved the validity of our thesis.

One step which must be taken at the outset is to discard the *merely* juridical character of citizenship. Because if we were concerned with a contradiction between the increasing bureaucratisation of the State, opposed to certain juridical forms, we would have no *political* contradiction (that is, one between antagonistic social forces), and the contradiction would be resolved through the obsolescence of these juridical forms and their more or less rapid supplanting. If, alternatively, the political contradiction does exist, it is because citizenship is more than a mere juridical form; it is an *ideology* which is shared by the social subjects who are threatened by the growing bureaucratisation. Where, then, within what we have defined as the democratic ideology, can we locate the element which is contradictory towards bureaucracy? Clearly not in the set of juridical norms which govern the exercise of citizenship, since it is precisely these norms which make way, through the principle of representation, for the phenomenon of bureaucracy. What is in contradiction to the principle of bureaucracy is the specifically ideological element of the juridical norm, that is, the *juridical ideal of the citizen*. And not all the aspects of this juridical ideal, but only those which do effectively contradict the bureaucratic principle. But, as we have seen, the contradictory element within the bureaucratic pole was the general form of domination, the externality and the abstract coercion which is inherent to this form. Consequently, if the democratic pole is to be established on this same level of abstraction, and ought not to include more elements than those which define the contradiction, then democracy can only consist of the elimination of external coercion and the exercise of direct power on the part of the actual social subject. And so the question arises: who is this subject? This is the key point. In order to answer the question, we must first pose two problems: a) what do we understand by *subject*, and b) what are the conditions of a valid response?

a) It is necessary to be quite clear as to what we mean by 'subject'. 'Subject' must not be taken to mean a physically existing social agent, but rather one of the objective principles of the identity of such an agent. In this sense, social subjects belong to the sphere of ideology. Ideology consists, precisely, of a practice which produces subjects. As shown by Althusser[17], the specific mechanism of this practice is interpellation. I will not develop this point at length, since I have dealt with it in an earlier work, to which I would refer.[18] In this sense, 'citizen' is not the name of the agent — which, like all names, would refer to the whole set of the agent's features and not only to one — but is an interpellative structure. Likewise, 'man' in general is, as a characterisation of the agent, an indeterminate abstraction in Della Volpe's sense — and is therefore illegitimate — but it is clearly a determinate and effective abstraction when seen as an interpellation which, in certain social formations, can provide the social agent with a subjective principle of identity. Moreover, social agents respond to many interpellations which maintain a coherence in relation to each other; thus, every social agent is possessed of a subjectivity which is multiple rather than unique. It should be clear, therefore, that when we allude, at later points in the text, to the emergence of the 'subject', we do not refer to the social agent, but rather to some of the interpellations which constitute the agent as subject.

b) We have to establish, before answering our question, the conditions for a valid response. The first is that the democratic subject must exist on the same level of abstraction as the opposite pole of the contradiction. It would not make sense, for example, to say that the worker or the capitalist *as such* were in contradiction to the general form of the State. The second condition is that in the contradiction between the subject and the State, it must be *exclusively* the general form of domination which creates the contradiction, and not its specific form. In this sense a class contradiction, even when it presupposes forms of coercion on the part of the dominant class, is not a contradiction which presupposes a democratic subject, since it arises at the level of the specificity of a determinate mode of production. The third and final condition is that we must be able to show not only *what* is the subject which is antagonistic towards the general form of domination, but also *how* the contradiction arises.

One kind of response has been of the anthropological type. The bearer of the democratic principle in general could only be Man, as such, and given that his essence is liberty, it is clear that the existence of political society must necessarily constitute a form of alienation. This is the solution adopted by 'humanist' Marxism. But within it, the 'general democratic subject' has ceased to be an ideological subject, and has come to mean the essence of concrete individuals. The Della Volpean school, on the contrary, rejects this kind of perspective and refuses to accept the existence of a general human subject; but this leads it, as a result, to deny the existence, as a determinate abstraction, of the general form of domination. Hence the bureaucracy/democracy contradiction must necessarily, for Cerroni, be a contradiction of a concrete type of society. If, then, we wish to insist that the State pole of the bureaucracy/democracy contradiction is the general form of domination, and not just the capitalist State; and if, at the same time, we wish to insist that the democratic pole of the contradiction is not 'man' in general, then the only way to argue it — without falling into an idealist approach — would be to demonstrate a) that the contradiction which leads to the emergence of the general form of domination is inscribed in reality itself (that is, it is the ensemble of social antagonisms, and foremost, class struggle, which creates the autonomy of the general form); and b) that the democratic subject which arises from this antagonism towards the State has been produced by the contradiction itself (for if its existence were found to date from before the contradiction, and thus not to have been generated by it, it would not be possible to avoid falling into an anthropological dogmatism).

Let us resolve, first of all, the problem of the democratic subject: if the general form of domination consists of coercion in general, and if, as we have said, the democratic subject must be constituted at the same level of abstraction as the State pole, it is clear that the subject can only consist of the abstract principle of self-determination. Note that we do not refer to the self-determination of the individual as such, since this would imply acceptance of the view that the individual must be considered as a significant unit having certain rights with respect to the community, which would mean already to suppose a determinate type of community. The community, in such a sense, is an instance more abstract than the individual. The abstract principle of the self-determination of the community is, consequently, the content of democratic interpellation. Well, why should we accept the existence of this principle of the self-determination of the community? Is this not a way of postulating, in a normative form, the natural rights of communities to self-determination, and thus falling for the anthropological approach that we tried to avoid? If we study the problem in more detail, we will see that this is not the case; because the contradiction is not established between the physically existing social agent — the 'individual' or 'man' — and the State, but instead between the ideological subject in the interpellative instance, and the State. If the State were to dispossess the peasants of their lands, the ensuing conflict would not arise as a result of the State having violated a supposed natural right of the peasant communities to the ownership of the lands, but rather from the contradiction between the State's coercion and the ensemble of specific interpellations which constitute the peasant as an ideological subject. In the same way, if a 'citizen' of a liberal democracy is stripped of his civil rights, the contradiction is established between the State and the 'citizen' as an ideological subject, and not between the State and the physically existing social agent (or, to put it another way, the contradiction is established with the social agent as the bearer of an ideological structure which constitutes him as a subject). It is, therefore, possible to accept the abstract principle of communitary self-determination without having to postulate any immutable human essence. This becomes clearer still if one bears in mind that the principle of communitary self-determination does not imply any preconception as to the type of community in question. Within the said community there might exist several different forms of personal subjection, but to the extent that these form part of the system of interpellations which constitute the social agents as subjects, and to the extent that the subjects experience their subjection not as an antagonism but as a definitive part of what they are, their submission will not be perceived as an external imposition and no contradiction will exist. On the other hand, any 'external' coercion which is exercised, even though it might be less offensive to our Western canons of human rights than 'internal' subjection, will enter into contradiction with the community's ideological subjects and will give rise to a democratic contradiction.

It still remains for us to demonstrate that the democratic subject is created by the very contradiction which involves the general form of domination, and that it does not precede the latter. It would seem that the democratic subject, insofar as it expresses the principle of the self-determination of the community, exists prior to the contradiction, since the community upon which coercion is exercised must have pre-existed it. That the community should have to exist before the coercion, is obvious. In this sense, democracy is the defence of what one *already* is. Hence the utopian, nostalgic features which democratic ideology generally involves: the simplicity of community life, lost or threatened; and, when — as in the case of the Enlightenment — an effort is being made to lay down the bases of a democratic future, the myth of human nature: it is no longer a matter of defending a state of affairs which is threatened, but one of restoring man to what he essentially is. Myths of the State having arisen as the result of an original sin, and the consequent fall of humanity, clearly express this nostalgic element in democracy. But, on the other hand, the democratic subject can only arise as a result of the contradiction between the communitary principle and the principle of coercion; because the community expresses itself as a totality through the democratic subject, in terms of the general principle of self-determination. And this presence of the community as a whole can only occur to the extent that it is specifically negated. We can affirm, with Hegel, that to be conscious of something as a totality means to be aware of its limits; and to be aware of its limits means to be conscious of what lies beyond them. In this sense, the consciousness of self-determination *as such* requires an awareness of coercion. Democracy only exists as an affirmation in front of that which negates it. Without external coercion, the ensemble of interpellations which constitute the social agents as subjects would, of course, continue to exist, but there would be no democratic subject able to bring out the community as a general form, through the principle of self-determination.

From what we have said up to this point, it should be clear that the democracy/bureaucracy contradiction does not belong to the essence of capitalism, but should be considered independently of it. A separate problem, though, is the fact that the full development of this contradiction requires conditions that are only present under capitalism, a point which is worth dwelling upon for a moment. One of these conditions is that the State, which holds the monopoly of power in a society, has to present itself as an instance separate from the latter. This is the aspect upon which the greater part of the analyses have insisted. But that, as far as we can see, does not mean that this is an inherently capitalist contradiction. Any system of oppression which is imposed coercively upon a community, and which violates the interpellative structures which constitute the social subjects, will generate the democratic contradiction in question. Hence the predominantly democratic character of the ideologies which, in the third world, have fought the imposition of the State form by the imperialist powers. On the other hand, however, the full development of the democratic contradiction supposes the progressive penetration of the State into areas where social life had traditionally been outside its domain. This has taken place in mature capitalism, especially since the period of the transformation of the State subsequent to the 1930s crisis, with the appearance of the interventionist State, which has indeed penetrated more and more into areas which has previously escaped State regulation. This has led to a politicisation of political conflicts, and to a generalisation of democratic struggles which surpass the limits and the channelling capabilities of the system of parliamentary representation.

If we insist so much on the non-capitalist character of the democratic contradiction, despite the fact that its full development can only take place in capitalist society, it is basically for two reasons: a) because the characterisation of this contradiction as capitalist tends to render inexplicable the type of democratic struggle which is characteristic of the colonial and semicolonial countries, where there has been a generalisation of the State form as a by-product of colonialism, and where, nevertheless, the capitalist mode of production is not dominant; and b) because political errors might flow from the idea that democracy tends spontaneously towards socialism, and socialism towards democracy, and that consequently we should await the unification of the two as a natural process which might begin at either of the two extremes, and which would not call for a conscious effort at unifying them. And above all, it eliminates the fundamental question of political analysis: namely, that of the conditions in which such an articulation becomes possible. From what we have said so far, it is evident that there is no necessary relation between the socialisation of political power and the abolition of private property in the means of production. It is true that the latter is a necessary condition of possibility of the former, but the inverse is not certain. That state ownership of the means of production does not lead to a spontaneous tendency towards the socialisation of political power, is something of which the regimes of Eastern Europe offer only too much evidence to remind us. (Please note that we are not saying that the democratisation of these regimes is impossible, but rather that it has to be the result of an independent and antagonistic struggle against the State, and not the result of a spontaneous tendency of the State to eliminate itself.)

II

We have established, then, that Cerroni's argument (that the political contradiction which he analyses is a specifically capitalist contradiction) does not meet the conditions of validity which we detailed at the beginning. On the one hand, it is not possible to show that the concept of capitalism is a logically necessary condition for the emergence of the political contradiction. On the other hand, it is clear that the supposed relationship of double implication between the socialisation of the economy and the socialisation of power does not obtain, since the former does not imply the latter. So this leaves us with two contradictions, one of which is specifically capitalist, while the other finds in capitalism only the historical conditions for its full development. This, consequently, obliges us to pose the problem of the type of articulation which exists between the two.

Let us begin by pointing out that the tendency which is logically implicit in democracy, towards the elimination of the State as an antagonistic force, although it supposes communism, does not tend spontaneously towards the latter, for the simple reason that there is nothing inherent in democracy which leads it to the logical development of the contradiction one of whose poles it represents. There are various reasons for this. In the first place, it is because democracy negates the State as an abstract coercive force, as the general form of oppression. However, this State is not only its general form, but is always a concrete State which responds to a class logic. To put it in scholastic terms, democracy negates the State in its existence, not in its specific essence. This is why, when democratic ideological subjects are not articulated to class subjects — that is, to forces which establish a contradiction to the very essence of a specific State — they tend to express their resistance by way of abstract negations of oppression, from the uprisings of the nineteenth century to May 1968 in Paris, and not in terms of a long-term strategy which takes advantage of the contradictions in the system. In this sense, democracy, if left to its own devices, is subversive but not revolutionary. Bobbio has expressed this clearly:

'It is not a peaceful relationship, because democracy is subversive. And it is subversive in the most radical sense of the word, because, wherever it arrives, it subverts the traditional conception of power, so traditional that it has come to be considered natural, according to which power — be it political or economic power, paternal or priestly power — descends from above to below. Much more subversive, in a certain sense, than socialism itself, if socialism is understood in the restrictive sense in which it is still often understood, as meaning the transfer of ownership of the means of production from private hands to the State, which, again, is the institution of a form of power which descends from above. So subversive is democracy that, if it were to be realised to its fullest Rousseauian extent, then *this* and not the hypothetical classless society would spell the end of the State, society without a State (because the State, any State which has existed up to now, has never been able to do anything otherwise than through downward relations of power). . .."[19]

There is, however, another reason why democracy does not tend towards the logical resolution of its contradiction. We should consider, in this respect, the specific dialectic which exists between the general form of domination and the content with which this form is identified. The general form of domination must be expressed, like the general form of value, in a content which can be differentiated from the form. These concrete contents operate as symbols of the oppressive power. But, it should be recalled, not as symbols of the 'essence' of this oppressive power — in which case they would be symbols of a specific form of the State — but rather of its 'existence', of the very fact of its antagonistic presence. And, in turn, the democratic subject which arises as an antagonistic pole of this contradiction, as the expression of the negated community, must also find expression through symbols which can be differentiated from itself. And once again, the democratic subject symbolises this community in terms of 'existence', not of 'essence'. But this marks the introduction of an ambiguity on the level of the matter through which these subjects find expression, because this matter represents, on the one hand, its literal meaning, and on the other hand, symbolises the totality. Just as precious metals, on the one hand, have use values, and on the other hand, represent value in the form of money, so the symbols which represent the dominated community and the oppressor power represent, in turn, for the democratic subject, their literal contents and the respective communities as existing wholes. But this means that these symbols will become all the more democratic, the more that they are stripped of the function of representing their literal contents, and the more that their literal contents have become symbols of the totality. With this distinction in mind, we may come back to our problem of the spontaneous tendency of democracy towards the logical resolution of its contradiction. We must ask ourselves: (1) what is the general pattern of this logical resolution; and (2) what are the historic conditions that would make it possible.

With respect to the first problem, we have already given the basic elements of a response. The logical resolution of the contradiction means the suppression of the general form of domination, that is, of the State as such. Since we know that the contradiction exists at the level of ideology, this supposes that that the subjects *recognise* in the democratic symbols the explicit negation which they represent. In the case of a colonial power, for example, they must be aware that such symbols negate, in colonialism, the general, abstract principle of domination — of all kinds of oppression — and not just one specific form of oppression. (It might be argued: but in the case of colonialism, the contradiction is established directly with imperialism, and not with the abstract principle of domination! However, if we look more closely at the case we will see that this is not so. Note that we are not posing the problem of the historical genesis of the contradiction. A genetic explanation could establish the set of circumstances which made the emergence of a contradiction historically possbile, but it would not be able to *explain* the contradiction as such. We know that the accumulation of capital leads to imperialist exploitation, and that imperialist exploitation leads to an antagonism with the people colonised. But still, this set of historical circumstances — accumulation of capital, imperialism, etc. — cannot explain to us why imperialism meets with the resistance of the people colonised. Any merely genetic discourse eventually reaches a point where meta-empirical assumptions are introduced — such as the idea that it is natural for every man to resist oppression, etc. — in order to build up a background which will lend coherence to the sequence of the argument. If we attempt, then, to isolate the strictly contradictory elements in this confrontation between historical subjects, we must necessarily refer back to our earlier argument: imperialism is only contradictory towards the colonised community insofar as it constitutes a coercive force. That is, in the conceptualisation of the strictly antagonistic element, imperialism intervenes only as the bearer of the principle of domination. On the other hand, as far as the colonised community is concerned, we have to separate out all that we know about it and concentrate on the single feature which actually contradicts the principle of domination: and this can only be the abstract principle of the self-determination of the community. But since neither of these principles has a *direct form* of expression, both must find it through a form which can be differentiated from the principles themselves: and this is where the dual function of the democratic symbol and the symbol of domination, referred to above, has its origins.)

We have said, then, that the condition for the logical resolution of the democratic contradiction consists in the democratic subject's being able to recognise, in the democratic symbols, the implicit negation which they convey. But this demands that the symbolic meaning of these contents, through which the form of coercion and the form of self-determination finds expression, must become more and more autonomous vis-á-vis their literal meaning. And this, in turn, requires the generalisation of the various conflicts involving the general form of the State. It is only when these conflicts are multiplied, and when it is perceived that the various 'significant use values' through which the oppression is identified in each case, are actually expressing something similar, will the general form of domination assume its autonomy; and only then will we see the emergence of the various social subjects able to carry the democratic contradiction to its logical conclusion. But this, in turn, supposes that the mutual connection between the democratic symbols be articulated in the form of a general subject symbolising the moment of the articulation itself (otherwise, each democratic symbol would appear atomised, with reference to the specific content symbolising oppression in that particular area, and thus the social agents would be unable to recognise that, through each of those specific contents, some general equivalent is expressed). Thus we have established the general pattern of the logical resolution of the democracy/ State contradiction: the formation of a general democratic equivalent.

We should now examine the second problem: that of which conditions would make possible the logical resolution of the contradiction. We can observe, in this respect, that there is nothing which leads democratic symbols *spontaneously* to establish relationships amongst themselves such as would permit the emergence of the general equivalent. The democratic symbols of the anti-imperialist struggle in a dominated country, for example, do not tend towards the spontaneous establishment of a relationship of equivalence with the struggle for women's liberation. If such a relationship is established, it must originate from outside the democratic subjects themselves; it must originate from those forces whose antagonism is established not at the level of the 'existence' but at that of the 'essence' of a particular system of domination, and which, therefore, establish the basic articulations which define an ideological field: that is, from social classes. Consider the case of a class which is in contradiction to a specific system of domination, but whose interests do not lead it to favour the suppression of the State. This class will speak the language of democracy, it will interpellate democratic subjects, but it will endeavour to prevent the implicit contradiction with the general form of domination from being recognised as such. That is, it will attempt both to develop the antagonism which is implicit in democratic interpellations, and to limit it to certain areas. The form in which this is done consists of preventing the development of the democratic equivalent, that is, *making the literal content of the democratic symbol become the source of its symbolic value*. It is akin to seeking, in the specific nature of gold and silver, the origin of the money form. In our previous example of the colonial country, for instance, the confrontation with the foreign power takes place through a daily and antagonistic witnessing of the differences: different dress, different customs, racial differences, and so on. Each of these elements taken separately symbolises domination, in that each alludes to it as a totality which is not given by the mere literal meaning of the sign. The use of the symbol of 'racial difference', for example, by the dominated community in order to establish its own identity, does not prove a racist position, given that here race intervenes in political discourse in its symbolic function as an allusion to domination, and not just as its specific literal content. But if the native conservative classes of the colony were to try to bring about a democratic mobilisation aimed at attaining independence, what they would attempt is to weld the antagonism to its literal content in such a way that one becomes indistinguishable from the other. Race ceases to be a symbolic form alluding to domination, and instead becomes the very stuff of the conflict. Nationalism as a democratic ideology has given way to nationalism as a xenophobic expression. Consider the involution of many third world countries, where, in the period after independence, the conservative classes have tended to establish their hegemony over the popular masses which had been mobilised for the anti-imperialist struggle, and where democratic nationalism threatened to create a system of democratic equivalents linking up with other democratic internal conflicts: in these cases, it will be seen that the ideological transformation which we have described has been used as a blackmail, and a form of ideological terrorism, by the bureaucracies which had established their dominion.

In the case of the central countries, the establishment of a system of democratic equivalents is made difficult by other factors. Here, the democratic contradictions are many, and tend to find diverse forms of expression: regional conflicts with the central State, the subjection of particular groups of the population, struggles within the institutions, in the universities, in the schools, the struggle for the liberation of women, etc. The efforts of the dominant classes, then, are not directed towards neutralising a single democratic interpellation, but rather towards preventing, by way of the sectoralisation of these conflicts, the emergence of a system of democratic equivalents between the various sectors. If the working class, on the contrary, is to impose itself as the hegemonic class, it must do so through developing the potential of opposition to the State which is inherent in these antagonisms.[20] And this means, as we have said, that national minorities, students, women, etc., should be able to recognise behind the various forms which oppress them, the fundamental enemy which constitutes the common denominator of all such forms: the State. But the State is not only the general form of domination; it is also a specific form: it is a *capitalist* State. To combat it means carrying the struggle onto the level of the fundamental antagonism which reproduces it. Conflict at the level of the general form might give rise to outbursts of violence — even of national proportions, such as in May 1968 in France — but not to a long-term struggle for hegemony, a war of position, as Gramsci would call it. Hence, the struggle for democratisation — that is, for the socialisation of power — if it is to hold out any prospect of success, must link itself to the struggle for the socialisation of the means of production. Herein we see the only possible sense in which the socialisation of power and the socialisation of the economy mutually require each other: the socialisation of power requires, obviously, the socialisation of the economy, and the struggle against capitalism, taking place as it does in a context dominated by the democratic struggle against the State, can only hope for success if waged as a democratic and popular struggle. But this demands the analysis of an historical conjuncture which might create the *possibility* of an increasing convergence and fusion between these two contradictions, and this is something very different from saying that unity between the two exists already by definition, on the grounds that both pertain to the essence of capitalism. If this is so, it means that the fusion between democracy and socialism must begin already, in the context of capitalism, and not wait for the socialisation of the economy to lead, of itself, to the socialisation of power.

This said, we can now pass on to our position regarding the problem of the relationship between Rousseau and the young Marx. It is true, as Della Volpe and Colletti have affirmed, that in Rousseau's work we can find a formulation of the funda-mental contradiction of modern representative democracy, between the principle of the self-determination of the citizen and the bureaucratic principle of representation. But the great merit of Rousseau is that he situated this contradiction where it really lies — seeing it not as a contradiction between capitalist democracy and the bourgeois representative State, but as a contradiction between the democratic principle and the gen-eral form of domination. This identifies Rousseau as a theorist of radical democracy, rather than a forerunner of socialism. And what of the young Marx? Colletti affirms, as we have seen, that Marx's political theory, almost in its totality, is contained in Rousseau — and that he, together with Engels and Lenin, adds only the analysis of the economic bases of the withering-away of the State. This — especially in the case of the young

Marx — is precisely true, except that neither is this a question of a specifically socialist theory, but instead of a general theory of democracy, built up according to the Rousseauian pattern. Marx founds his theory upon an anthropological premise: Man is the subject of history, and the transition to a new society consists of the process of his disalienation. And the Althusserian critique of the young Marx is based exclusively on his humanist character, without recognising that here, too, is contained a specific political theory regarding the democracy/bureaucracy contradiction; and that this theory, stripped of the humanist clothing in which it is wrapped, forms a basic foundation for the construction of a Marxist political theory.

It has been necessary to embark upon this lengthy discussion concerning the specific theoretical status of democracy, because this leads us to the heart of the difficulties which have impeded the formation of a mature and coherent Marxist theory of the State. These difficulties might be summed-up by the following problem: that the characteristic, and widely noted, ambiguity in Marx's work taken as a whole, is not only the result of an epistemological break between the ideological thought of his youth and the scientific thought of his maturity, but also of the way that the former offers us a theory of the democracy/State contradiction which is not a specifically capitalist contradiction, whereas the latter offers an analysis of the contradiction which is constitutive of the capitalist mode of production. This twofold ambiguity — or this double break, if one prefers to see it in that way — has given rise to three systems of premises, from which there have arisen three types of Marxist approximation of the problem of the State.

1 Those who have taken up the anthropological problem of Marx's youth have tried, at the same time, to make an analysis of the political contradiction *specific* to capitalism, with all the subjectivist, voluntarist or liberal deviations which are the natural consequences of such an approach. In fact, on the basis of this kind of perspective, the emphasis will be centred on *human* alienation, both economic and political. However, reification is not an exclusively capitalist effect, insofar as it is a tendency implicit in every commodity-producing society: although only under capitalism do the conditions obtain which permit its full development. The contradiction with the general

form of dominantion, on the other hand, although it too develops to its fullest extent under capitalism, is likewise not a determination specific to the latter. As a result, all that which is specific to capitalism is missing, in this perspective, from the analysis of capitalist society. The theory thus ends up expressing its criticism of the penetration of the State — and let us be clear that the reference is to the general form of domination — into capitalist society, from the viewpoint of a radical democratism, and the class point of view tends progressively to be abandoned. One is reminded of the evolution which leads from Lukacs to Marcuse.

2 But, on the other hand, those who have taken up the scientific problematic of the mature Marx, tend to abandon the analysis of the democratic contradiction, together with its anthropological wrapping, found in the works of the young Marx. The result is that efforts are made to construct a political theory based exclusively on class contradicitons. This gives rise to some currents which fall for a vulgar form of economism (the Capital Logic school); and to others, such as Althusserianism, which, as we said at the outset, formally introduced the principle of overdetermination, but end up studying class antagonisms alone; and even to theories which are based on the mere coexistence of forms of State and types of economy (D. Zolo).

3 Finally, Della Volpeanism represented a moment of balance between these two opposed perspectives. Its merit is that it has not limited itself to the analysis of only one of the contradictions, nor reduced one to the other, but has presented them instead as *parallel* contradictions, each with its own specificity. In this sense the Della Volpean school — and Cerroni in particular — has produced some of the most intelligent and profound analyses to date concerning the dialectical relation between socialism and democracy. Nevertheless, as we have seen, by presenting both contradictions as specifically capitalist, these theorists have been caught up in a series of paradoxes and difficulties, and have tended to simplify the problem by taking socialism and democracy to be articulated in a relationship of mutual implication, thus denying the need to conduct a political struggle to articulate them in a determinate historical conjuncture.

III

From our analysis hitherto, it follows clearly that the development of the antagonisms whose dominant pole is constituted by the general form of domination is inscribed in reality itself, and that consequently this general form is not an indeterminate abstraction in the Della Volpean sense. It also follows that the same social agents who are constituted by this antagonism as democratic subjects, can also be constituted as class subjects on the basis of the antagonism which is inherent to the relations of production. In this sense Engels' analyses, according to which the marginality of the Munzerite plebeans with respect to any class position was the source of their antagonism towards the general form of oppression, demand that we draw a basic distinction. If the historical fact of this marginality is seen as an *analytical advantage*, which allows us to perceive in its pure form the emergence of a popular-democratic ideology, then the approach will be justified; it would be erroneous, on the other hand, to consider this historical fact as the necessary condition for the emergence of any popular-democratic ideology, given that social agents who are constituted as classes on the level of the relations of production also form part of the 'people', and, on the level of the relations of domination, are also constituted as democratic subjects. Only a crudely reductionist perspective, which saw class contradictions as the origin of all the determinations of the social agent, would see any incompatibility in this twofold subjective determination of the agent.

A further conclusion which follows from our analysis is that the articulation between democracy, the representative State, capitalism and socialism, is rather more complex than the habitual tendency to establish necessary relations of implication or opposition between these concepts at the definitional level might have led us to suppose. Let us look at this in detail.

1 Let us consider the relationship between democracy and the representative State, first of all. Democracy does not by definition have to express itself through the representative State and the juridical form of citizenship. If by 'democracy' we are to understand, as we have previously proposed, the abstract principle of communitary self-determination, we should note

that there is nothing in the latter which would require citizenship as a necessary form. In order for the latter to arise with a democratic character, the general form of domination has to manifest itself as the explicit negation of the rights of the *individual*, but this supposes the existence of a particular type of community in which the social agents are interpellated as individuals. On the other hand, there is nothing to guarantee that the juridical form of citizenship, even when it is an interpellation which constitutes certain democratic ideological subjects, should be the only channel through which democratic subjects are constituted in a specific social formation. If the general form of domination manifests itself in contradiction with other communities — national, racial, or occupational minorities, etc. — then the democratic subjects which emerge from these contradictions will not be interpellated in terms of the general form of citizenship. Moreover, in a social formation in which the interpellation of social subjects as individuals has reached significant proportions — i.e. when social agents recognise themselves as holding certain individual rights — there is no reason to suppose that citizenship should not coincide with democratic ideological subjects. And to conclude, in a society upon which the liberal State has been superimposed, without being the product of the organic development of the particular community, citizenship will be a mere juridical form and will not constitute the specific interpellation of any democratic subject.

2 On the other hand, there is no necessary implication — on the definitional level — between democracy and socialism. It is true that there is a relationship of compatibility, in the sense that the final resolution of the democracy/bureaucracy contradiction is incompatible with a class society. But this does not mean, as we have already seen, that a socialist society — that is, a society in 'transition' to communism, which has abolished private ownership of the means of production — tends spontaneously towards the consummation of democracy. Nor does it mean that there exists any kind of necessary correspondence between democracy and capitalism: Bobbio errs on this point, in maintaining that until today, there has only existed a correspondence between democracy and capitalism, and that socialism has not in any sense been democratic.[21] The correspon-

dence suggested by Bobbio exists only to the extent that we refer to a very precise community of democratic ideological subjects: to those formed by the Western type of 'citizenship'. But if we refer to the democratic subjects of ideological communities characteristic of the peripheral world, we will observe that the contradiction which produces these subjects does not, at least in the first instance, involve the negation of citizenship.

3 Finally, nor is there a necessary relationship of correspondence between citizenship, or parliamentary forms, and capitalism. Here we touch upon a key point, one which has given rise to lengthy debates: are parliamentary forms essentially and necessarily bourgeois? Another problem ties in with this: is a parliamentary path to socialism possible? If by parliamentary forms we mean the Parliament as the kernel of the liberal regime, together with all the features which constitute such a regime, it is obvious that these could not possibly be other than capitalist forms. But here again, we are side-stepping the real problem, because we are postulating that parliamentary forms as such *necessarily suppose* the ensemble of ideological, institutional and political features which occur connotatively united to parliamentary forms in a bourgeois regime. But if we abandon such an aprioristic approach, and concentrate on the concept of parliamentary forms as such, we will find nothing in them which necessarily implies capitalism. It is obvious that parliamentary forms are not compatible with communism, insofar as they are representative forms, whereas communism is based on direct democracy and the abolition of the very principle of representation, but there is nothing in them which would make them incompatible with socialism. It should be noted that the argument that socialism implies the dictatorship of the proletariat, would not be a valid response; because, as emerges clearly from the Marxist texts, the hegemony of the proletariat is only 'dictatorship' to the extent that the State has not yet been suppressed, given that every State, *even the most democratic of republics*, is always a class dictatorship. And just as the dictatorship of the bourgeoisie can be effected through parliamentary forms, there is no reason to object in principle to the maintenance of parliamentary forms in a socialist State.

It might appear that with this merely logical analysis of Marxist categories, we debase them and rob them of their richness and their historical dimension. But I think that in fact the exact opposite is the case. Because by reducing these categories to what can logically be derived from them, one consequently widens the range of phenomena which it is necessary to explain historically. If we believe that between A, B and C there is an essential or definitional relationship, then nothing need be explained in historical terms. The presence of any one of these elements will necessarily imply the presence of the others. If, on the contrary, the logical analysis of each of these concepts were to show that there is no necessary relationship of implication between them, then the presence of the three together constitutes a *conjuncture*, which requires an historical explanation. *The increasing formalisation of the logical analysis of categories is, thus, the unavoidable precondition for a progressive historisation of our understanding of social reality.*

But there is another element which must be added to this. Semiology has shown us the extent to which current language *naturalises* purely connotative relationships between signifiers. And this naturalisation and atemporalisation of social relationships is not, of course, innocent: it represents the very process through which a class hegemony is imposed. The more that the dominated classes end up accepting the linkage between contents which the dominant discourse presents as necessary, the more complete the hegemony becomes. If, for example, the dominant discourse presents as essential the articulation between democracy, private property and liberalism, the dominated sectors eventually accept that between these three elements there is also a relationship of mutual implication. They conclude, then, by expressing their protest through the rejection of all three at the same time, thus illustrating their acceptance of the system of connotations through which bourgeois hegemony is constructed. This explains why the building of a socialist alternative has always had to begin by making the break with a vicious circle made up of two dimensions which form, strictly speaking, a closed system of alternatives: *social democracy* and *ultra-leftism*. In the case of the former, it is accepted that democracy is necessarily united to the system of connotations which articulate it to bourgeois discourse, and, because of the wish to be democratic, the discourse is accepted as a whole. In the latter case, the same acceptance is the point of departure, and, since one wishes to be revolutionary, one ends up rejecting democracy. Social democracy and ultra-leftism are symmetrical expressions of bourgeois hegemony. If, on the contrary, one aims to break this vicious circle and disarticulate the system of connotations in which bourgeois hegemony is based, a very different strategy is called for. It is obvious that it is the political mobilisation of the masses which disarticulates the discourse of domination. But the intellectual task which must accompany this mobilisation has to consist of showing that what has been presented as a natural and necessary correlation is no more than a set of connotative articulations resulting from an historical conjuncture. And the precondition for this historisation of our understanding of social reality is, as we have said, the logical analysis of the categories which make such an understanding possible.

IV

Let us conclude, then, by looking at the main phases in the development of Marxist thought in relation to the problem of the general form of domination.

1   In the period up to 1848, and, to a lesser extent, up to 1870, the theme of democracy had not disappeared from the concerns of Marxism. The reason is that the cycle opened up by the French Revolution had not yet fully closed, and the dominant classes had not identified themselves wholeheartedly with the bourgeois republic. As a result, the dominant classes had not totally absorbed liberalism, and neither had liberalism absorbed democracy. The non-ascribed, non-class character of democracy formed the intellectual and ideological climate in which the revolutionaries lived. Socialists were, still, the extreme left of democracy. This is still the era of the young Marx, and of 'permanent revolution'. The problem of the State is present, and the State is still its 'general form', i.e. indeterminate oppression.

2   The period from the foundation of the Second International up to the Russian Revolution and the advent of fascism, was marked, on the contrary, by the eclipse of the State as a theme

in politics. This is the era of the liberal State, during which democracy is progressively absorbed and neutralised by bourgois hegemony. Gramsci clearly noticed the change in the terms of the problem:

... The political concept of the so-called 'permanent revolution' arose before 1848, as the scientifically elaborated expression of the Jacobin experience from 1789 to Thermidor. The formula is characteristic of an historical period in which the great mass political parties and the great economic Trade Unions did not yet exist, and society was still, so to speak, in a state of flux in many respects. In the period subsequent to 1870, with European colonial expansion, all these elements change; the internal and international organ-isational relationships of the State become more complex and solid, and the 'forty-eightish' formula of 'permanent revolution' becomes elaborated and superseded in political science, with the formula of 'civil hegemony'. The same thing happens in political art as happens in military art: the war of movement becomes increasingly a war of position; and it can be said that a State wins a war only when it prepares for it, minutely and technically, in time of peace. The solid structure of modern democracies, considered either as a State organisation or as a complex of associations in civil life, form, in political art, something like the 'trenches' and the permanent front-line fortifications in the war of position: they render only 'partial' the element which had earlier been the whole war, etc. . . .[22]

Democracy has ceased to be a non-ascribed ideological value, and has fitted itself firmly into bourgeois discourse. Democracy and liberalism mean the same thing. This hegemonisation of democracy by bourgeois discourse also finds expression in socialist discourse; given that democracy seemed welded to liberalism, and that the liberal State was the type of State through which the bourgeoisie was imposing itself in Europe, the conclusion was reached that democracy was a bourgeois ideology. This is the stage when the paradigms typical of class reductionism were formed; even if they pre-sented themselves as a logical system of mutual implications, they did no more than rationalise the type of connotative articulation which the historical experience of Europe had established between heterogeneous contents. And since the State did not have the function of articulating heterogeneous elements, but rather of imposing, through homogeneous apparatuses, the dominion of one class — it was concluded that the State was a mere instrument. This was the position both of Kautsky and Bernstein; Kautsky maintained that democracy was bourgeois because it was welded to liberalism, and Bernstein held that, since democracy was a general human value, the liberal State was not bourgeois. Clearly, while all historical determinations were thus being attributed to class alone, the theme of the State as the general form of domination had to disappear.

3 The third phase begins with Leninism. This is the moment when the reductionist perspective begins to break up, and the theme of democratic antagonisms re-emerges in the field of Marxist thought. For Lenin, the world economy is not a mere economic category, as it had been for the Marxism of the Second International, but it also has a political dimension: it is an imperialist chain. And any crisis which arises in one point of this chain affects its other links, through a dislocation of the balance of forces between the classes, which might precipitate a revolutionary advance even before the objective conditions have matured from the point of view of a stageist logic, in the manner of Kautsky or Plekhanov. And this means that the contradictions generated by capitalism include not only the contradictions implicit in the relations of production, and between these and the productive forces, but also contradictions resulting from the uneven development of capitalism, from increasing antagonisms between the living conditions of the masses and the progressive bureaucratisation of power in the stage of monopoly capitalism. That is, democratic antagonisms in the strict sense in which we have earlier defined them. The reflections on Lloyd Georgism, for example, or about the dislocations in political control of the masses as a result of the war, figure among Lenin's sharpest analyses, and illustrate his clear understanding of the nature of democratic antagonisms. This analysis concludes with the affirmation of the priority of the political, since it cannot be expected that a certain degree of maturity of the productive forces will of itself produce the required results on the political level. The working class, in this new perspective, should no longer closet itself off within a class perspective and wait for the maturity of the objective conditions to lead it to a revolutionary denouement, but must instead be a hegemonic class, that is, must place itself at the head of the masses which are launched into political struggle by the dislocations created by world capitalism in its monopoly

phase. Hence the democratic and popular character which, according to Lenin, the proletarian revolution must have. However, it is necessary to point out the limitations of Leninism: Lenin is considering a new situation with the intellectual tools forged in the reductionist tradition of the Second International, and despite the transformation undergone by Marxist language under his influence, this does not go far enough to grasp the specificity of the new antagonisms which are developing before his very eyes: this is to say, that in Lenin we do not find a theory of the specificity of democratic antagonisms. The result is that the democratic struggle is not analysed in its most essential trait — its polar opposition against the general form of domination — and that all that is conceptualised in democratic struggles are the social classes which intervene therein. As a result, the principle of class is subjected to an extreme tension, in the sense that 'classes' have to perform tasks and strategic manoeuvres much more complex than was supposed by the simple and peaceful stageism of Kautsky or the Mensheviks. This leads to a militarisation of political language — defensive and offensive strategy, steps forward and steps back, the vanguard, the tactical alliance, and so forth — which is profoundly foreign to the political language of the Second International, and which would lend its characteristic style to that of the Third, and which finds perhaps its most complete formulation in Trotsky.

4 We can see, then, that Leninism as a whole is penetrated by an internal contradiction: on the basis of a purely class logic, it attempts to account for antagonisms which surpass class contradictions. The old and the new are interlinked without fully absorbing each other, and the result is an increasing use of paradoxes and metaphors. We are thinking of formulae such as 'unequal and combined development'; its explicit aim is to break away from a crudely stageist conception, and to show that conflicts which in theory ought to present themselves in successive stages, are overdetermined in a concrete historical conjuncture. But the very word 'combined' is clearly referring to this same stageist paradigm which it intends to combat. That is, the new can only be thought of as *different* from the old, and the old retains its positive value as a point of reference.

Any advance from this situation would require, as a precondition, that one begin to consider the nature of democratic antagonisms in their own specificity, and avoid identifying them with the class struggle. If the crisis of the First World War contributed the experience which made possible the reception and assimilation of Leninism, fascism led to a generalisation of democratic antagonisms which permitted advances in breaking with class reductionism. The resistance against fascism, firstly, and then against German occupation, and the consequent formation of popular and national symbols of resistance which afforded a subjective identity for the popular masses in democratic struggle, demanded of the socialist forces a step beyond Leninism. *That is, these forces had to conceive of a working-class hegemony which consisted not only of directing the allied classes, but of creating a growing unity between socialism and the popular and democratic subjectivity of the masses.* In Dimitrov's report to the Seventh Congress of the Communist International, we find the first steps, albeit imperfect and hesitant, towards a reorientation in this direction.[23] Gramsci's solitary reflections, and their re-elaboration by Togliatti after the Second World War, created in Western Europe an historical and intellectual matrix out of which it becomes possible to initiate a non-reductionist reformulation of Marxism. In the other extremity of the capitalist world, Mao laid down the bases for a popular and national movement which in practice broke with reductionism, and which, through the theorisation of a set of antagonisms — principal and secondary contradictions, the principal aspect of the contradiction, etc. — escaped the consideration of a purely class-based perspective, and created the political and intellectual space for an analysis centred on the specificity of democratic antagonisms.

The second main phase in the break with class reductionism occurred as a result of the wave of anti-authoritarian movements, at various levels of society, which shook the capitalist world in the 1960s and 1970s. The increasing bureaucratisation of society found a response in the politicisation of social conflicts and a sharpening of antagonisms, which broke from the satisfied image of the neocapitalism of the 1950s, founded on the myth of unlimited integration and the 'end of ideologies'. This new type of antagonism made even more evident the problem which, as we have seen, is recognised in an initial form by Leninism; the problem that the class struggle takes place on an historical terrain which is increasingly dominated by democratic antagonisms. While the fundamental antagonism which reproduces the system continues to be class exploitation, the bureaucratisation of society more and more displaces the areas of political conflict towards the field of democratic antagonisms. Seeking a new form of politics which would enable the articulation of the two types of struggle is the major preoccupation of Marxist theory and practice in the coming decades, because the present situation, apart from the notorious danger of reorientation in an authoritarian direction, also offers the possibility of a socialist and democratic future. We said earlier that the formation of a general democratic equivalent is the condition necessary for the struggle for direct democracy and the withering-away of the State, and that the precondition for the formation of this general equivalent is the generalisation of democratic antagonisms, and their unification with the struggle of the working class. Well, perhaps never before in the history of the working-class movement and of socialism have these conditions been produced together to such an extent as they have been in Europe over the last two decades.

The future of socialism in Europe depends on the transformation of this possibility into reality.

NOTES

1 This essay has been translated from the Spanish manuscript by Mike Mullan.
2 N. Bobbio, 'Esiste una teoria marxista dello Stato?', in *Il Marxismo e lo Stato* (Rome, 1976) pp. 1–17.
3 U. Cerroni, 'Esiste una scienza politica marxista?', in *ibid.* pp. 39–51.
4 N. Poulantzas: *Political Power and Social Classes* (London, 1973) p. 20.
5 D. Zolo: *State Socialista e Liberta Borghese* (Rome, 197–?).
6 For a good general English introduction to the Della Volpean school, see John Fraser, *An Introduction to the Thought of Galvano Della Volpe* (London, 1976).
7 Umberto Cerroni, 'Democracy and Socialism', in *Economy and Society*, Vol. 7, No. 3, p. 241.

8 *Ibid.* p. 244.

9 U. Cerroni, *Teoria Politica e Socialismo* (Rome, 1973).

10 L. Colletti, *From Rousseau to Lenin,* (London, 1972) especially Part III.

11 U. Cerroni, 'Esiste una scienza . . .', *op. cit.* p. 48.

12 D. Zolo, *La Teoria Comunista dell'Estinzione dello' Stato* (Bari, 1974) p. 85.

13 In an earlier version of this article, I had referred throughout to the 'general form of the State', meaning — as the text makes clear — the general form of domination. However, this was open to the objection that, since the present European debate tends towards a broader interpretation of the concept of politics, which has led to criticisms of the notion of the 'State apparatus'- being the sole centre of power and domination, the use of the word 'State', as it appeared in the text, could give rise to misunderstandings, when in fact the notion of the 'general form of the State', used here, was meant to be identified with domination and power in general and could not be tied in exclusively to any specific State apparatus. This danger led me to make certain modifications in the text, and to refer to the 'general form of domination' in place of the 'general form of the State'. Nevertheless, it should be pointed out that this second term might equally lead to another ambiguity: the implication that the Marxist idea of the withering-away of the State refers to State apparatuses in a restricted sense, instead of taking in the whole ensemble of the apparatuses of domination. On the contrary, as we have argued in the text, the withering-away of the State in Marx means precisely the withering-away of domination and power as such, and does not imply the elimination of every institutional apparatus.

14 U. Cerroni, *Teoria Politica e Socialismo, op. cit.*

15 'Towards a Theory of Populism, in *Politics and Ideology in Marxist Theory,* (London, 1977).

16 F. Engels, *The Peasant Wars in Germany* (Moscow, 1956) pp. 59–60.

17 L. Althusser, 'Ideology and Ideological State Apparatuses', in *Lenin and Philosophy and Other Essays* (London, 1971) pp. 160–70.

18 'Fascism and Ideology', in *Politics and Ideology in Marxist Theory, op. cit.*

19 N. Bobbio: 'Quali alternativi alla democrazia rappresentativa', in *Il Marxismo e lo Stato,* p. 28.

20 Regarding this conception of hegemony, see Chantal Mouffe, 'Hegemony and Ideology in Gramsci', in *Gramsci and Marxist Theory,* (London, 1979). Regarding the new conception of politics implicit in this idea, see Christine Buci-Glucksmann, 'Eurocommunisme et problèmes de l'Etat', in *Dialectiques,* No. 18–19, Spring 1977; and the same author's 'Discutere lo Stato. Sui compiti attuali di una critica marxista della politica', in *Il Manifesto,* 31 October, 1978.

21 N. Bobbio, in *Il Marxismo e lo Stato,* pp. 19–37.

22 A. Gramsci, *Quaderni del carcere* (Milan) Vol. III, pp. 1566–67.

23 G. Dimitrov, 'The Fascist Offensive and the Tasks of the Communist International, in *Selected Speeches and Articles,* (London, 1951).

Time and Information in Political Theory
KENNETH MACDONALD

IF political theory be an attending to the terms of political discourse and we wish to advance that attending, and, presumably, the discourse, we have an embarrassment of means. We might argue that progress is attained through more meticulous attending. For example, on a cursory reading, Hobbes' usage of 'authority' might seem to relate to modern 'power and authority' distinctions. But then we can note that Hobbes (except in his theological phases) avoids, as he would not were he deploying modern usage, 'authority over', and collapses 'authorize' into 'act as the author of', so that it becomes to our ears virtually a pun. Arguably, much of Hobbes' position depends upon this deliberately literal-minded translation. The next step, remembering Cornford's (1935) notion of the 'unwritten philosophy' would be to note that Hobbes' contemporaries do not cavil at this usage — they do not see it as novel. Acid critics do not hesitate over 'authority': 'the Prince acteth by the people's authority in things lawful ... for they be authors of his lawful power' (Ross, 1653:21), or again: 'let us suppose ... that the people by covenant have set up a particular person to be a Monarch, and so made themselves authors of all his acts' (Lawson, 1657:17). Which brings us well away from the notion that: 'Authorization, unlike representation, is peculiar to Hobbes' (Orwin, 1975:26). What to us is a central Hobbesian move appears no move at all in context. Such disentangling of Hobbes is trivial, but does tie to wider interpretative issues (the philosophy can then be seen as closer to applied jurisprudence than to the theory of possessive individualism) and hence modifies our perspective on the development of political discourse. There are other attendings to the logical geography of concepts (such as Rawls' focus on primary goods rather than utilities) which have more immediate impact. On the other hand we might hold that progress in political theory comes from attending to, and incorporating, non-normative theory and accounts within the normative (for example Berlin's 'negative liberty' uncomfortably disattends to the constraints imposed upon actions by the unanticipated consequences of the behaviour of organisations and institutions other than the state). And so on. Any such categorisation of ways begs a plurality of questions about the nature of social explanation (all varieties). Leaving these questions be, this chapter centres on one other way theory might advance. It might advance by attending to an aspect of political action which is ignored or slighted (and perhaps at one level not even part of political discourse) and yet can be held to matter. The task will then be to indicate the significance, neither grandiloquent nor subliminal, of attending to this aspect.

The aspect that we have in mind is, as might be guessed from the title, 'time'. Actions are ordered in time. That they are so ordered is held to be an integral aspect of these actions. The order of actions cannot profitably be reduced to attributes of the actors (for the permutations of 'n' acts is 'n' factorial, which for non-trivial 'n' is a very large number). Act A before act B is different from act A after act B — though we shall have to specify in what this difference inheres. Stopping the car and getting out is not equivalent to getting out and stopping the car; going to university now is not the same as waiting till next year; fraternity as a goal may change in value if liberty is attained first; and so on. The flavour of the obvious examples is micro- rather than macro-political (macro events perhaps being more self contained). At the end of the chapter we return to aspects of 'futurology' and 'the year 2000', but begin with individual action.

Much of our daily day account of ourselves does pay attention to time (if asked about ourselves we readily lapse into autobiographical narrative). And social science accounts that adhere to the detailed stuff of actors and their accounts present sequence as salient. For example Goffman in *Asylums* observes, not just with reference to the inmates, that: 'An important aspect of every career is the view the person constructs when he looks backward over his progress . . .' (Goffman, 1961:135). The classic empirical instance may be *The Polish Peasant in Europe and America* with its strong assertion that: 'We are safe in saying that personal life-records, as complete as possible, constitute the *perfect* type of sociological material' (Thomas & Zananiecki, 1958:1832). But the concern with sequentially ordered data does not survive into theoretical and quantitative social science. A claimed absence is not easy to document, and is susceptible of a plethora of trivial disproofs. But at one extreme we have Durkheim and Mauss in *Primitive Classification* talking about 'classifications' (unordered groups) rather than 'orderings', and though the detailed text demonstrates that what they find are 'systems of hierarchised notions' (Durkheim and Mauss, 1969:81) they do not deploy the asymmetry. An example with a different flavour would be *The American Voter* (Campbell *et al:* 1960) where the event sequence language of Section 1, with its talk of 'funnels of causality', fades when the actual analysis is tackled. And a recent article under the promising title: 'The variable order of events in the life course', simply reduces sequences to attributes and examines the characteristics of 'men who order their events non-normatively' (Hogan, 1978:585). The empirical field has not changed much since reviewed six years ago (Carr-Hill and Macdonald, 1973). As we argued then and later (Macdonald 1976a) some of the blindness may be because available and dominant quantitative techniques handle well the interrelationships of attributes but cannot handle sequences with unstable orderings, so political scientists have not seen what they could not talk about. 'What we cannot speak about we must pass over in silence', holds only for logical 'cannot'. The few strategies that are currently available have representations so esoteric that they require extensive computation and data for their estimation, and so seem not to map onto the experience of subjects and hence their actions. Whatever the reason, event sequences, though central to our untutored accounts of social reality, are not handled by our more theoretical abstractions. Were they handled, they might, for example, affect our ontology, since many concepts have static referents. Immigrants, pensioners, and, presumably, voters 'look solid enough as groups in the statistics formed on the "pile of snapshots" model of social change, but evaporate before the eye on the longitudinal "bunch-of-life-histories" model' (Elster, 1978:145). And attending to time can modify some of the conclusions conventionally expressed: for example, 'Conventional demand theory ignores the impact of past consumption on present tastes. . . .' (Manning, 1978:72); or a novel attempt can be made 'to link consumption behaviour to expected lifetime by making expected lifetime dependent on the consumption pattern chosen' (Hughes, 1978:63). And so on. Our present concern is to ask whether attending to the 'ordered in time' aspect of acts would have implications for normative accounts of politics. (A topic not much examined, though there are suggestive remarks in Elster, 1978:39–42, 162.)*

There is a body of literature (originating with Whorf 1956) the exploitation of which is by now hackneyed, arguing that western European linear conceptualisation of time as spatial order (implicit in most of our everyday usage) is but one culture's way of structuring (and a way not particularly apt for some of its needs, such as discourse on the theory of relativity). But talk of events 'ordered in time' does not presuppose a particular conceptualisation. For, in a social science context, the temporal asymmetry manifests itself as an informational one (remember the Hopi delineation of tense through differing modes of verification, or, one might say, pertinent information). Information might indeed be used as a definition of temporal asymmetry: in principle we can know the past and not the future — 'It may help here to recall Humphrey Lyttleton's rejoinder when someone asked him where Jazz was going "If I knew where Jazz was going I'd be there already." ' (Winch, 1958:93–4). That the future is yet 'to be constructed' imposes peculiar constraints and requirements on the pertinent information. Differing event orderings in time produce different information patterns, and different information needs.

* Jon Elster's *Ulysses and the Sirens: Studies in rationality and irrationality* (Cambridge University Press, 1979), which appeared after the present chapter had gone to press, carries typically provoking and stimulating discussion of some pertinent issues — in particular, time-preferences and precommitment strategies.

And the realisation that orderings, though asymmetrical, are not determinate is central in areas other than time. When thinking of 'cause' a useful metaphor is an interconnected network of events, any one of which, if a source of (or subjected to) perturbation, produces a radiating spread of consequences and is then seen as *the* cause (the image of a net, spread flat, being lifted by *any* one of its interstices). Space, like time, manifests itself in social contexts not directly but through information. Migration flows (within or between states) for example should not be seen as occurring across social distances if clear information flow exists across the space (patterns of seasonal migration around ports, prior to steam, providing one obvious example). Migration patterns within Britain show that the mapping between space and 'perceived' space (i.e. the information about space) is not univalent, for in space, as in time, propinquity does not imply relation ('the eighteenth century' and 'Britain' are, except at an empty formal level, equally suspect theoretical entities). But for time, as against space, the ordering is a necessary though not sufficient condition in determining the informational order. Further, a temporal asymmetry may occur in one of a plurality of orders, but, having occurred, it cannot be revoked as a spatial relation (on other than an extreme coherence theory of truth) might. And, while defining social time in terms of information entails possible incompleteness in temporal orderings (arising from imperfect information, and particularly non-information), temporal succession can be held central to moral choice in a way that spatial relations, for example, are not. It has been neatly said that there is 'no temporal succession of events in a deontically perfect world' (Lenk, 1978:27) and the existence of moral action (and hence political theory) as we know it is predicated upon deontic imperfection so defined.

Temporal ordering then, applied to political choice, would appear to lead to a stress on information (as the social correlate of time) and on the evaluation of choices rather than the evaluation of end states (the political world presents itself as choices, not as states). So first let us look at the place of 'information' in the 'moral', and then explore whether this informational component is reducible to information about end states, or whether language for evaluation of action is distinct from language for evaluation of states.

Moral action ties to 'information' not simply through the argument that moral action implies time which (socially) is defined in terms of information. There is also a direct link. If we adopt the simplistic strategy (Macdonald: 1976b) of saying we can distinguish between formal definitions of normative concepts and their instantiation, accepting its crudity (Lukes: 1977) but claiming its utility, we can locate foci of moral disagreement. We may disagree on formal definition ('liberty is not a *group* attribute'), on instantiation of the definition ('*argument* is not persuasion'), on facts of the case ('bull was *not* in the china shop') or on perceived consequences ('decreased taxation does not increase incentive'). Our paradigms of moral disagreements are the first and second, or trivially the third, but I would claim (an empirical claim) that most of our daily 'moral' disagreements are in fact disagreements about predicted consequences; if challenged we produce detailed 'factual' claims as to the 'factual' consequences of the action. Certainly there are real areas of moral disagreement, but most of what we identify in ordinary discourse as such dissolve, if pushed, into predictive disagreements (rule utilitarians were right to see moral rules as decision licences under uncertainty, but wrong to reduce actions to states). Arguments over the propriety of positive discrimination hinge on the perceived consequences (bootstraps or grievance). Arguments over resource distribution hinge on the consequences (contrast arguments over a private sector in medicine *if* it could be shown that such a sector had *no* detrimental effect on other care). Even the notion of 'real interests' carries considerable empirical baggage. No claim is made that all disagreement dissolves on 'informational' agreement (the private medicine example is pertinent), but that the bulk so does. 'Information' being not just 'knowing that', but also the detailed cognitive structuring of the world. An example from Cherlin (1978) may illustrate: faced with accounting for apparent increased instability from first to second marriages, he suggests that remarriage is incompletely institutionalised, we lack the categories. For example, 'there is no term a child living with his mother can use to describe his relationship to the woman his father remarried after he divorced the child's mother. And, not surprisingly, the rights and duties of the child and this woman towards each other are unclear.' (Cherlin, 1978:644). Cherlin's own verbal confusion (he means: 'married', not 'remarried') helps make his point. Whilst such structurings are pertinent to the assessment of both decisions and states of affairs, there are varieties of information whose content is more visibly determined by the sequence of events: 'two individuals with the same probability beliefs may nevertheless have different probabilities for the same event . . . because they have observed different other events' (Arrow 1978:3). And on a stronger Bayesian model, the probability beliefs themselves would be functions of histories. Towards the end of this paper we shall see that the decomposition of moral statements into informational claims has useful clarifying force when considering the evaluation of future states, and helps solve the problem posed by what Elster calls the 'endogenous change of preferences'. ('As we strive for short-term improvement we are ourselves changed so that our notion of what *is* an improvement may not remain the same.' Elster, 1978:39.) At the moment let us focus on the fact that decisions, including moral decisions, are taken on the basis of incomplete information about the future, and this information is integral to the decisions.

The view of morals in general as being peculiarly concerned with actions, not states of affairs has a long (though gappy) history. It may be at its clearest in Aristotle; not the Aristotle who talks about proportional justice, but the one who avers: 'the virtues we get by first exercising them, as also happens in the case of the arts as well. For the things we have to learn before we can do them, we learn by doing them, e.g. men become builders by building and lyre-players by playing the lyre; so too we become just by doing just acts, temperate by doing temperate acts, brave by doing brave acts.' (Aristotle, *Ethics*: 1103a). This implies a context dependent (act dependent) assessment of moral action, as being a non-formalisable skill: '. . . anyone can get angry — that is easy — or give or spend money; but to do this to the right person, to the right extent, at the right time, with the right motive, and in the right way, that is not for everyone, nor is it easy' (Aristotle, *Ethics*: 1109a); though Aristotle himself is not entirely consistent on this matter: 'some [actions] have names that already imply badness . . . nor does goodness or badness with regard to such things depend upon committing adultery with the right woman, at the right time, and in the right way, but simply to do any of them is to go wrong' (Aristotle, *Ethics*: 1107a). The question then is what interesting things can be said about actions that cannot be said about states. One debate is around the status of 'rights' talk. 'Rights' is not intrinsically an ordered or sequential concept, so there would seem no objection in principle to incorporating 'right maintenance/violation' statements into descriptions of states of affairs (if temporal order of rights is in general unimportant, where it matters it can be included as an attribute without generating factorial numbers of attributes). 'Rights' are relational in linking states to genitors, but do not capture temporal relations (though they are affected by them). Williams' (1973:108f) discussion of 'integrity' in relation to utilitarianism is closer, though again the temporal aspect is not emphasised. An example may help. In a perceptive essay on Jane Austen, Trilling (1955) locates part of her importance as lying in her presentation in English literature for the first time of a concept of 'bad faith'. The characters she presents for disapprobation are so not by being malevolent (or even maleficent) but, for example, since they address the heroine by her Christian name without following through the matrimonial implications of the act. Spelling this out is not straightforward. One of the criteria is connectedness or continuity or, possibly, progression: such action evaluations do not translate readily to state descriptors. Some of the theorists of 'social action', such as Grathoff, have given a defining role to 'social temporality' ('All arisal, enlargement or variation of social types starts with incipient events', Grathoff, 1970:109), but the difficulty of tying down, without lapsing into the metaphysical, what the proper descriptor of such action might be, is a real difficulty and one reflected in awkwardnesses around actual usages.

It is possible to point to substantive areas where our reluctance/inability to talk of action as against states does lead to analytic and evaluative weaknesses. One of the more interesting developments in social policy has been the growth of 'experimental social administration' (Halsey 1974; Smith

1975) — exercises such as 'head start' in the United States, and EPA and CDP projects in Britain — deriving from a realisation that political action concerns the creation of alternative futures, whilst conventional social research concentrates upon interrelations in the present state, which may be poor guides to behaviour in another. Yet the statistical techniques applied to 'action research' have been techniques for assessing end states (treatment worked/didn't) *not* techniques for assessing actions. The field (action) researchers have felt (justifiably?) that more was going on than the measures located. Some of the unease is reducible to inaptness of the formal model (intercorrelations of social effects in the world are not dissolvable facts about the world as they might be held to be for growing corn) but some attaches to the fact that the researchers focus on end states whilst the actors must deal with choice of action. This failure of the second-order commentary is not peculiar to action research (one of the commoner daily moral fallacies is to discredit a choice which led to disaster — 'I should never have married him/her' — though the choice, qua choice, was the right choice). That the methodology of action has not caught up with the action can be seen from the flaccidity of recent contributions (e.g. Goldstein *et al* 1978; Powley and Evans, 1979).

The conceptual myopia of concentrating upon states rather than actions is not peculiar to political theory. As Sen (1979) notes: 'The entire social choice literature is almost exclusively concerned with ranking states, or with choosing between states, rather than ranking or choosing between actions. . . . If actions consisted in choosing between fully described social states then a "social choice function" would indeed have covered the problem of choice over actions. But many actions — indeed most actions — are not of this type.' There would be no claim that comparison of actions would escape the problems which beset comparison of states (might attract fresh). But if we are engaged in the piecemeal construction of the future our political tools should reflect this. The Aristotelian impossibility of pre-evaluation ('the things we must learn before we can do them, we learn by doing them') is sharpest in those areas of decision-making where what I want is 'what the others would want' (planning outings with friends is the most familiar example; and the literature suggests that the evening decisions of American group-marriages founder on the problem; at a more serious level it is the problem of the individual actor who wishes to vote explicitly for Rousseau's general will). Many decisions in small corporate polities involve a 'depending upon what the rest think' clause which cannot be located prior to the decision (and ofttimes, as we know to our costs, not afterwards). At a more general level any systematic attending to 'public opinion' or attempt to evaluate hypothetical goods or bads enters the same problem (attitude to the provision of nursery care for offspring of working mothers depends upon how others opt, since acceptability is a real dimension of assessment). These are the sharper instances, but the non-existence of the future holds widely, and while the concept of 'possible worlds', which in any case is invoked by statistical causal statements (Macdonald, 1976c:87), may be helpful, attempting to describe the world as if choice were based on states can lead us to misperceive it. A small example might be the child-rearing practices of the kibbutzim. These we tend to see as clearly ideologically focused towards specific ends. But listen to first-hand account of their genesis: 'it was a difficult problem. How were the women both to work and look after children? Should each mother look after her own family and do nothing else? The men did not seem to feel strongly either way. But the women wouldn't hear of giving up their share of the communal work and life ... Somebody proposed that the Kibbutz should hire a nurse ... we didn't hire a nurse but we chose one girl to look after the lot of them ... And so this system developed ...' (Bettleheim, 1969:19). This actual account is less sharply 'ultimate end' tied and closer to a view of action as adaptation to the present in the light of the knowledge of the present, a very Aristotleian view. And that in turn has implications for considering how things might have been otherwise. Though the outcome 'possible worlds' (presence/absence of Kibbutz child-rearing arrangements) are radically different the point of departure may be trivial, the precipitating separation infinitesimal (a concentration on events which generate states, rather than on states, might affect the formulation of the problem of counterfactuals). Which may be another way of querying whether the correct moral evaluation of the pivot should be in terms of the outcome. With a different terminology Arrow (1974) reaches an analogous result; recent theoretical literature on irreversible investment under uncertainty suggests 'that the random accidents of history will play a bigger role in the final equilibrium. Once investment has been made and an information channel acquired, it will be cheaper to keep on using it than to invest in new channels' (Arrow, 1974:41).

If then politics is concerned with ordered actions it is pertinent to ask how do we set up a structure of information — and what type of information it should be. Political theory tackles questions of power and justice but, since politics is after all claimed to be the art of the possible, it should also tackle questions of information. How would you organise a polity (assuming it to be docile) to generate that apt information for the best decision (assuming us to be agreed on the nature of the 'good'). The prior question is what is 'apt' information. With different political organisation the structure of information has differing impact: contemporary 'official secrets' trials for example have centred not around 'spies', but around the collation of information available (if abstrusely) in the public sphere — were the opponents of the State other States the information would have already been assembled by them; but if the opponents are terrorists, lacking library researchers, then attempts to prevent the collation become intelligible. Further, since decisions are ordered in time, evaluation of decisions does not collapse into evaluation of states, so information is not simply information on states. Selecting an example, almost at random, Bernick (1978) expresses the 'hope that political theorists will give greater attention to the matter of self-esteem' as a basic concept, for '. . . it may be that advances in individual self-esteem are contributions to civilisation even greater than advances in material conditions' (Bernick, 1978:118). Clearly, if considering a given increment in self-esteem and a given increment in material conditions, the sequence of increments affects essentially (in a good medieval sense) their value, so atemporal, or more strictly, a-sequential, assertions of the form given by Bernick are (by not specifying the relations) meaningless. The sequence matters, as also does the sequence of the information. The worry is that this argument leads to an 'attending to intimations' (Oakeshott, 1956). To this question, of whether if we wish to act wittingly we must act conservatively, we return. But let us here adduce another strand in the traditional Burkean political argument, with parallels to notions of the intrinsic importance of continuity in individual acts which we met in Trilling's example. One of Burke's objections to revolution is that: 'By this unprincipled facility of changing the state as often, and as much, and in as many ways as there are floating fancies or fashions, the whole chain or continuity of the commonwealth would be broken. No one generation would link with the other. Men would become little better than the flies of a summer.' (Burke, 1790:193).

This notion of information and its continuity as a good in itself, the notion that it is essential to human life that it be tied through time, has gone out of fashion. Possessive individualism, ('The solitary and isolated hunter or fisherman, who serves Adam Smith and Ricardo as a starting point, is one of the unimaginative fantasies of eighteenth-century romances *à la* Robinson Crusoe' Marx, 1857:124.), dissolves temporal as well as social relations. The absolutisation of the market (Barber's 1977:15, phrase), might be seen precisely as a device to reduce relational terminology. Again Bell (1974) by setting 'information' as the new commodity of post-industrial society, to be made and bought and sold, produces analyses which may fit (that 'may' is a separate argument) but in doing so loses what is novel; the straight-forward empirical difficulty of maintaining information, once generated, as a private good (witness patenting of algorithms) may be a pointer to conceptual misalignment. And though there are interesting questions around the 'freedom of information' debates and issues of whether 'privacy' is a primary good or a consequential, the language in which they are couched reifies. The treatment of time as a scarce resource has extended the areas of economic analysis (see, for example, the overview in Becker, 1976:141–7), but in general by making time a substitutable good without sequential characteristics. And so on.

Again, while I have asserted that it seems wise to ask 'how should the polity be organised to generate apt information?', two of the most discussed recent contributions to political theory have systematically disattended to the issue. Rawls' (Nozick we deal with later) cavalier attitude towards his much criticised broad definitions of the 'least favoured' — 'I suppose that either of these definitions, or some combination of them, will serve well enough' (Rawls, 1972:98) — is, with its suppression of information, a case in point. In contrast to his unitary vision of the disadvantaged, detailed contemporary research on minorities locates the detrimental effect of concatenations of attributes. For example, Smith and Whalley (1975) in an excellent report on racial minorities and public housing stress the impact not of discrimination but of cumulative disadvantage on several dimensions. ('For example, Asians tend to have large families, but councils tend to have few properties with four or more bedrooms; therefore Asian occupants will have a lower than average chance of being rehoused, not because of their race, but because of their family size', Smith and Whalley 1975:13.) If this analysis be correct, and generalisable as seems to other social problems, then there are (*pace* Rawls) implications for the ways in which we attend to the business of politics. The conclusion reached by Smith and Whalley after examining how in fact a sensitive policy issue is handled is that: 'Positive management control can only be exerted if there is adequate information about all the main aspects of the system. The lack of such information has made it difficult to trace the consequences of present policies for the minority groups, and the same difficulty would have arisen whatever group had been studied.' (Smith and Whalley, 1975:115). A world whose characteristic political problems are of this form, and where we are faced with choices, generates a moral (or at least political) obligation to acquire information which is not at ease with the requirement that 'the veil of ignorance excludes all but the vaguest knowledge of likelihoods' (Rawls, 1972:155). Which is not to deny that moral requirements to acquire information present their own paradoxes ('Aristotle said that you can be held responsible for your ignorance, but how can you know how much you should know?' Elster, 1978:162). Rawls is of course consistent in denying the import of the temporal (informational) position of the chooser: 'In the case of an individual the avoidance of pure time preference is a feature of being rational. . . . The mere difference of location in time, of some things being earlier or later, is not in itself a rational ground for having more or less regard for it' (Rawls, 1972:293).

The argument of the present paper is that temporal order is not a discountable fact, so it becomes necessary to argue against the claimed irrationality of pure time preference. And we can make some defence (as Elster, 1978:78, from a different viewpoint does). One set of arguments, as with arguments around counter-factuals, might involve appeal to internal relations — nominally similar events in different time positions invoke different internal (constitutive) relations, and so are strictly different, and this pure time difference might entail a time preference. The case might be supported by demonstrative exposition (shades of debates on the coherence theory of truth), but its weakness for our present purpose is that internal relations, even if ceded, do not address the direction of the ordering; they merely say it may be rational to prefer A at time t to A at time $t+k$ as being different. More potent are arguments explicitly referencing order. One family centres around the indeterminancy of the future. It may be rational for me to display pure time preference for time t over time $t+k$ because the occurrence of time t is, to me, more certain than $t+k$; or because the occurrence of good, in a world with scarcity of goods and plethora of bads, is more certain at t than $t+k$ (birds in hand and bushes); or because the judgment 'good at time t' is more secure than the judgment 'good at time $t+k$' (secular change, or unpredictability, or endogenous change of preferences). Perhaps strongest is the argument that the present leaves traces in the future, changing and modifying it ('*Nam in omni adversitate fortunae infelicissimum genus est infortunii, fuisse felicem*'). The implications of this for any particular issue are up for discussion; you may choose to have your poetry reading before or after the push-pin; but it would be rash to dub you irrational for preferring one ordering to another, and the chosen ordering can be argued for ('you can only truly appreciate poetry when you bring to it the experience of a lived life'/'the rolling stanzas of Tennyson sustained me through the closing reaches of the game'). The serious point is that grounded discussion is possible, and that the reasons will, as a central and inevitable part of their justification, reference the temporal sequence. Temporal asymmetry

154 The Frontiers of Political Theory

(of effect, or consequence, or memory, or information) is present and grounds for time preferences. Admittedly in a narrow trivial sense pure time preference is irrational: it would be difficult to argue for allocating all jam to time t; but it is not irrational to have views on the time allocation of jam. And the rational component of such views need not be reducible, as Rawls would have it, to treating all time points as equal. The ramifications of an experience at the start of one's adult life are absent if the experience is moved to the end. In part it is a question of whether the future is different from the past: 'It is to be noted that nothing that is past is an object of choice, e.g. no one chooses to have sacked Troy; for no one *deliberates* about the past, but about what is future and capable of being otherwise. . . .' (Aristotle, *Ethics:* 1139b).

Temporal asymmetry in information, which we have already introduced partly as a defining measure, may be sharper in the case of 'moral' information. It would be the psychoanalysts' (as against the behaviourists') protection from experimental disconfirmation (akin to the query whether Mill's man who has experienced both push-pin and poetry can evaluate experiencing only one). In a different context, Kant, discussing the occurrence of a 'constitution governed by natural right' observes that 'a phenomenon of this kind which has taken place in human history *can never be forgotten*' (Kant, 1798:184). But the most famous example, engagingly discussed by Ryle (1958), is of course Aristotle: 'But yet it [practical wisdom] is not only a reasoned state; that is shown by the fact that a state of that sort may be forgotten but practical wisdom cannot.' (Aristotle, *Ethics*: 1140b). I am not here concerned to pursue the notion of a unique pivotal event, merely to note its occurrence, and suggest that attending to time and information may alert us to portions of traditional political thoery which, though downplayed in our summary textbook accounts, were for the writers important concerns.

Temporal relation (continuity) is not equally present in all actions, and it is possible to design social structures to minimise it. Discontinuity would reduce life to a single-stage Markov stochastic process, where an entity carries no record of past states (and, *a fortiori*, no ordered record) and its future action flows solely from its present state. Such discontinuity would however discomfit much of our terminology. For example, it is in order for Fried (1977:185) to take as a manifest fact, not requiring support, the view that: 'The kinds of entitites to whom values, preferences, choices, and the realisation of these can be attributed are human bodies that persist over time, the continuity of which is the continuity of the self. Thus an entity that existed only momentarily . . . would not form a recognisable unit for the ascription of our concepts.' And the continuity presupposed is, for the interesting ascriptions, not simply of spatial cohesion but of information. The most familiar individual level instance is in child rearing, where not only does the family act as a memory bank for the child, reminding of past acts, and providing reassuring regularities, but also, in Newson's (1978:12f) phrase, the evolutionary potential of a protracted time horizon modifies and constrains parental action (some things have to be more considered, others can be less, if they are not unique but recurrent). Continuity of groups over time has by some been held to be less obviously meaningful a concept (and hence even less a good). Plamenatz (1963:318) attacked Marx on class interest thus: 'John at seventy is the same person as John at seven. It makes sense to say that, given his character, his situation, and his prospects, this rather than that was or will be his true interest. . . . But it hardly makes sense to speak of a class in this way. . . .' Yet the continuity of a person is not a datum, but something to be striven for. The claim is not that human behaviour must necessarily be apprehended under the category of continuity, but that attributes which might be regarded as 'truly human' (begging questions), and within these the criteria of the desirable, reference such continuity. It enters into our moral evaluations: I have a friend whose past skills are not manifested in her present; a much reduced life-history could support her present performance. And that becomes a pejorative evaluation, which does not dissolve into a statement on 'lack of full potential', but retains reference to lack of continuity. I have retreated into the first-person anecdotal because we do not know enough about the detailed stuff of daily evaluation to decide whether the response is common or idiosyncratic. Continuity for polities or other political entities is as unproblematic or problematic (returning to the

Plamenatz quotation) as it is for persons. The generations of such continuity lies behind some conservative arguments: 'A man full of warm speculative benevolence may wish his society otherwise constituted than he finds it; but a good patriot, and a true politician, always considers how he shall make the most of the existing materials of his country.' (Burke, 1790:267). Its desirability might be held to be implied by any cumulative view of knowledge: '. . . reason does not itself work instinctively . . . if nature has fixed only a short term for each man's life (as is in fact the case) then it will require a long, perhaps incalculable, series of generations, each passing enlightenment to the next' (Kant, 1784:42–3). Notice that it is difficult to say 'time, information and hence continuity' without appearing to talk of progressive accumulation, or simply 'progress'. To this we shall return. The present point is that, granting cumulative knowledge to be important, while for some knowledge this might be attained by establishing an atemporal data-bank with individual discontinuity, it is less clear that social knowledge is thus isolateable. Burke, for example, is in no doubt that 'where the great interests of mankind are concerned through a long succession of generations, that succession ought to be admitted to some share in the councils which are so deeply to affect them'. (Burke, 1790:282). Whatever one's views on that issue, it does point to a set of real problems (of obligations to future generations, and of obligations of promise-keeping to the deceased) which do not dissolve into state evaluations. That polities exist over time presents issues that would not arise if they did not. Such continutiy is claimed as a moral dimension, not as being unable to engender immorality: 'It is this thinking which I think gives rise to the greatest tragedies of history, this sense of commitment to a past purpose which reinforces the original agreement precisely at a time when experience has shown that it must be reversed' (Arrow, 1974:29); though I would in turn argue that such rigidity comes from attending to ends and not actions, even though such a shift of emphasis does not dissolve the entire problem, (Arrow himself is more ambivalent than the isolated quotation suggests).

An elective emphasis on continuity does pose problems for political evaluation. Traditionally the requirement that we act wittingly and connectedly has been associated with a 'conservative' approach to politics. And in practice it may well be that, as a recent study of the relation between academics and the American 'great society' has concluded, 'research tends to be a conservative force because it fosters scepticism and caution' (Aaron, 1978: foreword). The observed cohabitation of ideas does not entail a logical connection, but the pressure is a real one, and the problem awkward. And the pressure towards conservatism is stronger than the analogy that 'on a misty hill the wise man takes small steps', for dealing with evaluation entails problems that are not fully described by simple indeterminacy of distance. The future goods that are most intractable may be public or social goods. The incentive problem for the provision of public goods and the avoidance of 'the tragedy of the commons' is familiar, and can be (Taylor, 1976) related to much of traditional political theory. But for some public goods (and perhaps for an increasing proportion of such goods) the problem lies in identifying them. The appearance of novel areas of decision presenting uncharted consequences (it is likely that shortly we shall be able to predetermine the sex of infants, with social consequences only faintly echoed in societies practising selective infancticide) make obvious and dramatic examples (and note how the creation of a possibility creates an obligation). The classic example is the inadequacy of market mechanisms (even assisted by medical insurance) to return accurate information on medical need, or, reciprocally, on medical 'product' quality. Part of the problem arises from the difficulty of foreseeing the aggregation of individual decisions, what Schelling (1974) has called the 'ecology of micromotives'. An asocial example would be the traditional computer 'game' modestly named 'Life' (Gardener, 1971), where a random scatter of monads in a two dimensioned space, given simple 'birth' and 'death' rules tied to individuals and the density of their neighbours, and then iterated, yields complex and longlived aggregate patterns, which appear to the uninstructed viewer to follow aggregate laws. Schelling, who does not reference 'Life', presents the example of a checker-board with black and white counters; each, not unreasonably, has a preference for an adequacy of similar coloured neighbours (e.g. 1–2 neighbours, one of same colour;

3–5, two; 6–8, three). For a range of detailed scanning strategies, and of initial proportions (you can try it by hand) the innocent wish results in a segregated society. There are analogues with our earlier 'possible worlds' discussion (radically different worlds may have trivial points of departure), but such outcome modification does make location of 'end' problematic. 'We may want sociability more than ever yet we cannot, individually and separately, express that want in a way that secures it' (Hirsch, 1977:81). Part of the difficulty of aggregation is the difficulty of locating future wants — which is to some extent the originality problem ('Originality is the one thing which unoriginal minds cannot feel the use of . . . If they could see what it would do for them, it would not be originality', Mill, 1861: 123) but more important is the want dependency of wants. If the difficulty of translation between individual wants and those aggregated be granted, the sociability problem does not reduce to the 'tragedy of the commons'. It is unfortunate that popular discussion of Hirsch (1977) has elided his argument to 'positional goods' (though primacy could be a temporal positional good), for his book contains much interesting work on the detailed relation between social structure and the pattern of desirable wants, which, as with travel to work, are then susceptible to 'changes in the efficiency of converting the input' (Hirsch, 1977:56). In a less institutional vein it might be argued: 'The chief thing the common sense individual wants is not satisfaction for the wants he has, but more and better wants . . . true achievement is the refinement and elevation of the plane of desire' (Knight 1935:23, quoted Hirsch 1978:61). Knight's formulation might be held ethnocentric, (though it is easy to think of diverse examples), but the argument is logical as well as empirical. Hobbes, though he ties it to his theories of motion, locates the point: '. . . the felicity of this life consisteth not in the repose of a mind satisfied . . . Nor can a man any more live whose desires are at an end, than he, whose senses and imaginations are at a stand. Felicity is the continual progress of the desire, from one object to another' (Hobbes, 1651:63). Though Hobbes presents it as prescription, it could stand as description; it is after all the empirical and conceptual flaw of utopian experiment. A state of affairs implemented generates evaluations additional to those in our present; as Mannheim remarks (1938:113), 'political thought cannot be carried on by speculating about it from the outside', a sentiment that finds an echo in Wolin's (1961:63) criticism of the *Republic*. Which gets us back to the question of public opinion, and the difficulty of evaluating counterfactual preferences. Future judgments may subvert the past choices which brought the future into being. Witness for example the conceptual difficulties of evaluating education policies over time (Halsey, Heath and Ridge, 1979). So it becomes important to ask how are moral and political judgments made, and what categories are attended to by the choosers.

Such emphasis runs counter to Rawls: 'The essential point . . . is that in justice as fairness the parties do not know their conception of the good, and cannot estimate their utility in the ordinary sense' (Rawls, 1972:155). His account systematically disattends to context. A stress on action would reintroduce context. The problem has not been entirely ignored, though perceptive solutions are hard to come by. Miller (1976:253) gestures in the right direction ('. . . I shall try to show that substantive ideals of social justice . . . take radically different forms in different types of society.') but his resulting typology (primitive/hierarchical/market) is too general to give leverage on changing issues within our world. The work of Alves and Rossi (1978), on fairness judgments of the distribution of earnings is too general, in interpretation and technique, to be helpful here. Dworkin *et al* (1977:13), discussing the organisation of markets, point at the issue — 'For . . . decisions not only reflect our current preferences and desires but, via their implementation, affect in a profound manner the kinds of persons we shall become' — but fail to cash this insight. From a very different stance Barnsley (1972) recognises that there is a problem but makes little progress. I see no evidence to subvert the findings of a recent American review: 'we know relatively little from contemporary social science research about the factors that lead some people to accept — or at least to tolerate — inequalities and that lead others to feel grievances and struggle against them' (Bell and Robinson, 1978:236). And the problem (not peculiar to justice) is not 'how are actions tagged to the evaluations?' but 'how do the evaluations arise?'.

Faced with an inelectably counterfactual future and the claim that continuity might lead to conservatism, and worries over the contextual nature of information, one radical attempted solution would be explicitly to structure a polity to minimise the temporal interconnections of judgments and downplay the role of information in evaluation. Part, for example, of our unease at the extreme literalism of Hobbes on 'authorise' with which I began this paper, arises from his complete dissolution of the question 'how should the state ascertain what to do?' ('They that have sovereign power may commit iniquity; but not injustice or injury in the proper signification', Hobbes, 1651:116), and its purging of alternative information structures ('lesser commonwealths in the bowels of a greater, like worms in the entrails of a natural man', Hobbes, 1651:218). The final sections of Nozick (1974) can be seen as an attempt to achieve precisely this dissolution of interconnections. Having asserted (shades of Mannheim) that 'one cannot determine in advance which people will come up with the best ideas, and all ideas must be tried out (and not merely simulated on a computer) to see how they will work' (Nozick, 1974:315), Nozick presents as his solution a framework within which independent utopian experiments can be conducted. This structure need not, on Nozick's part, be entirely stipulative. Technology, as interpreted in west-coast America, might, on its interpretation, entail irrelevance of the past, so discontinuous experiments would be appropriate. But, if I am correct in disbelieving here in strict technological determinism, there being other modes of social organisation compatible with the technology, then it is still open to us to criticise the entire presentation as prescription. Apart from the hackneyed problems of a structure to maintain the absence of structure, the most obvious criticism (from within British culture at any rate) is that he has provided for a plurality of experiments, but made no provision for these to inform each other (our present concern being with sequential transfer, though Nozick makes no provision either for contemporaneous). If the criticism is held to be not obvious or not pertinent there are two demonstrative strategies. One is to appeal to the cumulation of illustration which this paper has attempted, to show that continuity through time can be held to be an important (if often ignored) element in both normative and non-normative accounts of reality. But such presentation of a point of view is at best suasive. A more direct argument would be to appeal to the literature on past 'commune' experiments. To read accounts of such (resolutely disattending to the entertaining not-quite-realised experiments — Coleridge and friends on the banks of the Susquehannah, Lawrence and Russell and friends together in one community) is to acquire a dominant impression of lack of transfer of information and learning. The reinvention of the wheel, the syndrome known to computer programmers as 'not invented here', the generational transience of most experiments — all these raise doubts about the enterprise, though we may well feel strongly sympathetic to particular communitarian goals. The utopias do not themselves invite presentation as a record of human progress. There is no evolution (though certainly there is change). Precisely this lack of evolution enables Nozick to envision turning back the clock: 'given people's historical memories and records . . . an already rejected alternative . . . can be *retried*' (Nozick, 1974:317). But (and this may reveal cultural bias) there is to the British ear a certain absurdity in the implementation of a culture learnt from records (the jokes about the natives — e.g. the American Indians — reading the anthropologists to learn how to behave are uneasy jokes, and not all the unease is guilt at cultural extirpation). Only in Nozick's discontinuous world does the past leave no traces. If we are to handle problems of continuity and decison-making some strategy other than defining the problem out of existence is called for.

Before presenting that tentative solution, which is an application of points made earlier, let me take a final sideways exploration. ('On a huge hill/Cragged, and steep, Truth stands, and he that will/Reach her, about must, and about must go'). Two central British sociologists, recently, discussing progress deployed a metaphor which has been much cited (e.g. Halsey, 1978:92). 'The image that we are trying to suggest is that of a marching column with the people at the head of it usually being the first to wheel in a new direction. The last rank keeps its distance from first, and the distance between them does not lessen.. . . The people in the rear cannot . . . reach where the van *is;* but . . . they can hope in due course to reach where the van *was.*' (Young and Willmott, 1973:20). Hayek, who is undeterred by the fact that 'writers who value their reputation among the more sophisticated hardly dare mention progress without inlcuding the word in quotation marks' (Hayek 1960:39), also presents a unilinear march of progress: 'only from an advanced position does the next range of desires and possibilities become visible' (Hayek, 1960:44). Certainly progress can be in some sense a social fact — for example, as Adam Smith in a pre-echoing of relative deprivation, remarked: '. . .it is in the progressive state, while the society is advancing to the further acquisition, rather than when it has acquired its full complement of riches, that the condition of the labouring poor, of the great body of the people, seems to be the happiest and most comfortable. . . .' (Smith, 1789:90–91). There are, familiar, relativist problems in the identification of moral progress. I would suggest that applying the claim made earlier, that most moral judgments are elided factual predictions, both enables us to talk of progress and effectively subverts the tidy column image of Haydek and Young and Willmott.

Information may be disruptive (remember Ibsen) and knowledge may be lost — witness the fate of Greek scientific catapult manufacture (Soedel and Foley, 1979) — and at times we may be clearer about the future than the past, but time $t-k$ can transmit knowledge to time t which in principle time $t+k$ cannot. 'More' knowledge need not be 'better' knowledge, but at least it is a consistent asymmetry. Translating moral statements to informational claims does not remove the problems of 'progress', but at least it ties it in to a familiar family of puzzles (are paradigms incommensurable? — if yes, how do we argue against a move to revive Greek physics, if no, do we need paradigms to compare paradigms, as in the third man argument of Parmenides?). If the problems of moral 'progress' can be elided to the puzzles around any notion of 'cumulation' then we can evade peculiar discomfiture on saying 'moral progress', whilst at the same time discrediting the simplistic vision of a marching column faithfully following the pioneers. There are difficulties of simplistic assumptions that the ruling ideas are the ideas of the ruling class (see for example Joseph, 1977, on the politics of 'good and 'bad' information), and our awareness that knowledge in general cumulates erratically should make us hesitate over an image of the advance scouts wheeling, for some progress entails the relocation of the advance. More seriously, to mine the metaphor would require a Spenserian mythic landscape whose properties were inhabitant-dependent (Macdonald 1971:122–3), for the space through which the actors move (as indeed with apolitical information) is affected by the movement. As Hirsch (1977:167) perceptively puts it: 'What is neglected is that by the time the sought after ground is reached by the rear of the column the ground will have been affected by the passage of the column itself.' And whilst this is precise with respect to positional goods — the pleasure Lord Nuffield's products (I mean cars) gave to those who first acquired them is no longer with us — it also holds more interestingly (and in a way that subverts the spatial image) for plans that fix the future (transport forecasting being the traditional area where we 'fix the future', [Gershuny, 1978]) by implemented evaluations, though there are many others, such as housing [Dennis 1970]. Cumulation of information and action upon it (as with science) determines which future information shall be pertinent. The disagreement with Young and Willmott rests upon their substantive premise: 'we would put much greater emphasis upon another phenomenon, the similarity of people's needs, and their constancy over time'. (Young and Willmott, 1973:21). That this paper would wish to deny.

If any of the foregoing argument holds it has implications for the old question of the proper relation between social science and political theory. Part of the task of political theory is to clarify evaluations which, if acted upon, may bring into being a non-existent state of affairs. Social science might be able to help by specifying what evaluations of action might be made in the fresh state of affairs. If we are right to hold that much moral differentiation is based on differential information then there is 'a need for more research' on the relation between social structure and information. A thoughtful discussion of the obverse relation — using such concepts as information channels and 'codes' and the costs of their acquisition and creation, appears in the central chapters of Arrow (1974).

The advantage of deciding that (most) moral claims are disguised information claims, is that if we say 'values change with differing social context' whilst the assertion may evoke sympathetic agreement, we are left at a loss as to how to specify (predict or assess) the relation. If however we say 'information differs with differing social context' then we have to hand a set of familiar tools — underemployed tools, in that we know far too little about existent moral evaluations and their context; but at least we can see where to begin. The attraction of the enterprise, if we can handle it, is that it begins to provide tools for long-term social planning which allow us to escape the problems of conservatism and the want dependency of wants.

Since papers in this volume bear the twin obligations of pointing where the frontiers of political theory may have some give (though it is to be ascertained whether the flexing covers an irregularity or a doorway) and of noting the central problems on the way, it may be worth stressing that the problems of evaluating action for the future possess that combination of real-life and logical centrality that characterises the classic political issues (duty, justice, freedom . . .). It presents a logical problem, whose roots are entwined with our epistemology, and whose irresolution is an impediment to action. 'I think . . . that the problem of preference formulation and endogenous preference change is the greatest obstacle to complete freedom'. (Elster, 1978:162). Elster, who provides one of the more suggestive specifications of the perplexity, himself decides that there is no solvent. It may be worth quoting his pessimism at length: ' . . . even if I know (in a general manner) *that* my present actions will have an impact upon my future character, I may be unable to tell how they will change my preferences.. . . . I argue that this is an inescapable condition of *la condition humaine.*. . . . The impossibility of having specific knowledge about the impact of present behaviour upon future character traits does not stem from uncertainty about the environment, nor from practical difficulties in establishing the relevant causal connections. We are dealing with an absolute impossibility . . .' (Elster, 1978:46). An impossibility I propose we can dissolve by the prosaic strategy of spelling out the connections between actions and information.

And at this point, in the infuriating fashion of writers of programmatic papers, I point into the distance and stay at home. Though, in fairness, the claim is not that we now know which way to travel, but that it is possible to specify what we would need to know in order to travel. It might here be helpful if I gave some illustration of the types of sociological gaps and discussions I have in mind. The examples themselves do not speak directly to major political issues, and are a magpie truncated collection to give the flavour of the gaps in our knowledge, which require filling, and some possible accounts, which require developing. I would feel better equipped to act as a political theorist, in a world where we deliberate 'about what is future and capable of being otherwise', if these were less problematic. That at least is the claim. It is the uncertainty as to which changes are necessary if we are to implement our moral ideals; ' "Must the whole world be converted into a cotton factory?" protested William Hazlitt in his criticism of Owen's plan.' (Harrison, 1969:53). A recent Reith lecturer (Halsey, 1978:160f) interestingly suggests revitalising 'Fraternity' alongside 'Liberty' and 'Equality'. But if fraternity is to mean more than the 'treatment as equals' implicit in the two universalistic virtues, then as a particularistic virtue (not imposing universalistic obligations) it is not clear that we know the mechanisms for its creation, or, if created, the consequences (this apart from the problems of whether, as with pleasure, it can be pursued in the abstract). We do not know enough about the cashed ground rules for moral stances. Even on the textbook universal taboo of incest there is room for hesitation: 'There was more incest in the past and it was always fathers and daughters, never brothers and sisters. It happened when mother had too many children, or when mother was ill, or when mother was dead. And very often it didn't matter a bit. The daughter usually proved very fond of the father and there would be no sign of upset on the family. No, I think it was quite an understood thing that a daughter would take on the father when the mother was ill or dead' (Mrs. Annersley, magistrate, as reported by Blythe 1969:244). Though this is at best suggestive evidence it does suggest the issue may be open. Moral philosophy, even the 'analyse the OED' variety, is little help in locating the issues which actually do exercise people (and we should identify these, and how they arise, before acting). Do you for example find the following a mite unexpected?: 'There was also some opposition to the savings criterion (in supplementary benefits) because one's savings were felt to be a very private affair, and revealing them to strangers was found objectionable. Certainly in several group discussions [for the enquiry], informants were far more forthcoming about such matters as their marital breakdowns, than about the amount of their savings.' (Supplementary Benefits Commission, 1978:61). That same enquiry (a too-rare example of the sociography that is a prelude to accounts) noted that the public at large sees more impropriety in the meticulous acquisition of entitled benefits than the (illegal) 'moonlighting' whilst receiving benefits. And before acting on unemployment pay we need to know more on regional variations in the perception of unemployment (regional variations in general being an underexplored topic — again related to disattending to contextual effects on information and judgments). Perception and evaluation of the social services requires clarification before we embark upon rewriting the relation between the State and other institutions. Why, for example, is social work customarily assessed in terms of its benefit to the client, when both observation and theory (social services as government provided family surrogates) suggest the main help is often to those on whom the client would otherwise be relying for support. To manage innovation we need to spell out how/why the world is seen as it is. Do we, for example, know enough to apply Hirsch's egalitarian strategy of reducing the *incidental* benefits from positional precedence (reduce university teachers' salaries too far and the bright people depart, leaving those of us who entered for their company bereft of a positional good)? Or take an example in a somewhat different vein. In eighteenth-century Scotland, adoption of one scientific advance — innoculation against smallpox — was, at first sight surprisingly, most readily accepted not in the centre but in the sparsely populated periphery. This can be accounted for: 'It has been pointed out that it was in areas where the disease came round so frequently that its killing effect was almost entirely confined to children that adults had a strong religious objection to interfering with

God's will by incurring smallpox artificially . . . [whereas] . . . in parts of the Highlands and Hebrides and Northern Isles· smallpox appeared only occasionally, at intervals of about thirty years, with devastating effects among adults as well as among children.' (Flinn, 1977:291–2). It may be that Flinn's explanation is weaker than some alternatives (e.g. clergy, instrumental in innoculation, more attended to on periphery) but its form, tying moral perception to context and know-ledge, is to be applauded. It is, as Leavis would say, 'not irrelevant that' many of the examples that might be adduced centre on the 'family' (ignoring the vexed question of the status and utility of that concept) as an information defining nexus, and there is room for much work on the information-mediated connections between the systems of production and reproduction. An example on perceived probability of divorce: 'Couples are reluctant to invest in skills or commodities 'specific' to their marriage if they anticipate dissolution: having children and working exclusively in the non-marriage sector are two such marriage related activities. That is, the rise in women's labour force participation rates and the fall in fertility in the past two decades have partly been caused by, as well as being cause of, the rise in marital instability' (Becker *et al*, 1977:1142). And lacunae are so plentiful; one example: studies of decisions regarding family size (arguably central nexus of the individual and the social) still appear to reduce to observing: 'birth rates change because norms change', and all the attendant miseries involved in the identification of norms separate from behaviour (when they may well be descriptive of behaviour) sit precisely at the door of such locutions. A closer look at the information available to individuals might help; as might also noting that rearing, spread in time, is more amena-ble to changing definition than bearing. (O'Neill, 1979:38, points in the right direction: 'debates about population con-trol are misconceived if we forget that people bring children up as well as bring them into the world'.) And so on. The positive examples are randomly chosen and are small examples. But all the topics are amenable to research; if we saw such enterprises as central social science we could accumulate knowledge. Though notice (although not the business of the present paper) that a social science which would adequately account for such issues would straddle the current artificial boundaries between sociology, politics and economics and require the skills of political philosophy (*cf.* Barry, 1979). The examples are examples of gaps social science must fill if it is to be pertinent to political theory; there is little virtue in pretending to greater ignorance than we should possess.

The argument of this paper has been that time, which presents itself as information, is central to the definition of social life. This leads to an emphasis on actions as against states, and on the evaluation of actions as being, in contrast to the evaluation of states, ineluctably context bound (at odds with Rawls). Part of the context is temporal relation and continuity (at odds with Nozick). The requirement that we wittingly specify the future, coupled with the claim that most moral statements are surrogate information claims, specifies a particular view of the proper relation between social science and political theory. It is this last which is the main substantive conclusion of the paper: it suggests that social science can help the theorist out of what Elster (1978:162) has called 'the greatest obstacle to complete freedom' by beginning to spell out how information about social structure (and hence evaluation) is tied to that structure. As for the rest, the argument, whatever its other flaws, is too short to convince; I shall be satisfied if it has helped put 'time' back on the agenda.

Let me end speculatively on a minor political issue. Many of us have an untutored negative reaction to the demise of a culture (the damage of oil-related development on the traditional fabric of the Shetlands, or, differently — though it is interesting to try and specify the difference — the 'immigrants swamping our inner cities'). We react positively to the continuance of culture and are reassured to find traditional Hebraic ritual in west-coast America. It is difficult within the standard terms of political discourse to argue for such intuition (contemporary Shetland fishing skills would not be pertinent to fishing after the oil runs out, the American west-coast is such a strange phenomenon that traditional knowledge of the past is no help in 'silicon valley'; and so on). But if continuity, and continuity of information, is central (in the sense I have attempted to indicate) to decision-making, then that might be the start of an argument that culture matters.

NOTES

Aaron, H.J. (1978) *Politics and Professors: The Great Society in Perspective* (Brookings, Washington).

Alves, W.M. and Rossi, P.H. (1978) 'Who should get what? Fairness judgements of the distribution of earnings', in *American Journal of Sociology* 84:541–564.

Aristotle *Nicomachean Ethics,* trans D. Ross (Oxford University Press, 1925).

Arrow, K.J. (1974) *The Limits of Organization* (W.W. Norton & Co., New York, 1978).

(1978) *Risk Allocation and Information: Some Recent Theoretical Developments* (Institute for Economic Research, Queens University, Ontario: mimeo).

Barber, B. (1977) 'Absolutization of the market: some notes on how we got from there to here,' in Dworkin *et al, Markets and Morals,* (Wiley, New York).

Barnsley, J.H. (1972) *The Social Reality of Ethics: The Comparative Analysis of Moral Codes* (Routledge & Kegan Paul, London).

Barry, B.M. (1979) 'Editorial' in *Ethics* October, 1979.

Becker, G.S. (1976) *The Economic Approach to Human Behaviour* (University of Chicago Press).

Becker, G.S., Landes, E.M. and Michael, R.T. (1977) 'An economic analysis of marital instability', in *Journal of Political Economy* 85:1141–1187.

Bell, D. (1974) *The Coming of Post-Industrial Society* (Heineman, London).

Bell, W. and Robinson, R.V. (1978) 'An index of evaluated equality: measuring conceptions of social justice in England and the United States', in *Comparative Studies in Sociology* 1:235–270.

Bernick, M. (1978) 'A note on promoting self-esteem', in *Political Theory* 6:109–118.

Bettleheim, B. (1969) *The Children of the Dream* (Thames and Hudson, London).

Blythe, R. (1969) *Akenfield: Portrait of an English Village* (Allen Lane, London).

Burke, E. (1790) *Reflections on the Revolution in France,* ed. C.C. O'Brien (Penguin, London, 1968).

Campbell, A., Converse, P.E. Miller, W.E. and Stokes, D.E. (1960) *The American Voter* (Wiley, London).

Carr-Hill, R.A. and Macdonald, K.I. (1973) 'Problems in the analysis of life histories', in *Sociological Review Monograph* 19:57–95.

Cherlin, A. (1978) 'Remarriage as an incomplete institution', in *American Journal of Sociology* 84:634–650.

Cornford, F.M. (1935) 'The Unwritten Philosophy' in *The Unwritten Philosophy and Other Essays* (Cambridge University Press, 1967).

Dennis, N. (1970) *People and Planning* (Faber, London).

Durkheim, E. and Mauss M. (1969) *Primitive Classification,* ed. and trans. R. Needham (Cohen & West: London).

Dworkin, G., Bermant, G. and Brown, P.G. (1977) *Markets and Morals* (Wiley, New York)

Elster, J. (1978) *Logic and Society: Contradictions and Possible Worlds* (Wiley, New York).

Flinn, M. *ed.* (1977) *Scottish Population History* (Cambridge University Press).

Fried, C. (1977) 'Difficulties in the economic analysis of rights', in Dworkin *et al, Markets and Morals* (Wiley, New York).

Gardener, M. (1971) 'Mathematical Games', in *Scientific American* 224(2): 112–117.

Gershuny, J. (1978) 'Transport forecasting: fixing the future', in *Policy and Politics* 6:373–402.

Goffman, E. (1961) *Asylums: Essays on the Social Situation of Mental Patients and other Inmates* (Penguin, London).

Goldstein, M.S., Marcus, A.C. and Rausch, N.P. (1978) 'The non-utilization of evaluation research', in *Pacific Sociological Review,* 21:21–44.

Grathoff, R.H. (1970) *The Structure of Social Inconsistencies: a Contribution to a Unified Theory of Play, Game and Social Action* (Martinus Nijhoff, The Hague).

Halsey, A.H. (1974) 'Government against poverty', in M. Bulmer ed. *Social Policy Research* (Macmillan, London, 1978).

(1978) *Change in British Society* (Oxford University Press).

Halsey, A.H., Heath, A.F. and Ridge, J.M. (1979) *Origins and Destinations: Family, Class and Education in Modern Britain* (Oxford University Press).

Harrison, J.F.C. (1969) *Robert Owen and the Owenites in Britain and America* (Routledge & Kegan Paul, London).

Hayek, F.K. (1960) *The Constitution of Liberty* (Routledge & Kegan Paul, London).

Hirsch, F. (1977) *Social Limits to Growth* (Routledge & Kegan Paul, London).

Hobbes, T. (1651) *Leviathan*, ed. M. Oakeshott (Blackwell, Oxford, 1960).

Hogan, D.P. (1978) 'The variable order of events in the life sequence', in *American Sociological Review* 43:573–586.

Hughes, W.R. (1978) 'Lifetime utility maximisation when the consumer's lifetime depends on his consumption', in *The Economic Record* 54:65–71.

Joseph, P. (1977) 'The politics of "good" and "bad" information: the national security bureaucracy and the Vietnam war', in *Politics and Society* 7:105–126.

Kant, I. (1784) 'Idea for a universal history with a cosmopolitan purpose'. (1798) 'The contest of faculties', *Kant's Political Writings*, eds. H. Reiss and H.B. Nisbett (Cambridge University Press, 1971).

Knight, F.H. (1935) 'Ethics and the economic interpretations' in *The Ethics of Competition* (Allen & Unwin: London, 1951).

Lawson, G. (1657) *An examination of the political part of Mr. Hobbs his Leviathan* (London).

Lenk, H. (1978) 'Varieties of commitments: approaches to the symboliz-ation of conditional obligation', in *Theory and Decision* 9:7–39.

Lukes, S. (1977) 'A reply to K. I. Macdonald', in *British Journal of Political Science* 7:418–419.

Macdonald, K. I. (1971) 'Allegorical landscape in the *Faerie Queene*', in *Durham University Journal*, 32:121–124

(1976a) 'Causal modelling in politics and sociology', in *Quality and Quantity* 10:189–208.

(1976b) 'Is "power" essentially contested?' in *British Journal of Political Science* 6:380–382.

(1976c) 'Residential segregation in United States cities: a comment', in *Social Forces* 55:85–88.

Manning, R. (1978) 'Resource use when demand is interdependent over time', in *The Economic Record* 54:72–77.

Marx, K. (1857) 'Introduction to a critique of political economy', *The German Ideology*, ed. C.J. Arthur (Lawrence & Wishart, London, 1970).

Mill, J.S. (1861) *Utilitarianism* (Dent, London, 1960).

Miller, D. (1976) *Social Justice* (Oxford University Press).

Newson, E. (1978) 'Unreasonable care: the establishment of selfhood', in G. Vesey ed. *Human Values* (Harvester Press, Sussex).

Nozick, R. (1974) *Anarchy, State and Utopia* (Blackwell, Oxford).

Oakeshott, M. (1956) 'Political education' in *Philosophy Politics and Society* ed P. Laslett (Blackwells, Oxford).

O'Neill, O. (1979) 'Begetting, bearing, and rearing' *Having children: philosophical and legal reflections on parenthood* ed. O. O'Neill and W. Ruddick, (Oxford University Press, New York).

Orwin, C. (1975) 'On the Sovereign Authorization', in *Political Theory* 3:26–44.

Plamenatz, J. (1963) *Man and Society II* (Longmans, London).

Powley, T. and Evans, D. (1979) 'Towards a methodology of action research', in *Journal of Social Policy* 8:27–46.

Rawls, J. (1972) *A Theory of Justice* (Oxford University Press).

Ross, A. (1653) *Leviathan drawn out with a hook* (London).

Ryle, G. (1958) 'On forgetting the difference between right and wrong' in A. I. Melden ed. *Essays in Moral Philosophy* (University of Washington Press, Seattle) reprinted in J.J. Walsh and H.L. Shapiro, *Aristotle's Ethics* (1967) (Wadsworth, Belmont).

Schelling, T. (1974) 'On the ecology of micromotives' in *The Corporate Society* ed. R. Marris (Macmillan, London).

Sen, A.K. (1979) 'Personal utilities and public judgements: or, what's wrong with welfare economics' in *Economic Journal* (forthcoming).

Smith, D. and Whalley, A. (1975) *Racial Minorities and Public Housing* PEP Broadsheet No. 558 (PEP, London).

Smith, A. (1789) *An Inquiry into the Nature and Causes of the Wealth of Nations* ed. E. Cannan (University of Chicago Press, 1976).

Smith, G.A.N. (1975) 'Action Research: experimental social adminis-tration?' in Lees, R. and Smith, G.A.N. eds. *Action Research in Com-*

munity Development (Routledge & Kegan Paul, London).

Soedel, W. and Foley, V. (1979) 'Ancient catapults' in *Scientific American* 240(3): 120–128.

Supplementary Benefits Commission (1978) *Report on research on public attitudes towards the Supplementary Benefit System.* (Central Office of Information, London: mimeo).

Taylor, M. (1976) *Anarchy and Co-operation* (Wiley, London).

Trilling, L. (1955) *The Opposing Self* (Viking Press, New York).

Whorf, B.L. (1956) *Language, Thought and Reality* ed. J.B. Carroll (MIT).

Williams, B. (1973) 'A critique of utilitarianism' in J.J.C. Smart and B. Williams, *Utilitarianism: for and against* (Cambridge University Press).

Winch, P. (1958) *The Idea of a Social Science* (Routledge & Kegan Paul, London).

Wolin, S.S. (1961) *Politics and Vision* (Allen & Unwin, London).

Young, M. and Willmott, P. (1973) *The Symmetrical Family* (Routledge & Kegan Paul, London).

Social Justice and the Principle of Need[1]

DAVID MILLER

ONE of the issues that perplexes and divides liberals at the present time is whether policies that aim to distribute resources according to need are appropriately seen as required by social justice, or whether they are more properly understood by reference to other values like humanity and social utility. All liberal societies do as a matter of fact pursue social policies that aim to relieve the more urgent needs of their members, and few people in these societies would wish it otherwise; but there is less agreement about the principles which underlie the provision of relief. Do the recipients really have a just claim to the resources they receive? Would it be unjust, as opposed to simply inhumane, if a government were to decide, perhaps for economic reasons, to dismantle its health service, or stop giving unemployment benefit? Possibly these questions seem academic in the light of the wide practical agreement that seems to exist over provision for need. Yet it would be unusual if differences of principle did not at some point emerge as differences in practice, and I shall try to show that this happens in the present case. Whether or not we regard provision for need as a matter of social justice will affect a) the moral importance we attach to such provision; b) the form of provision we prescribe; and c) the way we understand the relationship between the recipient and the agency which provides — whether this be an individual, an institution, or 'society' considered as a whole. For this reason it is of crucial importance for liberals (and others) to decide whether need is a proper ground of social justice, and I shall here attempt to defend the view that it is, in opposition to some recent arguments that will be considered in due course.

We must begin by looking briefly at the notion of need itself, and at what is meant by 'the principle of need'. An elementary distinction that is sometimes missed is that between individual and social need. When we refer to individual need to justify a policy, we are pointing to a lack or deficiency on the part of one or more persons which can be overcome by providing those persons with the appropriate resources. 'Social need' has a different logic. If we refer to the social need for doctors to justify increasing the number of places available in medical schools, or paying doctors higher salaries, we are using an argument that is utilitarian in form; the welfare of the whole of society is being used to justify providing opportunities or incentives for particular individuals. 'Social need', then, refers to the more important aspects of social utility (utilities whose absence would be particularly damaging), and it does not in general justify distributing resources according to individual needs (though, like utility in general, it may occasionally justify such a policy). Our concern here is with individual need, rather than social need, as a political principle.

It is widely agreed that in considering the concept of need, a distinction must be drawn between needs and wants or desires. Not everything that a person wants to have can properly be called a need, and equally a person may fail, through ignorance or for some other reason, to desire something that he does need. Needs, then, have to be ascribed to a person at least in part independently of his wants; but there are two schools of thought about how this is to be done. One school advances a norm-related conception of need. Reference to need, it is said, presupposes a conventional standard of living; to the extent to which a person's level of resources falls below that required by this standard of living, he is said to be in need.[2] If 'adequate housing' includes the possession of a fixed bath, hot-water tap and inside w.c.,[3] a person whose house lacks one or more of these facilities will be said to need them. Clearly the norm itself will be conventional and socially relative; as a society becomes more prosperous, the standard of adequacy will rise (defenders of this view are not always so ready to recognise the converse implication: the poorer society is, the more limited will 'needs' become).

The advantage of this approach is that it produces a manageable and easily applied notion of need, and for that reason it is useful to policy-makers and administrators. Once the appropriate norm has been set, 'need' is relatively easy to identify, and (in theory) to remove. From a political point of view, however, this conception of need has a conservative-liberal bias, for it restricts the scope of need to the conventional minimum standard of living in any society. Any individual claims above the minimum are regarded, not as needs, but as something else. The implication is that only a small proportion of social resources are required to satisfy needs, and the remainder can be distributed through market mechanism, as rewards and so forth.

The other school of thought prefers an individual-related conception of need. The view here is that, while the distinction between needs and wants must be preserved, needs vary from individual to individual, and cannot be estimated without taking account of individual peculiarities. Even in the case of a basic need such as food there seems some justification for this approach, for the intake of calories etc., necessary to maintain bodily functions clearly varies from person to person. When we turn to less basic needs, the case becomes still clearer. 'Need' may here be taken to refer to what is necessary to the individual in order to carry out his central aims and aspirations, the aims and aspirations that make up his 'plan of life'.[4] Because plans of life vary greatly, so too will needs. Monks, for example, whose central aim is to acquire and practise certain religious virtues, will on that account have relatively slender material needs. Musicians, who aim to achieve a high standard of performance, will need well-constructed instruments. To prevent this notion getting out of hand, some limitation will have to be placed on what can count as a 'plan of life' for the purpose of assessing a person's needs (*bon viveurs*, for instance, cannot expect to be assessed under that description). But in any case it is useless to pretend that this conception of need makes for administrative ease. Its purpose is better construed as providing a goal towards which social aspirations may be directed — namely the full satisfaction of needs, as compared with the minimal satisfaction of needs which is the aim of current welfare policy. How a society which aimed to satisfy needs in this expanded sense might be organised has never been satisfactorily explained, but it would certainly be possible to move somewhat closer to the goal than we are at present. Whereas conservatives and liberals are likely to favour the norm-related conception of need, socialists will prefer the individual-related conception, which is appropriate to their aim of distributing all or most of society's resources according to need.

Most of the following argument does not require that a choice be made between these two conceptions of need, and readers will be able to place their preferred interpretation on the term. What both views have in common is an understanding of need as a lack or deficiency — in the first case, as the gap between an individual's resources and the social norm, in the second as the difference between what an individual ideally requires to carry out his plan of life and what he actually has. In both cases it seems appropriate to represent need as a negative quantity when attempting to measure it. For instance we might (arbitrarily) choose −100 to represent complete destitution, and 0 to represent fulfilment of the social norm (using the norm-related conception) or complete individual fulfilment (using the individual-related conception), with figures in between representing the percentage of any person's needs that are left unsatisfied. On the first interpretation of 'need', *most* individuals in comparatively affluent societies will score 0 (they are at or above the social norm), whereas on the second virtually no-one will reach 0 (though in such societies they will stand some way above −100). Without supposing that we can use such a scale with any precision in real cases, we may use it for the analytical purpose of formulating a distinction between aggregative and distributive principles of need. The aggregative principle is simply that the sum of individual need-scores should be made as small as possible; less formally, that total need should be minimised. Thus suppose we are considering four individuals whose needs can be represented as follows:

$$\begin{array}{cccc} A & B & C & D \\ -10 & -50 & -30 & 0 \end{array}$$

The aggregative principle supports any redistribution of resources that lowers the total need-score (−90). Thus it endorses a change to:

A	B	C	D
-10	-40	-20	0

But also a change to:

A	B	C	D
0	-60	-10	0

and in fact would be indifferent between these two changes.

The formulation of a distributive principle of need is a little more difficult. The usual slogan, 'to each according to his needs', suggests, by its similarity to the corresponding formula 'to each according to his merits', that the distribution of resources should be proportional to need. Thus, in our example, B, who is five times as 'needy' as A, should get five times as many need-satisfying resources, and so forth. However, I suggest that this interpretation only makes sense if we assume that the result of the distribution is that everyone's needs are satisfied, so that each person finishes with a need-score of 0. If this doesn't happen, a different interpretation is required.

Suppose, for instance, that I have just a single bread roll to share between a starving man and a man who is ordinarily hungry. I judge that the former is ten times more needy than the latter, using the above convention. Should I then divide the roll into eleven portions, giving ten to the starving man, and one to the man who is just hungry? The effect, let us assume, would be to leave the starving man still in greater need than the hungry man had been before he received his fragment of roll. It would seem more reasonable to give the whole roll to the starving man, and indeed (if more rolls were available) to continue distributing to him alone, until he had reached the point at which his hunger was similar to the second man's, and from then on to distribute equally. The aim would therefore be to equalise the extent to which needs were satisfied by distributing resources to those in greater need, and I suggest that this interpretation best captures the spirit of the slogan 'to each according to his needs'.

The distributive principle of need can therefore be formulated as follows: minimise the inequality in individual need-scores. To make this more precise, we need a way of measuring inequality. Several measures have been proposed,[5] but perhaps the most intuitively plausible is the mean difference in individual scores. This measure involves taking each pair of individuals in turn, calculating the difference between their scores and averaging the results. Thus if we let AB designate the difference between A's need-score and B's, AC the difference between A's and C's, and so forth,[6] we have, taking the original figures, AB = 40, AC = 20, AD = 10, BC = 20, BD = 50, CD = 30. The mean difference is 170/6 = 28.3.

The distributive principle of need would endorse a change to, say:

$$\begin{array}{cccc} A & B & C & D \\ -20 & -30 & -10 & 0 \end{array}$$

(Mean difference 16.7)

but also to:

$$\begin{array}{cccc} A & B & C & D \\ -50 & -60 & -40 & -30 \end{array}$$

(Mean difference also 16.7)

This shows that the distributive principle of need is unlikely to be accepted on its own as a guide to policy, but must be supplemented by an aggregative principle of some kind — at the very least to act as a tie-breaker between distributions with the same degree of inequality (for instance the two cited above), but more probably to stand in a more general trade-off relationship to the distributive principle. Some people might even feel at this stage that the distributive principle had nothing at all to commend it: surely, they might say, the point is to eliminate hunger altogether, not to ensure that people are equally hungry. However it is worth remembering a) that sometimes hunger cannot be eliminated (at a given place and time), in which case it may well be proper to attempt to 'distribute' it equally; b) that 'need' in our diagrams does not necessarily represent basic human need: if an individual-related conception is being used, the level at which basic needs are satisfied might be represented by −75, and the comparisons we have been making might be between the relative satisfaction of A's need for books, B's need for musical instruments, and so forth. Here it at least makes sense to weigh equality of need-satisfaction against *total* need-satisfaction, and even to give priority to the former. But to see why we might count equality of need-satisfaction as a value in the first place, we must turn to the concept of social justice.

II

The particular purpose of this section will be to distinguish the concept of social justice from other concepts such as benevolence and humanity in such a way that the problem of relating the two principles of need to social justice is brought into sharp focus. That justice does not comprise the whole of morality, and that social justice does not comprise the whole of social morality, is by now fairly commonplace. It is also widely recognised that the main division in individual morality lies between justice and benevolence, and in social morality between social justice and ends such as humanity, welfare, and social utility. The basis of division is fundamentally the same in both cases, and it seems to me to consist in two connected features. First, justice is directly concerned with the distribution of benefits and burdens among individuals, that is to say with the share of benefits and burdens each individual receives, whereas benevolence and its social analogues are concerned with the overall amount of benefit and burden received by the population in question, and not with the distribution per se; distributive questions are only indirectly relevant to benevolence, for instance insofar as the manner in which a given stock of goods is distributed may affect the total amount of satisfaction derived from it. Second, if we denote the practitioner of justice or benevolence as the agent, and the people on whom these virtues are practised as the recipients, there is a difference in the quality of the relationship between agent and recipient in a case of justice and a case of benevolence. In a case of justice, the recipient is said to be owed something by the agent, or to have a claim to what is due to him, whereas in a case of benevolence he is not. Let me expand a little on these distinctions.

The distributive character of justice may be brought out by observing that to act justly towards someone, we must begin by identifying the relevant features of his person and conduct, and then we must match our treatment of him to those features. In some cases the matching can be performed directly from a knowledge of the features in question, whereas in other cases a comparison must be made between this person and other people who might also be recipients of our distribution.[7] Thus if the relevant feature is a right which the person has acquired (for example by entering into a contract), this already indicates what is due to the person, and the treatment which justice requires can, in the absence of competing claims, be read off directly from a knowledge of his right. In contrast, if I am rewarding people according to their deserts from a fixed stock of goods, to know how to treat any particular person I have to compare his deserts with those of everyone else, and calculate what his proper share of goods should be. But although the matching process may take different forms, there is in each case a relationship to be established between a personal feature and a form of treatment, such that the treatment is said to be due to the person in virtue of that feature.

When we act benevolently, no such matching process takes place. We must of course learn enough about the recipient of our benevolence to ensure that the action is successful — that it gives pleasure or relieves pain. If we give someone a present, we want to know that he will appreciate it; if we are trying to cure an illness, we must discover what medicine will be effective. But here the relationship between features of the recipient and the action we take is simply a causal one: his features make a given form of action effective or ineffective. There is no matching to be done in the sense outlined above.

From the fact that justice is concerned with the distribution of benefits and burden among individuals, it does not of course follow that all distributive principles must be considered as principles of justice. We have still to establish what features of people may properly be taken as grounds of just treatment. Thus the fact that there exists a distributive principle of need does not entail that this principle is a principle of justice; it will only be so if need is a proper ground of just treatment. The analysis up to this point does suggest, however, that the distributive principle of need cannot simply be subsumed under benevolence or humanity, since the principle embodies a concern for the comparative treatment of individuals which is lacking in those virtues; it requires that resources should be distributed according to the relative needs of the recipients. (On the other hand, the aggregative principle of need, requiring us to minimise total need, clearly expresses an important part of both virtues.) We shall return to this question later.

Turning now to the second contrast between justice and benevolence, wherein does the difference in the relationship between agent and recipient reside? Focusing first on the agent, should we say that justice is a duty whereas benevolence and humanity are not? This proposal seems to narrow the scope of 'duty' excessively, for any relief of suffering, whether or not required by justice, appears to be a duty, and we might even want to speak of duties not to maltreat animals, which clearly could not be duties of justice. A more refined proposal is made by Mill when he suggests that we should distinguish between duties of perfect and imperfect obligation (the former alone being duties of justice). The first explication that he offers of this seems unsatisfactory, namely that duties of imperfect obligation are 'those in which, though the act is obligatory, the particular occasions of performing it are left to our choice'.[8] This suggest that benevolence is always casual, whereas in fact any encounter with a person in serious need immediately activates our duty of humanity irrespective of our choice. But a second attempt at explication is closer to the mark: 'duties of perfect obligation are those duties in virtue of which a correlative *right* resides in some person or persons.'[9] We must, in other words, focus on the recipient of the duty, rather than on the agent. A duty of justice corresponds to a right in the recipient, though a right in a very loose sense which I should prefer to describe as a claim, to distinguish it from a right in the narrower sense as something that arises from a rule or a transaction. In this broad sense we say that a person is entitled to just treatment, meaning that he has a claim against the agent to his just share of resources. This claim can be expressed, if the recipient chooses, in several ways. He can *demand* his fair share of benefits, he can *complain* if he fails to receive it, he may be able to take steps against the agent to guarantee performance. In the case of a duty of humanity, however, although the agent may be morally bound to perform the duty, the recipient has no claim to the benefit he receives, and cannot legitimately engage in any of the claiming activities just described. He may ask the agent to benefit him, and may think badly of him if he fails to do so, but he cannot insist that his request be met. Compare, for example, asking someone for a loan with claiming a sum of money that has previously been promised. Or compare asking for a pay rise because you want to send your wife abroad for a rest cure with asking for a pay rise because your skills are not being adequately rewarded.

One consequence of this distinction between justice and benevolence or humanity is that, in a case of justice, the relationship between agent and recipient remains an equal one, whereas in a case of benevolence or humanity, the agent acquires a kind of moral superiority over the recipient; the recipient has to supplicate the agent for the benefits he receives, and, if his request is granted, is afterwards indebted to his benefactor. If this interchange occurs regularly, an unequal relationship will be established which is likely to weaken the recipient's self-respect — a fact which will turn out to be of some important when we come to compare justice and humanity as justifications of social policy.

III

I now wish to make two positive claims about the relationship between social justice and the principle of need, and then to consider some arguments which purport to undermine these claims. The first positive claim is that, if justice consists in matching our treatment of people to their relevant qualities and actions, then need is a perfectly intelligible ground of justice. A person's needs are, first of all, quite clearly qualities of that person; it is possible to compare one person's needs with another's; and a comparison of needs will immediately indicate a relevant way of distributing resources among persons. Thus from a formal point of view, the distributive principle of need is perfectly appropriate as a principle of social justice (whereas many other principles — the principle of utility, for instance — can be eliminated on these formal grounds). The second positive claim is that the 'common moral consciousness' in contemporary liberal societies does in fact recognise need as a ground of justice; in other words, in practical discussions of economic or social policy, people will describe a policy as socially just on the grounds that it distributes resources according to need. It is, for example, regarded as socially just that the health services allocate medicine on the basis of need, and that social security is given to people who would otherwise lack any means of support. Taken together, these claims constitute a *prima facie* case for regarding the distributive principle of need as part of social justice.

The arguments I shall consider acknowledge the *prima facie* case, but go on to assert that the appearance is nonetheless an optical illusion. Although people do refer to the relief of need when maintaining that policies are just, it is said, they should not be understood literally. The reference to need conceals the fact that some other factor forms the real ground of justice in such cases. Consider the view of J.R. Lucas.[10] Justice, he believes, is centrally a matter of rewarding individuals according to their deserts. But since, for practical reasons, we have to order our societies by establishing fixed rules, justice takes on a secondary sense of entitlement under the established rules, which may conflict with desert. In special cases — for example in a 'mutual benefit society' — we may design the rules so that individuals are given benefits according to need. In such a case, then, individuals would have just claims to resources on the basis of their need, but the ground of these claims would be entitlement under the rules of the society rather than need *per se*. An equally needy non-member would have no claim. Lucas maintains that 'the same principle governs the National Health Service and various other aspects of the Welfare State'.[11]

Campbell makes a similar point.[12] Distinguishing between formal and material justice, he observes that we may decide (on grounds of humanity) to institute a scheme for the relief of need, but that once we have done so, individuals will have claims of formal justice to benefits which they could not have claimed on grounds of need alone. 'Thus, if there is a law to the effect that whenever A needs x then A is to be provided with x by the State, then A has a right to x and formal justice requires that he be provided with x.'[13] But besides recognising that needs can become relevant to justice when they give rise to entitlements via formal rules, Campbell also points to several ways in which need may become connected to desert. First, needs may result directly from deserving behaviour (for instance a need for medical treatment incurred by a courageous act). Second, needs may indicate that someone has received less benefit than he deserves (for instance poverty which arises because men are not given a fair reward for their work). Third, the satisfaction of needs may be a prerequisite of fair competition for rewards (for instance the satisfaction of basic needs for food, etc. as a condition of equality of opportunity in education). In these cases, referring to need to show that a policy was socially just would be a roundabout way of referring to desert; the fact that needs were unsatisfied would show that people had not been (or could not be in the future) treated according to their deserts. But, Campbell concludes, if need is linked neither to formal rights nor to desert, it has nothing to do with justice itself. The relief of need as such is a matter of humanity, not of justice. Lucas agrees: 'It is not an exercise of justice to give a man something merely because he wants it or needs it, although it may be an exercise of generosity or of liberty or of humanity so to do.'[14]

In assessing these arguments, it is important to recognise the correctness of their positive claim: needs can indeed become pertinent to social justice in the guise of rights or in connection with desert when otherwise they would not. It is also important to see that many social policies can be justified in alternative ways, and it may not be easy to decide which of these justifications is decisive in practice. The granting of unemployment benefit, for example, can be viewed in several different ways: as a humanitarian policy to prevent suffering; as the outcome of a social insurance scheme to which everyone contributes to guard against the risk of unemployment; as recognition of the fact that a capitalist economy needs a pool of unemployed labour, and that the unemployed therefore 'contribute' indirectly to production ('They also serve who only stand and wait', as Lucas puts it); and finally as a requirement of social justice. The justifying principles are, respectively, humanity, entitlement, desert and need. This makes it difficult to construct a watertight rebuttal of the Lucas/Campbell position, for any examples that are produced are liable to be reinterpreted to fit that position. Nevertheless the arguments that have been outlined above, ingenious though they are, do not seem to me to do full justice to the commitment which the 'common moral consciousness' has to the principle of need.

To begin with, if needs can only become a ground of social justice when they appear in the guise of rights, one cannot say of rules or practices that aim to distribute resources according to need that they are themselves just. Although one may say that a Welfare State, when it is established, creates just claims on the part of those in need, one cannot on this view say that the creation of a Welfare State is itself an act of social justice, or that a society which incorporates a Welfare State is more just than one without. This seems to me to contradict most people's beliefs about the Welfare State, which they regard as materially just, not merely as formally just (in the sense of giving rise to just claims when it exists). So at this point Lucas's treatment of the claims of need fails to match up to the generally accepted view.

Second, although the existence of unfulfilled need may often indicate that deserts have not been properly rewarded, not all cases can be interpreted in this way, nor even all those cases in which we think that questions of justice arise. Consider the example of medicine being distributed according to need. In making the distribution, are we obliged to distinguish between those who deserve medicine because their ill-health results from meritorious action or from an undeserved deprivation in the past, and those who do not? Is the distribution only just if we make this distinction? It seems to me again that most people would regard these questions of desert as irrelevant to the matter at hand, and would be perfectly happy to describe as fair a distribution which aimed to restore each person equally to health without any enquiry into the origins of their illnesses. Nor is the distribution fair merely because it re-establishes the conditions for equality of opportunity. Campbell's argument at this point seems curiously reminiscent of the attempts of nineteenth-century charity organisations to use desert criteria instead of need criteria in allocating poor relief. First, relief was only to be given to the 'deserving poor' —

those whose needs arose from factors outside of their control, not from personal deficiencies such as idleness or intemperance. Second, the extent of relief was to be limited to the minimum necessary to set the individual back on his feet again, so that he could rejoin the 'struggle for existence'. Thankfully, these attempts eventually foundered on the organisations' inability to distinguish between the 'deserving' and the 'undeserving' poor. Nowadays we are a little more enlightened in our attitudes. Although we seem reluctant to relieve needs above a fairly minimal level, for fear (it is said) that the incentive to work would be lost, we do recognise that need in itself gives a man a just claim to the share of resources which will raise him to the minimum. To reintroduce questions of desert in this area, which is the upshot of Campbell's argument, would be a retrograde step.

Campbell's intention is of course precisely the reverse of this. By making the satisfaction of needs a matter of humanity rather than of justice, he hopes to disentangle need and desert entirely. So we must now consider whether it is satisfactory to subsume the principle of need under humanity rather than justice. At this point the distinction between aggregative and distributive principles of need, explicated in Section I, becomes important. The aggregative principle of need — the principle that we should minimise the total of unsatisfied need in the population we are considering — seems a plausible way of formalising our duty of humanity in one class of cases. The distributive principle of need — the principle that we should equalise individual need-scores by redistributing in favour of those in greater need — might on occasion yield a prescription that was identical with that yielded by the aggregative principle, but there is no reason to think that it will in general (as we saw in Section I), in consequence of which it cannot be subsumed under humanity; for why should our duty of humanity require us to be concerned with the *relative* levels of need-satisfaction enjoyed by different people? That duty is a duty to relieve suffering; it is not a duty to be concerned about relativities.

Now Campbell does try to deal with the objection that humanity cannot accommodate the distributive principle of need, which (he appears to admit) carries moral weight. But the argument seems to me ambiguous.

Humanity does not require us simply to relieve the sum total of suffering, but to relieve the suffering of individual human beings and the obligation is greatest where the suffering is greatest, in that the person who is suffering most has first claim on the available resources. That is, beneficence as embodied in the principles of negative utilitarianism embodies the distributive principle that those in greatest need ought to receive most assistance, or, more specifically, that aid should be in proportion to need.[15]

Does Campbell mean that the minimisation of suffering does as a matter of fact require us to give most to those in greatest need, or that the minimisation of suffering is qualified by the independent (distributive) requirement that aid should be given in proportion to need? If he means the first, his argument is open to the objection that it is empirically implausible. Suffering may sometimes be minimised by adhering to the distributive principle of need, but it will not be in all cases. If we have to treat a number of sick men with a limited supply of medicine, will their total suffering necessarily be minimised if the neediest are given most medicine? Might we not make the (hard) decision to leave the worst cases untreated so that we can restore a larger number of men to reasonable health, and thereby minimise the total amount of pain? This would (in my view) be human but unjust. On the first reading of Campbell's argument, it would simply be impossible for the case to occur.

The second reading is more interesting. The question we must ask is how a distributive principle can become inserted into a duty which is not essentially concerned with distribution. Something like the following account may be proposed. Suppose I come into contact with a group of people who have needs that I can relieve with the resources at my disposal. At this point my duty towards them is a duty of humanity alone, not a duty of justice — they have no just claim on my resources. Once I have decided to relieve their need, however, questions of justice do arise. I must try to distribute my resources fairly, even though the people concerned had no prior claim on those resources. Some philosophers have referred to this as 'justice in the distribution of benevolence'. Feinberg puts the argument well: 'No person has a right to another person's charity, and yet if a charitable benefactor distributes his largesse to nine persons in a group of ten, arbitrarily withholding it from the tenth for no good reason, his behaviour seems in some important way unfair to the tenth.'[16] But *if* a person has no claim of justice to another person's resources, how can he come to have such a claim merely because nine other people are given benefits? This brings to light a crucial feature of Feinberg's example. If the ten people were considered as separate persons standing in no special relationship to one another, the tenth person would have no claim to benefit merely because the other nine had already done so. For example, if you tell me of ten equally needy people living in different countries, and I decide to help nine of them, I have done no injustice to the tenth, always assuming (what has yet to be decided) that I have no prior duty of justice to any of them. But in Feinberg's example the ten people are described as a *group*. This suggests that the benefactor creates, by word or deed, an expectation that each person is to be a beneficiary, and it is the non-fulfilment of this expectation that makes the treatment of the tenth person seem unfair. If this is correct, it follows that no distributive principle is actually included in the duty of humanity or benevolence; but that in acting benevolently we may place ourselves in such a relationship to the recipients of our benevolence that questions of justice arise — and then, of course, distributive principles come into play. Strictly speaking, then, there is no such thing as 'justice in the distribution of benevolence'. Benevolence and humanity, as principles, are distinct from justice and do not incorporate distributive considerations. But the practice of these virtues may (though it need not) create a new relationship between agent and recipient such that the recipient comes to have claim of justice on the agent. These claims of justice, however, arise from the relationship itself, and are not derived from the original duty of benevolence.

Our conclusion must be that duties of humanity and benevolence cannot account for the obligation we seem to feel, not merely to satisfy other people's needs, but to treat them fairly by giving more to those in greatest need and so to bring about a state of equality in the extent to which needs are satisfied. This latter obligation is an obligation of justice, and moreover one that cannot be reduced to our other obligations of justice, such as the obligation to respect entitlement or the obligation to reward desert. Yet the arguments we have considered, though they are ultimately unconvincing, do raise in a sharp form an important question we have yet to face: how does one man come to have a claim of justice on another on the grounds of his need? Is it the case that need in itself gives rise to claims of justice? Or must there be some stronger relationship between agent and recipient before such claims arise?

IV

It may seem that the conclusion we have just reached commits us to a straightforward answer to these questions. Unless need by itself gives rise to claims of justice, how can need be considered a ground of just distribution at all? But here we ought to reflect that a similar problem arises in the case of desert. Although desert is generally taken to be a proper ground of just distribution, it does not follow that each person's deserts give him a claim of justice against everyone else who might be able to satisfy them. On the contrary, the claims that desert creates are usually quite specific — one deserves such-and-such *from* a particular person or institution.[17] This fact can be recognised without reducing desert to a kind of entitlement. Perhaps the case of need is essentially similar. There seems something plausible in Lucas's assertion that the bare fact of someone else's need gives rise only to a duty of humanity on my part, not to a duty of justice, even if we think that the duty of justice may sometimes require us to distribute resources according to need. But Lucas only indicates one way in which need can give rise to claims of justice — namely when an arrangement is deliberately created with the aim of satisfying need (his example is a 'mutual benefit society'), in which case need becomes merely a condition of formal entitlement. Is this the only kind of relationship in which needs become relevant to justice?

Consider by way of contrast the family as a social institution. In the family it is acknowledged that one member's need gives him a fair claim to another member's property: although there is private possession, there is also an expectation that goods will be shared when the necessity arises. If we had to explain why this was so, we should refer to the quality of the relationships which (ideally, at least) prevail in the family — to the existence of strong emotional ties, activities performed in common, shared ends and so forth. Quite why relationships of this kind should give rise to a particular sense of justice cannot be demonstrated, but only understood. It seems clear, however, that if one stands in relation to another person as one stands towards one's parent, child or sibling, then that person will have a just claim to one's resources on the grounds of his need. For this reason, those who have wished to defend an interpretation of social justice as distribution according to need have often tried to extend the model of the family to apply to some wider social grouping, or even to the whole of mankind.

As, in a family, justice requires that the children who are unable to labour, and those who, by sickness, are disabled, should have their necessities supplied out of the common stock, so, in the great family of God, of which all mankind are the children, justice, I think, as well as charity, requires that the necessities of those who, by the providence of God, are disabled from supplying themselves, should be supplied from what might otherwise be stored for future wants.[18]

It is unlikely that such a simple extension of the model will be found very convincing. Nevertheless the example of the family serves as a useful corrective to the opposite view, which is that all social institutions must be conceived on the model of voluntary associations. For the family is clearly a non-voluntary institution. Although the choice of the marriage partner is to a greater or lesser extent voluntary, from then on one is bound in relationships not of one's own choosing. (Hegel gave a particularly effective demolition of the view that the family can be analysed in terms of contract.)[19] One does not choose one's brother, for example, but one has obligations of justice towards him which require one to meet his claims of need. These obligations are not assumed by any contract or act of agreement, or indeed by any voluntary act at all.

The idea that one can have obligations to a person by virtue of the relationship in which one stands towards him, even though these obligations have not been voluntarily assumed, is an important one even if the model of the family cannot literally be extended to wider social groupings. Although a person may belong to a number of voluntary associations which create no obligations to other members other than those explicitly laid down in the articles of association, it is clear that society itself is not properly conceived as a voluntary association; nor, despite recent attempts to present it as such,[20] is the state. We do not choose to join the society to which we belong or the state of which we are citizens. Before we are capable of choice we have already received immeasurable benefit from society and the state: sustenance, medical aid, security, the resources of language and culture. As members of society we continue to benefit from an unbroken scheme of social co-operation which we take for granted but which we could not do without. The image of the individual as an independent monad who contracts for everything he receives is simply a travesty. By belonging to society, therefore, we stand in a non-voluntary relationship to our fellow members which has at least something in common with the family, and which can plausibly be seen to create obligations of justice to our fellows when they are in need. These obligations are plainly less extensive than those within the family, reflecting the relative weakness of general social ties when compared to family ties, but they exist nonetheless. There is much to be said for Hegel's view that the state (in his broad sense) combines the unity and mutual obligation of the family with the fragmentation and mutual indifference of civil society. Recent attempts to revive a contractual theory of the state ignore the third moment of the dialectic.

I suggest, then, that if we reflect on the kind of relationships that exist in a normally-constituted society, we shall see that these relationships are sufficient to generate claims of justice based on need. We tend, however, to lose sight of this fact, for two reasons at least. The first is that we are rarely directly involved in provision for need which is usually channelled through the professional agencies that exist for this purpose. Cases like the giving of blood (which has been taken by Titmuss as a paradigm case of a social practice based on altruism)[21] in which there is a direct physical link between agent and recipient are comparatively rare. As agents, therefore, we miss the experience of providing for need; as recipients, we claim our benefits from particular bodies according to well-defined rules of qualification, and fail to recognise that these benefits are, properly speaking, social benefits, expressions of a genuine social obligation towards those in need. The second obliterating factor is that, in a capitalist society, most of our relationships with others are contractual relationships governed by a rule of equal exchange — we expect to make a return for what we get. It is therefore difficult to grasp that our society is also made up of relationships of a different kind, which make it appropriate for us to recognise that the claims of need give rise to a duty of justice. Those who have written on the social services have observed how the values of capitalism tend to distort the manner in which relief is provided for the needy;[22] and how people who regularly receive such relief tend to experience their position as stigmatising. Pinker argues that people who have already achieved a satisfactory status in the economic market are able to use the social services without stigma, whereas those in a position of economic inferiority will feel debased when they have to turn to these services, since they can make no return for what they receive; 'consequently most applicants for social services remain paupers at heart'.[23]

Clearly what is necessary here is to reinforce a sense of community such that people are more strongly inclined both to recognise obligations of justice to the needy and to make claims of justice when they are themselves in need. The most hopeful way of achieving this is by developing the idea of citizenship as a status which every member of society enjoys on an equal footing, and which links together legal, political and social rights.[24] Citizenship becomes a symbolic expression of the communal ties which certainly exist, but which tend to get obliterated for the reasons outlined in the preceding paragraph. It may be, as Pinker suggests, that citizenship at the moment means very little to those most dependent on the social services. If this is so, we shall have to find ways of making it more meaningful — for example by extending the scope of political participation so that users of the social services can have some say in how those services are organised and provided.

It should be apparent that an important element in the idea

of citizenship is that provision for need is regarded as a matter of justice rather than of humanity or benevolence. The reason for this is not simply that justice is generally thought to take priority over these other values, but that (as we saw in Section II) the relationship between agent and recipient differs between cases of justice and cases of humanity or benevolence. Where the recipient makes a claim of justice to some benefit, and the agent acknowledges this claim, there is no sense of inequality in the relationship; whereas a benefit that is provided from a sense of humanity creates an inequality between the two parties concerned. If this provision is repeated, the recipient is likely to feel stigmatised. Thus we can interpret the feelings of stigma experienced by many recipients of the social services as indicating that these people do not regard themselves as having claims of justice to the benefits they receive. Their sense of justice is predominantly formed by the contractual exchanges of a capitalist society, and in receiving benefits unilaterally they feel that they have become objects of charity. To remove the stigma, it is necessary to activate a different sense of justice, namely justice as distribution according to need; but this can only be done by finding some way of strengthening the feeling of community membership that makes such a conception of justice appropriate.

To summarise the argument of this section, I began with the problem of determining when the existence of need gives rise to claims of justice against those who can satisfy it. I argued that the answer lay in the relationship between (potential) agent and recipient. The family was used as an example of a relationship which made the relief of need a matter of justice, whereas in a voluntary association this would not normally be the case. A society, I argued, is not a voluntary association. Because it embodies non-voluntary and co-operative relationships, it has something in common with a family, and this gives its members claims of justice against one another on the grounds of need. However in socieities like our own, this aspect becomes obscured by the prevalence of impersonal and contractual relationships, and people no longer feel that they can make claims of justice on one another on the grounds of need alone. Thus to avoid stigma and to preserve self-respect when relief is claimed by those in need, it is necessary to re-establish our sense of community, and to reassert that such relief is a matter of social justice, not merely of humanity or benevolence. I hope, then, to have shown both that the principle of need is a proper part of social justice,[25] and why this is sometimes denied — why people sometimes think and act as though the relief of need were a matter of humanity or benevolence rather than justice.

V

As a short postscript to the argument, I wish to ask whether the conclusion we have just reached can be extended from the social to the global level. Are relationships between men from different societies such that their needs give them claims of justice upon one another? If this were so, then of course every case of need would by the same token give rise to a claim of justice against mankind at large. However, it seems to me doubtful whether the argument can be extended in this straightforward way. The facts about societies which were cited to establish that members of the same society had obligations of justice to one another do not apply to the world considered as a whole. Each national society embodies a high level of economic and social co-operation, possesses a single legal system, has in most cases a common language, and serves as the focus of intangible feelings of national identity. These features create the bonds of community which give rise to mutual obligations of justice. It cannot really be maintained that the world as a whole currently manifest analogous features. Obviously this is a matter of degree,[26] and as societies become more interdependent, economically and politically, a 'world community' may at last materialise. In the meantime it seems better to take a realistic view of cross-national relationships, and to say that the needs of members of other societies impose duties of humanity upon us, rather than duties of justice.

It may appear paradoxical that the question whether need gives rise to claims of justice or not should depend on the social membership of the person in need. For it seems on the face of it that to treat people differently according to whether they are, say, English, French or Indian is the epitome of injustice.

Doesn't justice require that our treatment of others should depend solely on their *personal* qualities, construed in such a way that nationality is excluded along with other features generally deemed irrelevant such as race and religion? However what has to be borne in mind is that the relevant characterisation of the person in need here is 'co-member of the same national community as the agent'. What differentiates an Englishman from a Frenchman in considering what I, as an Englishman, owe as a matter of justice, is not the fact of his being English in itself, but the fact of his belonging to the same community as I. If I were French, the claims of the two men would be precisely reversed. As has already been indicated, there is an analogy here with cases of desert. If someone goes out of his way to help me, he deserves some reward as an expression of gratitude; but this reward is deserved *from me*, and if I am unable or unwilling to provide it, there is no claim against the general public to supply the appropriate benefit. Likewise the needs of Frenchmen give them claims of justice against other Frenchmen, and the fact that those obligations may not be met (for whatever reason) does not impose a duty of justice on the members of other societies, though it may activate a duty of humanity.

This is not quite the end of the matter, however, for it overlooks the existence of duties of justice of another sort. Insofar as some countries have (now or in the past) been involved in the exploitation of other countries — by exploitation I mean the unequal exchange of valuable resources — the exploited countries have a just claim to reparation against their exploiters.[27] It seems likely that the amount of this reparation, if it could be calculated, would be considerable. We cannot be certain, therefore, whether needy inhabitants of foreign countries can appeal only to our humanity, or make claims of justice against us. Considered simply as human beings in need, their appeal must be to humanity; but as victims of past exploitation, they may rightly demand reparation for injustice.

Finally, since the extent of historical exploitation is now virtually impossible to calculate, we might suggest wiping the slate clean and propose a new principle to govern inter-societal relations in the future. A strong candidate for this role is

Rawls' difference principle — the principle that we should arrange inequalities so that the benefits of the worst-off are maximised. The units in this case would be societies, and an appropriate measure of benefit might be per capita GNP. Rawls' principle has rightly been rejected as a principle of justice, but here it would appear in its appropriate colours: as a rule of rational prudence which largely autonomous actors (societies) might adopt to govern their mutual relations, partly because of uncertainty about the future, and partly because the better-off societies had reason to believe that their material assets were less than wholly deserved.

Global justice, then, is not social justice writ large. The principle of need does not apply across social boundaries as it does within them. Indeed it may be better to recognise that societies co-exist in what is largely a state of nature, and therefore to propose rules of prudence to govern their relations, rather than to put forward principles of justice which must remain inoperable in the foreseeable future.

NOTES

1 An earlier version of this paper was presented to a panel on Liberty, Liberalism and Justice at the Conference of the International Political Science Association, Edinburgh 1976. I am grateful to my fellow panel-members, John Gray, Geraint Parry and Hillel Steiner, for their written and verbal comments on the paper.
2 See S. Benn and R.S. Peters, *Social Principles and the Democratic State* (London, 1959), Chapter 6, Section III; T.D. Campbell, 'Humanity before justice', in *British Journal of Political Science,* IV (1974).
3 See J. Parker, *Social Policy and Citizenship* (London, 1975) Chapter 7.
4 The meaning of this phrase, and the associated conception of need, are explained more fully in my *Social Justice* (Oxford, 1976) Chapter 4.
5 See H. Alker and B. Russett, 'On measuring inequality', in *Behavioural Science,* IX (1964).
6 In each case we consider the difference as a positive quantity, regardless of whether A scores higher or lower than B, etc.
7 The necessity of making this distinction is shown by J. Feinberg in 'Noncomparative justice', *Philosophical Review,* LXXXIII (1974).
8 J.S. Mill, 'Utilitarianism' in *Utilitarianism; On Liberty; Representative Government* (London, 1964), p. 46.
9 *Ibid.* p. 46.
10 J.R. Lucas, 'Justice', in *Philosophy,* XLVII (1972).

11 *Ibid.* p. 242

12 Campbell, *op. cit.*

13 *Ibid.* p. 3.

14 Lucas, *op. cit.* p. 229.

15 Campbell, *op. cit.* p. 15.

16 Feinberg, *op. cit.* p. 314.

17 See J. Feinberg, 'Justice and personal desert', in *Doing and Deserving,* (Princeton, 1970); Miller, *op. cit.* Chapter 3.

18 T. Reid, *Essays on the Active Powers of the Human Mind,* ed. B.A. Brody (Cambridge, Mass., 1969) pp. 423–4.

19 G.W.F. Hegel, *The Philosophy of Right* (Oxford, 1952), particularly paragraphs 158–69.

20 For instance, R. Nozick, *Anarchy, State and Utopia,* (Oxford, 1974).

21 R. Titmuss, *The Gift Relationship,* (London, 1970).

22 R. Pinker, *Social Theory and Social Policy* (London, 1971), Chapter 4; V. George and P. Wilding, *Ideology and Social Welfare,* (London, 1976), Chapter 6.

23 Pinker, *op. cit.,* p. 142.

24 See T.H. Marshall, 'Citizenship and social class', in *Sociology at the Crossroads* (London, 1963); Parker, *op. cit.,* Chapter 9. I have attempted to show how the political and social rights of citizenship may be linked together in 'Democracy and social justice', in *British Journal of Political Science,* VIII (1978), reprinted in *Democracy, Consensus and Social Contract,* eds. P. Birnbaum, J. Lively and G. Parry eds. (London, 1978).

25 My task has been to rebut the Lucas/Campbell view that the satisfaction of need is a matter of humanity alone, and to establish that it is properly seen as required by social justice. To achieve this, I have employed conceptual argument, and have also cited what I hope are relatively uncontroversial facts about liberal societies, in the wish to create as broad a base of support as possible for the positions advanced. To establish the stronger thesis that need is the *only* proper ground of just distribution, much more controversial assumptions about society would have to be made — for the kind of assumptions required, see Chapter 7 of Miller, *op. cit.*

26 C.f. C.R. Beitz 'Justice and international relations', in *Philosophy and Public Affairs,* IV (1974–5). Although I disagree with some of Beitz conclusions, I have found his paper very helpful in clarifying the issues discussed in this section.

27 Thus it is not my view that all duties of justice are restricted to the members of one's own society. The duty not to exploit others, and more generally not to cause them harm, is owed to all men considered merely as such. The argument I have advanced is aimed specifically at the duty to distribute resources according to need.

The Essentially Uncontestable Concepts of Power[1]
PETER MORRISS

IT is a striking feature of the contemporary approach to politics to demand conceptual rigour — a requirement in a philosophical tradition which I need hardly elaborate on here. Undeniably one of the key terms in the political vocabulary is 'power': one need only browse through the politics shelves of a moderately stocked bookshop to find a dozen books with the word in their very titles. Not surprisingly, then, considerable intellectual effort has been devoted to the task of determining the exact meaning of this term; and yet we seem further away now from an agreed definition than we were twenty, or even forty, years ago. Why, one wonders, has so little been achieved by all this mental effort?

Recently an attempt has been made to account for this lack of success by suggesting that 'power' is an essentially contestable concept, and that, as a consequence, disputes about the correct application of the term are inevitable.[2] But the notion of essential contestability has changed considerably since Gallie first introduced the idea over twenty years ago,[3] and it is by no means clear how it is now being applied. In its new, wider, form the essential contestability argument is a dangerous weapon that needs to be handled with care.

I consider that the object of conceptual analysis is to solve conceptual conundrums, to resolve disputes; not merely to explain how they arose. Saying that disputes about a concept like power are inevitable is not to advance our understanding very far; it amounts to either a dereliction of philosophical duty or an admission of failure. For the conclusion that there are philosophical disputes which cannot be resolved is one which should be reached with the greatest reluctance: every conceivable attempt at reaching a solution needs to be tried before the hunt can be finally abandoned. The onus of proof, in short, lies firmly on the shoulders of those who advance an essential contestability thesis.

In another paper[4] I have attempted to show how one recent attempt to demonstrate the essential contestability of 'power' fails. In this paper I approach the problem in a more constructive spirit, and try to produce an analysis of 'power' which goes at least some way towards resolving the disputes which have been associated with this term. For whilst I consider that it is not an advance to characterise 'power' as an essentially contested concept, I would not query for a moment that the term has given rise to heated debate as to its correct use. But what lies behind these contests are confusions, layer upon layer of them; and, moreover, needless confusions. The purpose of this paper is to isolate, and then remove, these confusions.

The first major source of confusion is that, although 'power' may be used in normative contexts (indeed, I shall argue that it often is), the term itself is still descriptive. I consider it essential for conceptual clarity to recognise the normative-descriptive distinction. It is of course true that in ordinary speech descriptive words often carry normative implications: for it would be incredibly tedious to be restricted to separate descriptive and normative vocabularies, so that each time one used a descriptive term one had to attach to it an appropriate normative qualifier. We are normally lazy, and develop linguistic habits that reflect this — habits which usually do no harm. But when confusion *is* created, one of the first steps should be to disentangle the different ideas lumped together under one term, and see to what extent the dispute is engendered simply by the two parties talking at cross-purposes.

The use of descriptive terms in normative contexts should not be allowed to cause problems: there is nothing evaluative in the concept of oxygen, even though I most certainly prefer the air I breath to contain it. Similarly, even if one has very strong views on what the distribution of power in a society ought to be, this does not make the concept normative. One first has to establish the existence and distribution of power within a society — that is, provide a description of it — before applauding or condemning it for conforming to one's hopes or fears.

A second, and related, source of confusion is that writers on the concept have tended to pack into it far more than is justifiable: claims which ought to be considered as empirical are crammed into the concept itself — whereby, of course, they tend to become true by definition. For examples of this, one need only consider the often-remarked division of contemporary theorists of society into two camps — loosely called consensus and conflict theorists — and compare their different analyses of 'power'. Both schools, it should be noted, consider 'power' to be a concept which is vitally important to the understanding of modern societies, and they have clashed on the issue of what the term means.

The definition of power usually adopted by conflict theorists, at least those of the American sort, is some variant of Dahl's,[5] to the effect that A has power over B to the extent that she can get B to do something that B would not otherwise do.[6] Insofar as B would prefer to do what he would have done but for A's intervention (and this is usually either assumed or written into the definition) then this definition necessarily entails conflict between the preferences of A and B. Conflict, under this account, is a definitionally necessary aspect of power: the study of power will also be the study of conflict.

Compare Parsons, who explicitly rejects this emphasis on power 'as power *over* others'. He states: 'My own emphasis is on power as capacity to get things done. Whether there is opposition or not is an empirically very important but theoretically secondary matter. My point of reference will be the *capacity of a social system to get things done in its collective interest.*[7] But why should one study solely the satisfaction of the social system's collective interest, and ignore the satisfaction of various individuals' private interests? Parsons is here choosing to ignore any consideration of power as involving conflict of interests or preferences: consensus is found by definition.

I do not deny that either of these definitions of power can be used in empirical research, and that this research could possibly be worthwhile. But when members of either school argue with someone from the opposing camp, and attempt to use their research on power to support their points, they will simply be talking at cross-purposes. I hope to show that there is no need to build empirical or theoretical assumptions into such a basic concept as 'power'; and that the term, shorn of these empirical implications, can be very useful in disclosing the relative significance of consensus and conflict within a society.

The third, and perhaps most important, source of confusion is the failure to recognise that there are *two* distinct concepts covered by the term 'power'. That this is not often noticed is a consequence of the unrefined state of much of the present academic political vocabulary — which is, to a considerable extent, still that of some early and influential behaviouralists, who cavalierly combined terms such as power, influence, control, and coercion into one category, and then endeavoured to find the one definition that 'lay behind' all these terms.[8] And even those writers who have recognised that there are two concepts of power have pointed this out as a preliminary to ignoring one of them.[9]

An instructive way of bringing out the difference between these two concepts is by considering the derivations of the two words 'power' and 'influence'.[10] 'Power', of course, comes from the Latin *potere* meaning to be able. 'Influence', however, is derived from the Latin *influere*, meaning to flow in, and refers to an astrological belief that a substance, emanating from the stars, flowed into people in the sublunary world, thus changing their behaviour — or at least affecting them in some way. Hence 'under the influence', and also 'influenza'.

I want to draw the conclusion from this that there is on the one hand a set of concepts which apply to situations in which someone is somehow affected — his actions, behaviour, thoughts, beliefs, desires, or perhaps something else, are altered. As a shorthand (and *only* as a shorthand) I shall call these *influence concepts*. But there is also another set of concepts (which I shall dub *ability concepts*) which describe the capacity of someone to obtain some end, outcome, or goal.

It is doubtless the case that social and political theorists of power tend to be rather less interested in those situations in which someone is influenced by alcohol or astral forces, in comparison with cases in which it is people (or social structures) that do the influencing. Similarly, abilities are more likely to be socially significant when other people are somehow involved. But this does not mean that ability and influence concepts collapse into each other when they are applied in social settings, for there are crucial differences of both grammar and emphasis. The logical subject of an influence concept is the person who has been affected, and the occurrence that the use of such concepts highlights is that there is someone who has been affected. It makes perfect sense to say that someone has been influenced, without mentioning who or what is doing the influencing: influenza acquired its name precisely because it wasn't known what the cause of the disease was. And it makes no sense to say that someone is influencing, without saying (or implying) who or what it is that is being influenced. On the other hand, the subject of an ability concept is the person, the A, who is obtaining something; it makes no sense to specify a B without an A ('someone is being abilitied'), but perfect sense to leave unstated who is necessary for A to have or exercise her abilities.[11]

There are, of course, many situations in which *both* sorts of concepts can be applied, and most of the 'paradigm' cases of power offered by social theorists fall into this category: paradigms of the kind 'A obtains X by making B do something which he wouldn't otherwise have done'. Here the first part of the sentence tells us of some ability of A (the ability to obtain X), the second that B is subject to an influence, and the sentence as a whole that it is through this influence that A has the ability.[12] It should by now be clear that to say that A has the power *to* do or obtain something is to use an ability concept, whilst to say that B has power exercised *over* him is to use an influence concept.

The difference in emphasis that these two families of concepts allow should enable us to make statements that are clearer. As a consequence, because a careful choice of the appropriate concept will distinguish the relevant from the irrelevant, we should be able to use this added clarity to simplify research programmes. Thus if I say that a trade union (or its leader) has the power to gain a large wage rise, I need not consider who, if anyone, will be affected. This could be by no means obvious: in the case of a nationalised industry which obtains the extra money required from the government, who in turn raise the money by borrowing on the international market, it is far from clear who is affected, and how. But it is still the case that the union's members have their wage increase.[13] Conversely, when there is no bread in the shops because of an industrial dispute in the baking industry, my diet is affected. An influence concept is appropriate here: it is not relevant which party was the cause of the dispute, and it may be very difficult and contentious to determine this. Neither need I imply that anybody is gaining anything for themselves. Nevertheless, I still have to go without my bread.

I have stressed that the logically prior form of an influence concept is in the passive, with the person influenced as the subject; but it must be obvious to all that we often use the locution 'A influences B'. Indeed, the most popular *definiendum* in definitions of power is 'A has power over B' — which, in my terminology here, is either a special case of 'A influences B', or simply synonymous with it. An analysis of 'A influences B' will provide us with at least the logical structure of an analysis of 'A has power over B'.

When we say that A influences B it necessarily follows that B is influenced. 'A exercises power over B', then, requires analysis in terms of an influence concept: B is influenced, and the cause of this is A. Frequently we will also specify in what way B is affected, thus filling out the influence concept further.

Sometimes this is all that is meant by 'A has power over B'. Dahl gives as one of his examples that when he requests his son to mow the lawn on Saturday mornings, this has the inevitable effect of inducing his son to go swimming when he would otherwise have stayed at home. He calls such an occurrence 'negative power' — although he has to admit 'that negative control of this kind is not ordinarily conceived of as power'.[14] Using the terminology developed here we can say, less confusingly, that Dahl's son is influenced, is influenced by his father, and is affected in that he goes swimming when he wouldn't otherwise have done.

In this case no ability is present, for Dahl fails to get his lawn mown.[15] But often (indeed, I would say, invariably) a sentence of the form 'A influences B' *also* attaches to A an ability to achieve something. This 'something' could simply be the way in which B is affected, or it could include causal consequences of the changes brought about in B. Whatever the case, the affecting of B is likely to enable A to obtain outcomes she could not have obtained on her own. Thus we can say that A influences B so as to obtain X, which is to say that A has an ability to obtain X, and that this ability involves affecting B. Mentioning B informs us of at least one person involved when A obtains X.

'A influences, or has power over, B', then, necessarily involves an influence concept, and may involve an ability concept; and we need no other sorts of concepts to give us an adequate analysis of statements of this form. Providing an analysis of 'power' as an ability and as an influence concept is, therefore, logically prior to analysing 'A has power over B', and also sufficient for enabling us to understand such sentences.

I would like to give just two examples showing, briefly, the lack of clarity that exists in discussion of power, and how it can have important political consequences. Firstly, a leading academic writer on power, Robert Dahl, is hopelessly muddled between these two sorts of concepts. In his theoretical work he gives the definition already cited, which is in terms of A's power over B — and, as I have just pointed out, treats it as an influence concept. But in his empirical work he switches, and equates a person's power with their success on matters of key importance: he 'consider[s] one participant as more influential [or powerful] than another if the relative frequency of his successes out of all successes is higher, or the ratio of his successes to his total attempts is higher.'[16] That is, he is here using an ability concept: yet nowhere does he point out that he has changed his interpretation of 'power'.

The second example is more important because it is from real politics rather than academic discussions. It involves the slogan 'Black Power', which encapsulates a platform aiming to give blacks the power to run their own lives: it represents a demand for autonomy. The originators of the movement never intended the slogan to imply that blacks should have disproportionate power *over* non-blacks — should somehow dominate them.[17] Indeed, one strand of the movement sought to remove as much contact as they could between white and black people; it advocated setting up black enclaves which were as self-governing as possible. White supremacists, however, have been able to make propaganda by equating power-to with power-over, and thereby claiming that black power and black domination are the same. It is regrettable that reputable, and liberal, academics, by considering power over others as the only sort of power, have unwittingly encouraged such distortions.[18]

Having located some of the mistakes which writers on 'power' have committed, it is now time to commence my own analysis. But there is no point arguing about the meaning of a concept in a contextual vacuum: such a procedure is little different from the dogmatic arbitrariness towards meaning for which Humpty Dumpty has become famous in philosophical circles. Arriving at a definition of a concept does not necessarily solve a dispute; indeed, if the definition appears purely arbitrary it can often engender further disputation. Stipulating a definition out of thin air and for no justifiable reason can never be an adequate solution to a conceptual dispute.

Nevertheless, Humpty Dumpty was quite right in claiming that it is we, and not words, who should be the masters; concepts are like tools (they are entirely man-made), and we need to fashion the tool to be as appropriate as possible for the job we intend it to do. It is for these reasons that I think Hart's approach to the concept of law is the one we should follow: 'Plainly the best course is to defer giving any answer to the query "What is law?" until we have found out what it is about law that has in fact puzzled those who have asked or attempted to answer it, even though their familiarity with the law and their ability to recognise examples are beyond question. What more do they want to know and why do they want to know it?'[19]

The appropriate questions, then, are 'What do we want the term to do?' 'Why do we feel the need for it?' and 'Why is it so prevalent in our language?'. I am not asserting that the meaning of a concept is discovered in its use — far from it — but that we can examine different interpretations of a word intelligently only if we know to what use the word is to be put.

The object of this exercise is thus not to produce a *definition* of 'power', but to advance towards the solution of problems involving the term. A term such as 'power' is a shorthand for previously understood ideas; such shorthand terms are obviously useful except and until it is unclear, or contentious, how they work as a shorthand. The solution to this lack of clarity is *not* to abandon the term, but to ask (again) what the reasons for developing such a shorthand term were (and are). We may well feel, after such an examination, that the use of just one term is misleading and that a larger number of such terms is needed — perhaps replacing, and removing, the original contentious term. Or (as I feel with 'power') such an examination will result in the removal of confusions, and allow us to retain the term, now purged of its misleading elements.

These strictures apply with undiminished force to 'political power'; for it is amazing that throughout the now voluminous literature there is so little consideration of how this term fits into our vocabulary. We have all the more reason to doubt those authors who have concluded that 'power' is too ambiguous, or unclear, to be useful,[20] because so little thought has been devoted to the question of the uses for which we require it — why the term has evolved in the first place. Our discussion of 'power' can start when we know what we want it to do — *then* we can start refining it more sensibly.

So what *do* we want a concept of power to do? Roughly, I think, three things — and undoubtedly this triple task has added to the confusions.

First, 'power' is used in predictive or instrumental settings. We expect little green men, on descending from their spaceship, to say to the first human they meet 'take me to your leader'. Somewhat analogously, an American or Soviet ambassador, upon arriving in a new country, could be expected to ask to meet 'the people who run things round here' — that is, the most powerful people. Powerful people are, then, those who can get things done; those one wants on one's side; those with 'muscle'.[21] If we want to predict what will happen we look to see what these people are doing; if we want to predict what will happen we look to see what these people are doing; if we want to affect or change the course of events then we either try to become one of these people ourselves, or seek their support. This is the 'power' of practical politics. We are not particularly concerned here about who is *affected*, or how; rather, we are concentrating on those who can obtain desired outcomes. This is clearly working with an ability concept.

Secondly, we use the word in the context of responsibility and blame. It is this context which recent writers who have claimed that 'power' is essentially contestable have emphasised; Steven Lukes, for one, assumes that 'The point . . . of locating power is to fix responsibility for consequences held to flow from the action, or inaction, of certain specified agents.[22] For (to quote from a writer with different political views) 'A man cannot be blamed for not doing what he was unable to do: a necessary condition of responsibility is power. Indeed, we often use the word "responsibility" to mean "power", as when a man says that he wants greater responsibility.'[23]

As this quotation shows, we have here the use of an ability concept: to have power or responsibility is to be able to do things. Conversely, as Lukes and Connolly argue, to be able to bring outcomes about is to be responsible for these outcomes and their consequences; and, perhaps more important, to be able to bring some end about whilst refraining to do so is to be responsible for this omission. Given their location of 'power' in this context, I am unable to understand why Lukes and Connolly both reject ability concepts in favour of an influence concept of power.[24]

Thirdly, we use the concept of power in the *evaluation* of social systems, in judging them; for people can, and do, value one distribution of power more than another. It is impossible here to write a treatise on the different things people can value in social systems; but it is enough to understand that one may be concerned here with either ability or influence concepts, or both together. Influence concepts are particularly important to liberals, and some socialists, and fit in with an analysis of freedom as the absence of interference from others, or as negative liberty. The restriction of freedom and liberty is, to liberals, one of the greatest of all evils — and, for them, to lack liberty is to be within the sphere of influence of others.

An alternative normative theory, such as that recently resurrected by Macpherson, argues that:

... the end or purpose of man is to use and develop his uniquely human attributes or capacities. His potential use and development of these may be called his human powers. A good life is one which maximises these powers. A good society is one which maximises (or permits and facilitates the maximisation of) these powers, and thus enables men to make the best of themselves.[25]

A writer holding *these* views would use ability concepts, and would investigate the presence, and distribution, of power to do things (or achieve goals).

That there are two conflicting normative positions is shown starkly in the following pair of quotations. Ted Honderich has written that:

Democracy gives to citizens only something which can best be described briefly in a negative way: a circumstance in which no individual or minority has as much autonomy, with respect to major policies of the society, as have individuals or minorities in other political practices. It gives to citizens not any freedom *of* power but rather a freedom *from* power.[26]

A similar analysis of society is used by Alasdair MacIntyre to support a very different emphasis:

The feeling of impotence that many have is not misplaced. They are impotent. But they are not impotent because they are dominated by a well-organised system of social control. It is lack of control which is at the heart of the social order and central governments reflect this impotence as clearly as anyone else.[27]

Thus one can judge societies either by the extent to which they give their citizens freedom from the power of others, or by the extent to which citizens have the power to meet their own needs or wants. To be impotent is to lack an ability; to be dominated is to be influenced; these are not the same and need not be found together. Conversely, Parsons is right to point out that when people co-operate, and work together to achieve their goals, their power (ability) is increased, whether or not any other group of people is significantly affected. There is no reason simply to assume that we live in a zero-sum world.

So whether one chooses to investigate influence or ability concepts it is imperative that one distinguishes explicitly between them throughout the research.

Most writers who recognise the distinction between power-over and power-to have considered that the correct analysis of power is in terms of power-over,[28] yet we have seen that this can only be an appropriate use in one context out of three. The mistake of excluding ability concepts has been encouraged by the importance of negative freedom in liberal ideology; it would seem that the prevailing liberal orthodoxy in political science has led many academics to consider that power can only be important when it involves power over others.

The rest of this paper consists predominantly of an analysis of power as an ability concept — the power to do or obtain something — and attempts to provide a sort of map of the concept.[29] For even when one clearly distinguishes between power-over and power-to, the ability concept can still be confusing: in part, as we have seen, because the concept is an umbrella-term, covering a large number of different uses. The map endeavours to show how different variants, or conceptions perhaps, can be distinguished — each one appropriate for a different task. Since I shall be, from now on, almost exclusively referring to the ability concept of power, I trust that it will not cause confusion if I use the term 'power' as a shorthand for this ability concept — to refer to someone's power to do something.

As a further preliminary, it perhaps needs to be made clear that the concept under consideration is not the same as constitutional or *de jure* power; it is descriptive of what people can, in fact, do — not what they are legally entitled or empowered to do. *De jure* power obviously has a logic akin to an ability concept (it is power *to*) but crucially different in that there is no necessary entailment that the possessor of *de jure* power can, in practice, actually obtain those ends which she is entitled to obtain. The analysis of this sort of power properly belongs to works on constitutional law; it is *de facto* power which will concern us here.

It is worth pointing out, though, that even such a basic distinction as this can create confusion. A well-received work on American politics contains the following surprising passage: 'Power is often illusory. In a democracy, those who have influence, wealth, and power may not be free to use it. The price of holding power may be self-denial. The penalty of using power may be to be stripped of it.'[30] This is nonsense. Power which is illusory, or cannot be used, is simply not power. It is decidedly less confusing to say that the realities of power often do not coincide with the situation as expressed in textbooks on the constitution. (Or perhaps the authors are intending to say that if one wants to have power in the future, it is dangerous to use it too blatantly now.) We have enough problems with 'power' as it is, without needlessly creating more through such sloppy use of language.

Let us first consider 'power' in the first context which I have mentioned: that of practical politics. Brian Barry has suggested that, whatever one thinks about the concept of power, the powerful people in any society must include those whom the CIA would want to bribe[31] — or, one should add, assassinate. The CIA agent's first concern would be to discover who actually runs things in the country to which he has just been posted; he would then have to determine to what extent bribery would be an effective means of securing help and compliance. Bribery is obviously preferable to assassination — it would have been a particularly dumb CIA operative who tried to assassinate King Hussein — but our focus here is not on the *CIA*'s attempts to exercise power, but on the things CIA agents would look for in locating power *within* whichever societies concern them. Hussein — and Castro, Allende, and others who figured prominently on CIA assassination lists — were all at the time actually exercising power. What they had in common was that they were not only *able* to secure a wide range of outcomes in their countries, they were actually securing them.

But the CIA obviously consider that it is also worth bribing people who are not *actually* exercising power, not because they cannot, but because they don't want to at the moment. They *have* power; and perhaps, if the motivation is provided by suitable amounts of cash or other incentives, they can be induced to exercise it. These people are unlikely to be worth assassinating, but they can yield considerable positive returns if intelligently handled.[32]

A third category of people features prominently in Philip Agee's book describing the workings of the CIA:[33] those whose power is latent. In order to plan for the future, a large number of contacts are maintained which are of no immediate use, but which might yield fruit later on; often agents are planted in the opposition parties and the trade unions in the hope that they will be able to manoeuvre themselves into positions of power. This power is latent in that it cannot be used right now — these people have to do certain things (or certain things have to happen to them) before they can be said to have power.[34]

Necessary for any sort of power is a sufficient level of competence: to be powerful it is not enough to have appropriate resources at one's disposal, one must know how to use them effectively. Somebody is incompetent if they have enough resources to do a job properly, but misapply them, and so fail; and, since to be powerful implies to be successful, if one is incompetent to do something then one lacks the power to do it. However, a person who is incompetent yet can learn how to employ her resources properly possesses power which is latent.

A simple illustration of these three sub-concepts would be the ability to speak a language. I could actually be speaking the language; be able to speak it whenever I wanted to; or be able to learn it whilst not being able to speak it at present. The central meaning is the middle one of these: a French-speaker is one who speaks (reasonable) French whenever she chooses to express herself in that language. Similarly with 'power'.

The central meaning of 'power' is to succeed in bringing about some given end whenever one chooses, whilst the other two senses are derivative meanings. Recognising the centrality of *having* power prevents us from making the mistake of concluding that because someone is not actually exercising power he is therefore powerless — an error all too common with behaviouralists. The connection between power and potential is clear in the common derivation of the two words; and all ability concepts describe a capacity, or potential, for obtaining something, and not exclusively the actual obtaining of it.

What needs emphasising here is that the counterfactual choice clause in the analysis of 'having power' (the 'whenever she chooses') is a true counterfactual. It is not just that whenever, as a matter of fact, she chooses to attempt to acquire X she succeeds in obtaining it; we require a far stronger condition to the effect that whenever she *might* choose X, *if* she chose it then, she would obtain it. Otherwise the account of 'power' would lay itself open to the well known objection that stoically not wanting to do things that one could not do would increase one's power. In order to avoid this, the choice counterfactual must be one including the whole range of (possible) wants, whether or not the things are actually desired at the time.[35] Ability concepts, then, refer to a capacity or potentiality which is there to be tapped (or exercised); all that is required to actualise them is the appropriate act of choice by A.

To return to the CIA: they want to discover not only the powerful individuals or groups of individuals, but also which are the most powerful *positions* within the country. It is worth planting an agent in the students' union, in the hope that he becomes president of this organisation, only because it is known that this position carries with it a considerable amount of power. A skillful incumbent of this position would be more powerful than a mediocre one; a complete incompetent might have no power at all; but nevertheless the power of the position itself is relatively constant.

The CIA, of course, will want its nominees to occupy the most powerful positions within the society, and will need to locate such positions. One account of the power of a position is that it is the power of a reasonably skillful, or average, incumbent. A slightly different version is developed by bargaining theory, and other versions of game theory: in this case, the most powerful position is said to be that which will give the highest pay-off given the *best* strategic behaviour by all parties. Whether one accepts an analysis which assumes perfect calculators or averagely fallible humans is not something which I want to go into here: it would seem to depend on the problem under investigation. It does seem plausible, however, that in this predictive context one will be more likely to want to work with the assumption that one has an average human being, whilst in more evaluative contexts the rational calculators of game theory may be more appropriate.

As we have seen, there are other uses of the concept of power: the second context is that of excuses and responsibility. The concept of power is relevant here because if someone is powerless to prevent something then it is, on the whole, wrong for us to praise or blame him when this thing occurs. It is usually omissions, rather than comissions, that are being considered, and that one was powerless to intervene is usually an adequate excuse. This is a consequence of the widely held principle of 'ought implies can', and its corollary 'cannot implies not-ought'. That is to say, one is only under an obligation to do something when one can do (has the power to do) that thing.

Suppose it is agreed that on a certain occasion A did not intervene to prevent the occurrence of some disaster, and she provides the defence that she was helpless to prevent it. In order to censure her it is necessary to show that she was able to intervene successfully, and the argument will probably be about whether this power was present. But whilst she stands condemned if the ability is established, this should not mislead us into thinking that the original charge against A was that she had the power to intervene (and that having this power is somehow wrong); for what A is being accused of is failing to intervene when she should have (and could have) intervened. It is important to keep clear that one is not being blamed for *having* power, but for failing to exercise what power one has.

The analysis of power which is appropriate in this context differs from the predictive one in several respects. First, we want to inquire further into incompetence: if someone is blamed for not doing X, it is often considered a feeble excuse for her to claim that, whilst she *could* have done X, she was in actual fact too incompetent or ignorant to do it. But being under an obligation to do X is different from being under an obligation to *know how to* do X, and the two should not be confused. So if A couldn't do X because she didn't know how to do it properly, and she was under no obligation to know how to do it, then she is blameless. But if she *was* under such an obligation, then her defence fails — provided, of course, that she was able to know how to do X.

Second, one could construct a more complicated defence: that one was for some reason unable to *try* to bring about X — it being acknowledged that the attempt to do X would have succeeded. If agoraphobia and kleptomania really do exist, then those people who suffer from them just *cannot* go into open spaces or refrain from stealing. The block is mental, rather than physical, but this does not make it any less of a block. What is meant here is that it is somehow *impossible* for the actor to choose a certain end, or do anything meaningful about putting her choice into operation. What the exact nature of this impossibility may be I do not know, nor do I have to say. For elucidating the nature of phobias and the like is a matter for psychologists and psychoanalysts, not for philosophical disputation.

We can thus provide an answer, however apparently question-begging, to Quentin Gibson's quandary: 'should we accept the policeman's statement to his psychiatrist that an impulse to stand quietly and watch the traffic jam deprived him of all power to give the signals?'[36] If the 'impulse' is part of some phobia, such that we conclude that he *could* not give the signals, then we must concur with his view that he lost the ability. The answer to the question, therefore, is that we should accept the policeman's statement if his psychiatrist does.

There is a further excuse that we can accept: *weakness of will* is a limitation on abilities if it is really beyond the actor's control. Some people have relatively weak bodies, and this lack of strength is a restriction on their abilities; other people are weak-willed, and this lack of will is equally a limitation on their abilities, and one which restricts the number of things they can achieve. We cannot, as a philosophical principle, decree that all such limitations on the will can be dismissed, while analogous limitations on the body are not. It is no doubt more difficult to observe somebody trying and failing to (say) give up smoking or refrain from stealing, than it is to see someone shoving against a door but failing to open it; but this does not mean that the former sort of failure is incomprehensible. The actor really does try, but the will breaks (or the attention wanders) and he finds himself over-riding his (genuine) long-term wants for his short-term desires. It is not that he did not try hard enough; it is that *however* hard he tried he would have cracked at some point. None of our minds are perfect, and it is significant that we talk of will-power and power of concentration, as well as bodily powers. This may be partly metaphorical, but does bring out that we think that our powers to will or concentrate are not limitless.

Here we are back with psychic states akin to phobias and other forms of compulsive behaviour. Most people who fail to do things do not fail in this way: they succumb through lack of effort. But some people doubtless fail to do some things because they literally could not do them. Nowadays we do not believe all failures are due to lack of effort; we believe in nonrational factors governing at least some choices, and that these factors are sometimes both beyond our conscious control and too strong to over-ride. To know whether this is what is happening we need the psychiatrist again.

Finally, what is the status of the plea that A could not do X because the cost of so doing would be prohibitively high? I think this defence fails, unless the cost actually prevents her from doing X. If the obligation A is under is simply to do X, she cannot use the cost to support a claim that the obligation is void through lack of ability — for she does not lack the ability. It is more than likely, though, that the implied terms of the obligation will include some reference to the limits to which A could be expected to go in order to secure X. If this is not the case, A can always argue that the obligation is unnecessarily harsh in requiring her to do X at such great costs — but the claim that the obligation is not a reasonable obligation is a purely moral argument involving no reference to A's powers.

There is another sense in which it might be thought that 'power' is used in this context. We often condemn people not for bringing about (or failing to prevent) some reprehensible outcome, but because their actions *themselves* were reprehensible. We tend to censure highway robbery, but not (mainly) because of the consequent redistribution of income; rather it is the *means* — the use of intimidating threats — to which we object. Our morality, then, requires us to look more closely at the *methods* people employ in attaining their ends.

It has been suggested[37] that 'power' is an essentially contested concept in part because of this allegedly irremovable link between 'power' and our deepest moral values. But this rests on a mistake, because this sort of moral censure has nothing to do with the term 'power'. We are considering here which actions are right, and which wrong, in one's interactions with other people: which involves, quite simply, the whole field of morals. I am not censured for being *able* to rape someone (if I should want to), but only for actually raping her. The rapist is, doubtless, exercising power when successfully engaging in rape; but our moral senses are outraged by this not because it is an exercise of power, but because of the sort of act involved. When discussing the rightness of wrongness of someone's actions, we require a morally appropriate vocabulary for describing these actions, and a set of moral beliefs for judging them; we do not require a redrawn concept of power.

More important politically than a consideration of blame and excuses is that people can value one *distribution* of power more than another: this provides our third context. Either ability or influence concepts may be considered here: we might be particularly concerned about people's relative ability to obtain certain ends, or interested in determining who, in the society, tend to be more affected by others' behaviour.

Reasons for paying attention to this latter question have been given so often that there is little point in my repeating them here. A respect for individual autonomy is widely shared in our culture, and autonomy demands that a person takes a decision unimpeded by the illegitimate interference of others. It follows that we need to distinguish those sorts of influence which are legitimate from those which are not: for to be persuaded by rational arguments to choose a course of action is very different (morally) from being coerced into doing the same thing.

It is worth stressing again that for B to be subject to the influence of A does not imply that A is intentionally, or even knowingly, influencing B: people can be affected as an unintended by-product of others' actions. The decisions that governmental agencies, large corporations, and many other institutions, take impinge in many ways on the lives of all of us, and all these effects need to be taken into consideration when assessing people's freedom from interference. In addition, B is in A's power when he might be affected by her actions, even though he is not so affected at present.

It is not clear to me whether it is possible to conduct a study to determine to what extent people are subject to the influence of others. Apart from the sheer magnitude of the task, I find it difficult to give meaning to the notion of a choice uninfluenced by others, which is necessary as a point of comparison. Modern society contains so much contact between people that a completely uninfluenced choice seems impossible to contemplate. This may be merely a failure of imagination on my part, but the result of it is that I am unable to see any way of using influence concepts on their own in this context. For these reasons I shall not consider influence concepts except insofar as they can provide important moral qualifications to a pure ability concept of power.

Faced with these overwhelming complexities, it is a relief to turn to the distribution of abilities. But why should anyone be interested in this way in power as an ability concept? The answer is strikingly obvious, but is one of the most systematically overlooked aspects of the power debate.

Most people have some view about the merits or morality of the way goods (including such intangible, but highly desired, goods as leisure) are distributed within their society; thinkers of a more radically egalitarian stamp, for example, have been appalled by societies in which a few people obtain far more things than others. Some writers, such as Lasswell, have simply defined the powerful as these people: 'The influential [or powerful] are those who get the most of what there is to get. . . . Those who get the most are *élite*; the rest are *mass*.'[38] This does not seem a useful approach for, as I have already argued, one can be powerful and yet not get very much if one does not exercise one's power. If the mass *could* get much more of 'what there is to get' but do not — because, perhaps, they choose not to exert themselves or just want other things — then we would make a different moral judgment than we would if the mass were truly powerless to improve their lot.

But the literature on the concept of power accepts this point and then goes beyond it: to ignore completely the distribution of goods *except* insofar as this distribution is consequent upon an exercise of power. This is a mistake: a mistake which we must be careful to avoid.

Let us continue to restrict attention to one outcome or state of affairs X — which can be thought of as the receipt of some object. To have the power to obtain X seems to entail that one can get it if one chooses. But it is also possible that one receives X, whether one chooses to or not. If we are interested in those people who *can* get X, then we must also be interested in those people who *do* get X. The former I describe as having active power; the latter as having passive power.[39] It is passive because they have no control over it; they do not have to *exercise* power in order to get X, for X just comes, like a free gift. That is, those who are presently obtaining X include both those who *exercise* power in order to get it, and those who do not, but simply receive it. (Of course, people may also be receiving X through flukes and chance occurrences, but we are not interested in these cases; we are only interested in relatively reliable outcomes.)

This formulation of passive power is, I think, my own, and yet it captures an essential aspect of power — one which all too often merely lurks in the background. Occasionally it reasserts itself, as in a recent, Marxist, study of contemporary Britain, which is concerned to stress the point that: '. . . individuals or groups may have the effective benefits of "power" without needing to exercise it in positive action.. . . What we have in mind is a passive enjoyment of advantage and privilege, obtained merely because of 'the way things work', and because these ways are not exposed to serious challenge.[40] Even Nelson Polsby, no adherent of Marxism, finds himself saying that 'many community "decisions" are unconscious, intended by nobody in the community, and yet have profound consequences for the shaping and sharing [sic] of community values.'[41] However, Polsby then proceeds to ignore all such decisions.

If the social system performs in such a way as systematically to advantage some individuals or groups, it certainly seems odd not to take account of this. It might even be that active power begins to pale into insignificance compared with the magnitude of passive power.

Passive power, though, does have both advantages and disadvantages compared with active power. The advantage is that one doesn't have to *do* anything in order to obtain the X: it comes of its own accord, and the beneficiary can spend her time in whatever way she finds most congenial. It is rather like an absentee landowner, who can live in comfort in the South of France on her income without ever needing to bother to visit the property if it doesn't suit her. The drawback is that if one changes one's mind and decides that one doesn't like X after all, that's just tough luck.

We may well, in addition, consider certain forms of power as morally distinct from others, and reflect this in our assessment of the total distribution of power. If, for example, A can obtain a great deal, but people give it to her willingly, even gladly, then we may well treat the resulting inegalitarian distribution of goods differently than if she obtained her wealth by highway robbery.[42] We need, then, a very brief discussion of the ways in which A could obtain the outcome in question.

A may be able to obtain X herself, unaided by others. Such a case is possible, and, of course, important to us; but socially relevant power presumably must involve some sort of interaction between at least two actors. We can continue to call the actor with the power 'A', and lump together all the other actors which are necessary for A to obtain X as 'B'. For convenience, I shall treat B as if it is a single actor; this simplification does not produce any distortion for the somewhat limited and exploratory analysis that I provide here.

A's power to obtain X involves, then, some sort of co-operation on the part of B; but why *should* B co-operate? I think that one can isolate four different sorts of reasons. First, B may fear that, if he does not co-operate, A will punish him in some way — or get someone else to punish him. At the moment I am not concerned with whether this fear is justified or not; the point is that it is there, and it is because it is there that B co-operates and helps A to bring about X. Secondly, B may hope that A will reward him for co-operation. These two cases have a lot in common, and can be taken together, because in both of them B co-operates because of the expectations that he has regarding A's behaviour following his actions: in both cases, B expects to be better off if he co-operates, and better off because of what A will do as a consequence.[43] Thirdly, B may do willingly what he thinks A wants, without expecting any rewards in return. This doubtless occurs when B is in love with A: gifts to one's beloved are, just occasionally, given without expectation of a quid pro quo. Political instances are those of a legitimate authority, obeyed because of its perceived right to command obedience, or a charismatic leader. Finally, B might be quite happy bringing about X anyway, because he, too, wants this to occur.[44] As a consequence, A also gets X. One might call this consequential power, in that A obtains her desired outcome as a consequence of B's freely chosen acts.

It may appear at first glance somewhat odd that the more powerful a person is, the more one would want him to fill the role of B; conversely, no one will try to coerce, bribe or trick someone who is completely ineffectual. The more powerful you are, the more others will try to use you for their own ends — to make you a B to their A. Hannah Arendt has tried to construct something akin to a paradox here:

> Oddly enough, the only person likely to be an ideal victim of complete manipulation is the President of the United States. Because of the immensity of his job, he must surround himself with advisers . . . who 'exercise their power chiefly by filtering the information that reaches the President and by interpreting the outside world for him'. The President, one is tempted to argue, allegedly the most powerful man of the most powerful country, is the only person in this country whose range of choices can be predetermined.[45]

But control over information differs from other resources only in being more hidden: the same point has been expressed more pithily, and clearly: 'to be a good memo writer [is] a very real form of power'.[46]

Consequential power is frequently passive, but one can have active power of this kind as well. This involves persuasion, manipulation, or the introduction of impediments: A may actively alter B's wants, B's perception of the objective situation, or the objective situation itself, in order to lead B to choose to bring X about. One sort of consequential power that is particularly important in politics is that which is a consequence of the rules of the political game;[47] this can give rise to both passive and active power. An example of the former is provided by Northern Ireland before the imposition of direct rule: the existence, and location, of the border with the South, combined with the rules of representative democracy, were sufficient almost by themselves to ensure that large benefits flowed to the Protestant population and were denied to the Catholics. An example of active power consequential upon rules is provided by the effects that changes in the rules governing primary elections to select Democratic presidential candidates had on the distribution of power within the Democratic Party; the authors of a recent article on these changes claimed that: 'If 1972 is an adequate guide, altering primary regulations ... could well determine which blocs will be influential [or powerful] within a party, thereby working fundamental (if unintended) change on that party.'[48]

Manipulation can be a particularly effective sort of consequential power. If B can be persuaded by some interested party that he really could not possibly want X — perhaps by being fed systematically distorted information about X or in favour of one of its main rivals — then A's power to prevent X is correspondingly increased. The power of capitalists to maintain capitalism is undoubtedly augmented if the main sources of information available to the proletariat, on which they have to rely in assessing the relative merits of socialism and capitalism, are in capitalist hands. This need not by itself make the proletariat any less able to bring about socialism should they decide to try to do so; but it does make them less able to want to try, and therefore the capitalists' position is more secure.

Whilst active manipulation seems clearly an exercise of power, some writers have wanted to distinguish authority and persuasion from power on the grounds that, if B complies willingly, this is somehow morally distinct from situations in which he is coerced. The same argument has been applied to my second motive for B: that in which he is bribed. Leaving aside for the moment the merits of these moral distinctions, I want to reiterate here that authority is no less power because compliance is willing, nor is power absent from the market place because, in the theory, the only exchanges to occur are entered into freely. Charles Merriam destroyed that argument over forty years ago, when he wrote: 'Power is not strongest when it uses violence, but weakest. It is strongest when it employs its instruments of substitution and counter attractions, of allurement, of participation rather than exclusion, of education rather than annihilation. Rape is not evidence of irresistible power in politics or in sex.'[49]

We can, though, agree wholeheartedly with this, and yet still imprison rapists while allowing Casanovas to go free. For, in this evaluative context, we might be unconcerned about the distribution of some forms of power — perhaps authority or persuasion — and instead concentrate on discovering those whose power depends on morally less defensible forms, such as coercion. It is here that influence concepts come in. But it is important to realise that we are making *moral* distinctions here, and not redrawing the boundaries of the concept of power.

My four forms of power provide a basis for drawing desired moral distinctions, but many would certainly want to divide these forms further. They could want to consider not only B's perception of the situation, but A's also: for B might co-operate because he feared punishment for noncompliance, when A never intended to carry out this punishment. Even here it might be thought important to distinguish between those cases in which it was *reasonable* for B to expect punishment, and those cases in which the fear would seem to be irrational. It is also probable that researchers might want to treat differently different sub-categories of my fourth case, in which B chooses without considering A's wishes — distinguishing between genuine coincidence of preferences and manipulation: although exactly how this is to be done is not immediately obvious. But this sketch of the possibilities will have to suffice for now: it is up to the individual researcher to distinguish the varieties of power he wishes to concentrate on, and to justify his choice.

A word needs to be said, however, on the so-called 'problem of anticipated reactions', with which the literature on power has been much concerned. I regard this as a pseudo-problem; or, to put it another way, anticipated reactions are so fundamental that it is misleading to suggest that they occur only on the periphery of the subject. I have suggested that B could co-operate with A for four broad sorts of reasons, the first two of which involve expectations about the response A will give to his actions, and the other two do not. When B's compliance is *not* dependent on his expectations of A's future actions then, of course, no question of B anticipating A's reactions occurs. But when B is co-operating through expectation of reward or fear or punishment, then B is *necessarily* anticipating A's reactions. Sometimes, naturally, it is easier to hazard a guess as to A's likely response and sometimes more difficult. When a highway robber waylaid a traveller, pointed a gun at the victim's head, and demanded money on pain of death, it didn't take a genius to guess that the threat was meant in earnest. On the other hand, I am told that one of the problems of walking in New York nowadays is distinguishing between beggars, panhandlers, and muggers; the nervy tourist tends to pay up whenever anybody requests his money.[50] New York's beggars, of course, are well aware of this, and can make good money playing on the fears of passers-by, without having to go so far that they run the risk of facing charges of demanding money with menaces. The very ambiguity of asking for money is a resource which beggars can use.

The snag with leaving one's threats or promises implicit is usually the reverse: being implicit, they might appear less strong, and thus secure less compliance. Since success is necessarily part of the definition of power — to utter a threat or a promise which is ignored is a sign of weakness, not power[51] — this simply means that *unstated* threats (and promises) are likely to be less effective than *explicit* ones — which is hardly novel, nor a problem at the conceptual level. More important, perhaps, is that if A leaves her *preferences* unstated, they may be misperceived by B — and this can be true even if B wishes to satisfy A because of his affection for her. That is, B might know that something is expected of him, but in the absence of a sign by A, might guess wrong. To the extent that this occurs, so A's power is diminished: she is being incompetent in not expressing her wishes clearly.

Until now I have been concerned with developing a conceptual map of A's power with respect to some specified outcome. Yet, contrary to some writers' claims, I think that we often want to say that someone is powerful, or more powerful than someone else, without adding a long list of things which they have the power to do. To be able to talk meaningfully of an individual's overall power is particularly necessary in this third context; for there is little point discussing the distribution of power within a society if we have to consider each outcome separately.

People are the more powerful the more important to them' the results they can obtain are; or, to put this another way, the more these results accord with their interests. Thus I think that

Poulantzas is very much on the right lines when he wishes to designate by power 'the capacity of a social class to realise its specific objective interests'[52] (although I see no reason why we should restrict the concept of power exclusively to social classes). Surprisingly enough, at least two pluralist works contain passages which are little different from Poulantzas': Lasswell and Kaplan considered that 'the ruling class is the class from which rulers are recruited *and in whose interests they exercise power*',[53] and Arnold Rose at one point attacked Wright Mills on the ground that 'the significant question is in whose interests the political élite acts'.[54]

But how does the notion of interests fit in with my conception of power? I think that conceptions of interest play a crucial role not in the *identification* of power, but in the *aggregation* of separate powers.[55] Thus, if we are content to say that A has the power to obtain X and Y, whilst B can get V and W, and just leave it at that, then there is no need to bring in any notion of interests. Yet if, as we are quite likely to, we want to say whether A has more power than B, or more or less power than she ought to have, then we have to weight the importance of the outcomes X and Y to A against the worth of V and W to B. We might decide that this can't be done. Or we might have some conception of human nature that allows us to evaluate the worth of these outcomes. How we might do this is not a matter that I want to get involved in here; the point is that however it is done, the basis of the judgment will be the same as a decision to the effect that A's interests are satisfied more than B's, or vice versa. A fully-fledged theory of interests would be necessary to perform such aggregations and comparisons; I don't possess such a thoery, and, luckily, I don't need one to elucidate the concept of power.

The practical result of this intrusion of notions of interests into ascriptions of power is that it is more than likely that two researchers with different ideas about interests will fail to agree on comparisons of power, even though they might be in complete agreement as to the outcomes each has the power to obtain. But this does not make the concept of power value-dependent. The concept of power can be accepted on all sides, and agreement secured that A has the power to bring about X, Y, and Z. However, the assessment of the actual distribution of power depends on an aggregation of these outcomes, and this will be dependent on a valuation of these outcomes — which, in turn, could easily depend on a theory of man. There is no reason why this theory should be *written into* the concept of power. Here, as elsewhere, it helps to be very clear about the location of the contests: disputes about 'interests' are not about 'power'; so that, whilst the concept of interest may be essentially contested (or may not: this is not a question I consider here) this, of itself, does not make 'power' an essentially contested concept.

The situation is somewhat similar to that of an election, viewed from within a liberal-democratic conceptual framework. All writers within this tradition agree on what an election is — the concept of 'election' is not contested. However, the actual mechanics of voting, and particularly the aggregation of the votes, produces severe disagreements: for example, on the merits of proportional representation as against the first-past-the-post system. Thus, whilst the *concept* of election is not contested, there may be severe disagreement as to how the winner should actually be chosen.

Nearly a century ago, Heinrich Hertz wrote the following trenchant passage on the problem of the nature of force or electricity:

. . .why is it that people never in this way ask what is the nature of gold, or what is the nature of velocity? Is the nature of gold better known to us than that of electricity, or the nature of velocity better than that of force? Can we by our conceptions, by our words, completely represent the nature of any thing? Certainly not. I fancy the difference must lie in this. With the terms 'velocity' and 'gold' we connect a large number of relations to other terms; and between all these relations we find no contradictions which offend us. We are therefore satisfied and ask no further questions. But we have accumulated around the terms 'force' and 'electricity' more relations than can be completely reconciled amongst themselves. We have an obscure feeling of this and want to have things cleared up. Our confused wish finds expression in the confused question as to the nature of force and electricity. But the answer which we want is not really an answer to this question. It is not by finding out more and fresh relations and conections that it can be answered; but by removing the contradictions existing between those already known, and thus perhaps by reducing their number. When these painful contradictions are removed, the question as to the nature of force will not have been answered; but our minds, no longer vexed, will cease to ask illegitimate questions.[56]

Similar comments could profitably be made about social scientists' problems with the concept of power, and one of the tasks of this paper has been to show how the painful confusions which prevent us asking the legitimate questions can be removed. I do not think it is useful to hide behind a smoke screen of essential contestability: to claim that we can never know what power is — or at least, never reach agreement about it — because of some property of the term.

Rather, I have tried to show that where disagreement does legitimately occur — as it undeniably does — the differences are not really about concepts of power, despite being phrased in this way. Two people can do research into different sorts of political problems, confusingly both using the same word 'power' for what they are investigating — and yet not be misusing the word or contradicting each other's findings. The 'power' of practical politics is different from the 'power' of political evaluation. Within the context of evaluating the distribution of power, different researchers, with different normative beliefs, will be interested in different aspects of power. Some will consider coercion a great evil and manipulation a matter of little importance — and concentrate on appropriate segments of power's conceptual map. Other researchers will disagree, and concentrate on a wider range of power phenomena. But it is confusing to see this divergence as something intrinsic to the *concept* of power; it is, rather, more fundamental: a deep-seated disagreement as to that which is politically, or ethically, more important. And the same far-reaching differences underlie the various approaches to interests that researchers could adopt when aggregating those things which people have the power to bring about. It is just misleading to say that the presence of these value-dependent elements makes 'power', itself, value-dependent. Conceptual clarity can be gained by showing how the one (ability) concept of power can be infused with different values: we can then sort out how many of the disagreements concerning the appearance or distribution of power are due to different factual interpretations, and how many stem from the different values of the researchers.

A 'map' of the concept of power

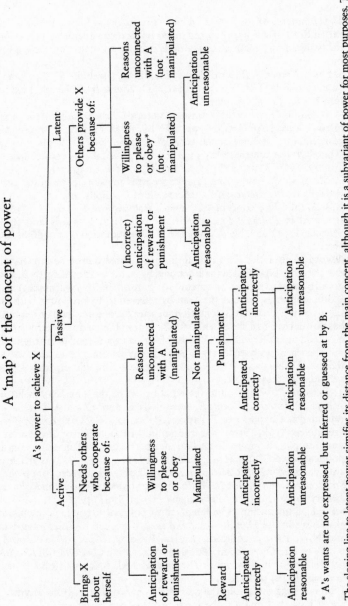

The sloping line to latent power signifies its distance from the main concept, although it is a subvariant of power for most purposes. The distinction between exercising and having power cuts across this map, but only applies to active variants of power.

* A's wants are not expressed, but inferred or guessed at by B.

NOTES

1 The comments of Joe Femia, Michael Freeman and Hillel Steiner on an earlier draft of this paper forced me to revise it considerably, I think for the better. I owe them a considerable debt for the help they have given me.

2 S. Lukes, *Power: A Radical View* (MacMillan, London; 1974) p. 9; and W.E. Connolly, *The Terms of Political Discourse* (D.C. Heath, Lexington, Mass., 1974) Chapter 3.

3 W.B. Gallie, 'Essentially contested concepts', *Proceedings of the Aristotelian Society*, 56 (1955–6) pp. 167–98; A. MacIntyre, 'The essential contestability of some social concepts', *Ethics* 84 (1973) pp. 1–9; J. Gray, 'On the contestability of social and political concepts', *Political Theory*, 5(1977) pp. 331–48; Connolly, *op. cit.* Chapter 1.

4 P. Morriss, 'Ordinary language, conceptual revision, or essential contestability?' (forthcoming); a discussion of Connolly, *op. cit.*

5 R.A. Dahl, 'The concept of power', *Behavioural Science* 2 (1957), reprinted in *Political Power*, eds. R. Bell, D.V. Edwards and R.H. Wagner (Free Press, New York, 1969). The quotation is at p. 80 of this reprint.

6 A word on notation. Throughout this paper I shall adopt the convention that the more powerful actor is denoted by A, the less powerful by B, and X will be used to refer to an outcome or state of affairs. I will make A and B different sexes, so that they can be referred to by pronouns without risk of confusion: Dahl's definition is easier to comprehend if it reads 'A has power over B to the extent that *she* can get him to do something that he would not otherwise do'. Philosophical examples tend to lay themselves open too easily to charges of male chauvinism; in an attempt to redress the balance, I shall make A female throughout, and B, the subordinate actor, male.

7 T. Parsons, ' "Voting" and the equilibrium of the American political system', in *American Voting Behavior*, eds. E. Burdick and A. Brodbeck; reprinted as Chapter 9 of T. Parsons, *Politics and Social Structure* (Free Press, New York, 1969). The quotation is from p. 205 of this reprint.

8 For example, H. Simon, 'Notes on the observation and measurement of political power', *Journal of Politics* 15 (1953) p. 501 n. 3. This article is also reprinted in *Political Power, op. cit.*; Dahl, 'The concept of power', *Political Power, op. cit.*; N.W. Polsby, *Community Power and Political Theory* (Yale University Press, New Haven, 1963) p. 3.

9 See F.E. Oppenheim, 'The language of political inquiry: problems of classification', in *Handbook of Political Science*, eds. F.E. Greenstein and N.W. Polsby, (Addison-Wesley, Reading, Mass., 1975) Vol. 1, p. 288 or F.E. Oppenheim, 'Power and causation', in *Power and Political Theory: Some European Perspectives*, ed. B. Barry (John Wiley, London, 1976) p. 103.

10 I am not suggesting that the derivations of words can *prove* anything about how they ought to be used; but they can be instructive.

11 Throughout this section I shall speak indiscriminately of *having* and

exercising power. Later I shall discuss the difference between these two ideas, and examine their relative importance; here, though, I am concerned with more basic issues.

12 I should perhaps repeat that I am using 'ability' and 'influence' in a wider sense than that current in ordinary usage; we would not consider it appropriate to say of someone whose actions changed because a gun was stuck in his back with the accompanying threat that the trigger would be pulled unless he complied, that he was *influenced*. Rather, I suspect, we'd say that this was a case of coercion. Nevertheless, my label of 'influence concept' is intended to apply to *all* such situations, *whatever* the reason for B to change his actions, or the cause of his being affected.

13 Assuming that we can ignore inflation, in that the inflationary effect of one union's wage increase is likely to have only a very small effect on the value of that rise. For the sake of this example, we can assume that all unions' pay negotiations are independent of each other, or sufficiently independent so that a pay rise is never, in itself, self-defeating.

14 Dahl, 'The concept of power', *op. cit.* p. 83.

15 He would seem, of course, to be able to make his son go swimming whenever he wants, but we can safely ignore this here. In any case, it could be that his son never does any one specific thing, but just finds *some* excuse to avoid mowing the lawn.

16 R.A. Dahl, *Who Governs?* (Yale University Press, New Haven, 1961) p. 333. There is also a similar passage on p. 66.

17 See S. Carmichael and C.V. Hamilton, *Black Power: The Politics of Liberation in America* (Penguin Press, Harmondsworth, 1968); and cf. J.D. Aberback and J.L. Walker, 'The meanings of black power: a comparison of white and black interpretations of a political slogan', *American Political Science Review* 64 (1970) pp. 367–88.

18 An exception is T.H. Marshall, 'Reflections on power', *Sociology* 3 (1969) p. 152.

19 H.L.A. Hart, *The Concept of Law* (Oxford University Press, 1961) p. 5.

20 J.G. March, 'The power of power', in *Varieties of Political Theory,* ed. D. Easton, (Prentice Hall, Englewood Cliffs, 1966); D.M. White, 'The problem of power', *British Journal of Political Science* 2 (1972) p. 490; R.E. Wolfinger, *The Politics of Progress* (Prentice Hall, Englewood Cliffs, 1974) p. 9.

21 Cf. Lee's description of the Citizens Action Commission, in Dahl, *Who Governs?* p. 130.

22 Lukes, *op. cit.* p. 56; see also Connolly, *op. cit.* Chapter 3 *passim.*

23 J.R. Lucas, *The Principles of Politics* (Oxford University Press, 1966) p. 119.

24 Lukes, *op. cit.* p. 31; Connolly, op. cit. pp. 87–8. See my paper referred to in note 4 for a discussion of Connolly's confused use of 'responsibility'.

25 C.B. Macpherson, *Democratic Theory: Essays in Retrieval* (Oxford University Press, 1973) pp. 8–9.

26 T. Honderich, 'Democratic violence', *Philosophy and Public Affairs* 2 (1973) p. 203.

27 A. MacIntyre, *Marcuse* (Fontana, London, 1970) p. 71; see also J.S. Coleman, *Power and the Structure of Society* (W.W. Norton, New York, 1974).

28 An exception, of course, is Parsons.

29 See diagram at the end of this paper.

30 R.A. Bauer, I. de S. Pool and L.A. Dexter, *American Business and Public Policy: The Politics of Foreign Trade* (Atherton, New York, 1963) p. 264.

31 B. Barry, 'The economic approach to the analysis of power and conflict', *Government and Opposition* 9 (1974) p. 189.
    B. Barry, 'Power: an economic analysis', in *Power and Political Theory*, ed. B. Barry, p. 67.

32 Compare the two different reputational methods, as distinguished by D.M. Fox, 'Methods within methods: the case of community power studies', *Western Poltical Quarterly* 24 (1971) pp. 5–11.

33 P. Agee, *Inside the Company: CIA Diary* (Penguin Books, Harmondsworth, 1975).

34 In addition, of course, the CIA can *give* power to relatively powerless but ideologically suitable groups, for example by providng them with money or weapons. Whilst this may use up a considerable amount of the organisation funds, it involves *changing* the distribution of power within the society, rather than locating the powerful. Groups which are worth aiding in this way must be latently powerful; the object of the aid is to realise this latency, and convert it into actual power, preferably of the first sort.

35 This is, of course, a rather simple account, and space prevents me from entering into any of the complexities which I here skim over: this is not the place to provide an account of counterfactuals. One required refinement is that A may be able to obtain X under some conditions, but not under others: the ability is to that extent restricted.

36 Q. Gibson, 'Power', *Philosophy of the Social Sciences*, I (1971) p. 109.

37 By Connolly, *op. cit.* Chapter 3 *passim,* especially pp. 97–8.

38 H. Lasswell, *Politics: Who Gets What, When, How* (Whittlesey House, New York, 1936) p. 3.

39 This is not a happy phrase, perhaps, and must be taken as an abbreviation of a longer, and more clumsy formulation. In this context I consider that those who receive X, even though no action by them is required, need to be classified together with those who are able to obtain X at will. Whether one calls the union of these two sets 'power' or something else is not important; but the problem we are concerned with here is one that has traditionally been discussed under this label.

40 J. Westergaard and H. Resler, *Class in a Capitalist Society: A Study of Contemporary Britain* (Penguin Books, Harmondsworth, 1976) p. 142. See also J.G. Deutsch, 'Neutrality, Legitimacy, and the Supreme Court: some intersections between law and political science', *Stanford Law Review,* 20 (1967/8) p. 255.

41 Polsby, *op. cit.* p. 133.

42 See, for example, Nozick's tale of Wilt Chamberlain, in R. Nozick,

'Distributive Justice', *Philosophy and Public Affairs* 3 (1973) pp. 57–60, or in R. Nozick, *Anarchy, State and Utopia* (Basic Books, New·York, 1974) pp. 161–4.

43   It is of course often difficult to distinguish between the threat to punish and the mere withholding of an expected reward; since I do not intend to offer suggestions here about how to distinguish threats from offers, it might be better to consider these two categories together. I have not done so simply because it will be seen that many writers make a moral distinction between compliance obtained through threat of punishment and that induced by an offer of a reward: it is up to such moralists to argue the distinction, not to me, but it is wrong for me to suggest that it is an impossible one to maintain.

Neither do I want to deny the possibility of someone employing a combination of threats and offers (called by Hillel Steiner 'throffers' [H. Steiner, 'Individual liberty', *Proceedings of the Aristotelian Society*, 75 (November 1974) p. 39]) such as 'Do X and I shall give you £1000, fail and I shall kill you'. In this context, 'throffers' are merely a special case of a combination of any two (or more) reasons for B's compliance — and I certainly do not want to be taken as implying that such combinations are impossible. In normal times, for example, we all obey the law *both* because we are afraid of punishment if we are caught breaking it, *and* because we recognise it as legitimate. My four categories are ones which can be logically distinguished, and sometimes we want to treat them differently, but motivations in real life are almost always mixed.

44   Or, more accurately, because B wants to bring about some Y (which may, but need not, be the same as X) where the actions he would perform in trying to obtain Y would lead to A's obtaining X.

45   H. Arendt, 'Lying in politics: reflections on the Pentagon Papers', *New York Review of Books* XVII No. 8 (18 November 1971) pp. 30–9. The quotation contained in this passage is by R.J. Barnet, from R. Stavins *et al.*, *Washington Plans an Aggressive War*, p. 199.

46   D. Halberstam, *The Best and the Brightest* (Random House, New York, 1972) p. 62; he is referring here to McGeorge Bundy.

47   For a discussion of power stemming from rules and routines, see G. Parry and P. Morriss, 'When is a decision not a decision?' in *British Political Sociology Yearbook, Vol. 1: Elites in Western Democracy*, ed. I. Crewe (Croom Helm, London, 1974) pp. 331–4.

48   J.I. Lengle and B. Shafer, 'Primary rules, political power and social change', *American Political Science Review* 70 (1976) p. 25.

49   C.E. Merriam, *Political Power: Its Composition and Incidence* (Whittlesey House, New York, 1934) p. 180.

50   I used to think that a mugger was a person who hit first and asked after, but apparently, at least in New York usage, mugging includes demanding money and using violence only if refused.

51   Even this has been disputed: by D.V.J. Bell, *Power, Influence, and Authority* (Oxford University Press, New York, 1975) p. 21 and *passim*.

52   N. Poulantzas, *Political Power and Social Classes* (New Left Books, London, 1973) p. 104. This passage is italicised in the original.

53 H.D. Lasswell and A. Kaplan, *Power and Society: A Framework for Political Inquiry* (Routledge & Kegan Paul, London, 1952) p. 206; my emphasis.
54 A.M. Rose, *The Power Structure: Political Process in American Society* (Oxford University Press, New York, 1967) p. 28. The passage continues 'and whether it is checked by the mass of voters and of interest groups . . .'.
55 A similar account of the significance of interests is suggested by F.E. Oppenheim, in his *Dimensions of Freedom* (St. Martin's Press, New York, 1961) pp. 201–2.
56 H. Hertz, *The Principles of Mechanics* (Dover, New York, 1956) (republication of 1900 edition) pp. 7–8.

Introduction to the Reading of Alexandre Kojève

PATRICK RILEY

I

ONE of the most visible phenomena on the frontier of post-war political philosophy has been a resuscitated 'left Hegelianism', and among contemporary left-Hegelians none has been so influential as Alexandre Kojève, whose brilliant *Introduction to the Reading of Hegel*[1] is viewed as a modern classic even by those who see it as a one-sided interpretation of Hegelian philosophy. Why 'left Hegelianism' in general, and Kojève's 'reading' of Hegel in particular, should have sprung up in France (beginning in the 1930s but fully flowering only after the War), is a question not as easily answered as some appear to think. Allan Bloom claims in his English-language edition of *Introduction to the Reading of Hegel* that 'Kojève is the most thoughtful, the most learned, the most profound of those Marxists who, dissatisfied with the thinness of Marx's account of the human and metaphysical grounds of his teaching, turned to Hegel as the truly philosophic source of that teaching';[2] but it is not at all clear how far Kojève's 'reading' of Hegel is really 'Marxist', despite the fact that Kojève makes the 'dialectic of Master and Slave' in the *Phenomenology* the 'key' to his interpretation of the whole of Hegel.[3] If there is (at least) a Marxist *component* in Kojève's 'reading', there is also an existentialist one — which is at its clearest in his insistence that the historical struggle between Masters and Slaves is a struggle *freely* entered into, without 'cause' or 'biological necessity';[4] and there is also what one would call a Nietzschean component in Kojève's hatred of all 'transcendence', of all 'escape' into a 'beyond' where there is (allegedly) no struggle, no Mastery and Slavery. This distaste for the 'beyond', so reminiscent of the *Twilight of the Idols*,[5] is the foundation of Kojève's hostility to Plato (and the realm of Ideas),[6] and of his lesser but substantial aversion to Kant (and the realm of things-in-themselves).[7] (One can, Kojève complains in the 'Plato' chapter of his *Attempt at a Reasoned History of Pagan Philosophy,* 'deny the possibility of all satisfaction on the here-and-now'. Thus 'the affirmation of religious satisfaction' — whether in Plato or in Kant — 'demands the affirmation of a "beyond" where the man can be satisfied who cannot be in the here-and-now'.[8] Put otherwise, Kojève continues, 'religious satisfaction cannot be anything else than an 'extinction' [nirvana] of the extended-duration of human empirical existence'.[9] Since, for Kojève, Hegelianism is a 'radically atheistic' philosophy which treats Christianity as only 'anthropologically' true — insofar as it stresses God-becoming-man[10] — Hegel avoids altogether the 'religious attitude' which believes in the 'impossibility' of man's being 'fully and definitely satisfied' in *this* world, 'in the world where he is born, lives and dies'. Hegel, indeed, for Kojève, is *the* philosopher of 'perfect' satisfaction in the ' "worldly" *hic et nunc*'.)[11] A complete 'picture' of Kojève, then, would stress not just the Marxian elements of his thought, but the existentialist and 'Nietzschean' ones as well: these elements, in themselves perfectly discrete, may well be able to co-exist, and even support each other (if one stresses, say, the 'voluntary' undertaking of a 'struggle' for Mastery whose upshot is the enslavement of those who find solace in a 'beyond'); but these mutually supporting discrete 'elements' add up to something more and other than 'Marxism' *tout court*.

With the posthumous publication of Kojève's *Kant* and of the last two volumes of his *Attempt at a Reasoned History of Pagan Philosophy*, one is finally in a position to sketch the outlines of this complete picture. The central and decisive Kojèvian work remains the magistral *Introduction to the Reading of Hegel*; but this can and should be supplemented, not only by *Kant* and *Pagan Philosophy*, but by several important articles which Kojève wrote for the journal *Critique* — above all 'Hegel, Marx and Christianity'[12] and 'The Political Action of Philosophers'.[13] It is only out of this entire ensemble that an accurate portrait of Kojève can be built up, so that one can begin to assess his status as the most eminent of contem-porary 'left Hegelians'.

II

In his brilliant and influential *Introduction to the Reading of Hegel* Kojève makes his treatment of the *Phenomenology* revolve around Hegel's great set-piece,[14] 'Master and Servant' (which he renders 'Master and Slave'). And in this treatment Kojève argues that for Hegel human society and human 'discourse' began when men were first willing to risk their 'animal' and biological existence in a 'fight to the death' for 'pure prestige', for 'recognition' by the 'other'.[15] The man who became the Master was he who was 'willing to go all the way' in this fight: the potential Master 'preferred, to his real, natural, biological life, something ideal, spiritual, non-biological — the fact of being recognised in and through [another] consciousness, of bearing the name "Master" '.[16] The (potential) Slave on the other hand, was the one who saw and feared his own 'nothingness' should he die in the struggle, and who 'recognised' the Master rather than die.[17] The Master, for his part, finds that he is not 'satisfied' with mastery, since he has risked his life for recognition by a mere Slave whom he uses as a 'thing'; the Master has the 'pleasure' of not having to work, but this pleasure is not a true *satisfaction*. 'To get oneself recognised by a Slave is not to get oneself recognised by a *man*'; hence 'the Master never attains his end, the end for which he has risked his very life'.[18] (It is for this reason, according to Kojève, that Mastery is ultimately 'tragic' and 'an existential impasse'.[19]) The Slave, who submits to and 'works' in the service of the Master, can ultimately find satisfaction in his work (by which he transforms the natural world of 'given being' and himself as well): through work, which 'negates' 'given being', the Slave overcomes the world.[20] 'The man who works transforms given being . . . where there is work there is necessarily change, progress, historical evolution.'[21] Though this progress and evolution involves alterations in the 'means of production', the essential change is in the Slave himself:

'thanks to his work, the Slave *can* change and become other than he is, that is — in the end — cease to be a Slave'.[22] For work, according to Kojève-reading-Hegel, is *Bildung* or education 'in a double sense of the word: on the one hand it forms and transforms the world, humanises it, by making it more adapted to man; on the other hand, it transforms, forms, educates man, humanises him in bringing him closer to the idea which he makes for himself' (the 'idea' of being 'free' and 'recognised').[23]

Since the Slave's 'overcoming' — of the natural world of 'given being', of his fear of the Master and of death, of slavery itself — is not historically complete until men choose their own work and become citizens of a 'universal and homogeneous' Hegelian state,[24] history is, *inter alia*, a history of 'slave ideologies' by which Slaves conceal their slavery from themselves. 'The transformation of the Slave, which will permit him to surmount his terror, his fear of the Master . . . is long and dolorous.'[25] At first, Kojève-reading-Hegel asserts, the Slave 'raises himself' through his work to the 'abstract idea' of liberty — an abstract idea which he does not 'realise' because 'he does not yet dare to *act* in view of this realisation, that is to struggle against the Master and risk his life in a struggle for liberty'.[26] Before 'realising' liberty, the Slave 'imagines a series of ideologies, by which he seeks to justify himself, to justify his servitude, to reconcile the *ideal* of liberty with the fact of slavery'.[27] For Stoicism, the first of the 'slave ideologies', Epictetus in his chains and Marcus Aurelius on his throne are 'equal' as 'wise men'; hence for the Stoic 'ideology' the chains do not 'matter'.[28] In Christian 'ideology' equality is of a different sort: all men are equal 'before God', whatever their earthly stations; but this is simply another escape to a 'beyond' (beyond the historical world of work and struggle) in which, though there are no 'masters', there is one 'universal' Master (God) to whom everyone is enslaved. Christianity, according to Kojève-reading-Hegel, 'does not take account of social distinctions, but leaves them intact. Equality is transposed into the beyond (men are brothers "in Jesus Christ"; that is, all slaves of an absolute Master).'[29] A modern bourgeois may, by contrast, appear to be 'his own master', but bourgeois ideology is simply a new slavery: one is now enslaved to property and to capital. 'The bourgeois does not work for another. But neither does he work for himself, taken as a biological entity. He works for himself taken as a "juridical person", as a private proprietor . . . he works for Capital.'[30]

And so long as there is slavery — whether to a Master, to God, or to Capital — man will never be truly 'satisfied' or truly free, since true satisfaction and freedom come from being 'recognised' as an equal by an equal, which is possible only in the Hegelian state. 'Man can only be truly "satisfied", history can only end, in and through the formation of a Society, of a State, in which the strictly particular, personal, individual value of each is recognised as such . . . by *all*.'[31] Such a state, *selon* Kojève, 'is only possible after the "suppression" of the opposition between Master and Slave'.[32]

This 'suppression', to be sure, is brought about mainly through the Slave's work. 'Only the Slave,' Kojève urges, ' "suppresses" his "nature" and finally becomes a Citizen. The Master does not change: he would rather die than cease to be Master. The final struggle, which transforms the Slave into a Citizen, suppresses Mastery in a non-dialectical fashion: the Master is simply killed, and he dies as a Master.'[33] But by this point, the end of history, the Slave is ready for the reality of freedom, not its mere 'imagination' (as in Stoicism or Christianity). 'The complete, absolutely free man,' Kojève insists, 'will be the Slave who has "overcome" his slavery. If idle Mastery is an impasse, laborious Slavery, in contrast, is the source of all human, social, historical progress. History is the history of the working Slave.'[34] In the 'raw, natural, given world,' he adds, 'the Slave is the slave of the Master. In the technical world transformed by his work, he rules — or, at least, will one day rule — as absolute Master. And this Mastery that arises from work, . . . will be an entirely different thing from the "immediate" mastery of the Master. The future and History hence belong not to the warlike Master . . . but to the working Slave.'[35] In another passage of his *Introduction*, Kojève enlarges and refines this view. 'History will end when man no longer acts in the strong sense of the term, that is, no longer negates, no longer transforms given being and social being through bloody struggle and creative work. And man no longer does this when what is Real [*le Réel donné*] gives him full satisfaction, by realising fully his Desire (which in man is a desire for universal recognition of his personality, which is unique in the world).'[36] Or, as Kojève puts it in 'Hegel, Marx and Christianity', history will end 'necessarily' at the moment when the desire for recognition is 'fully satisfied'. This desire will be satisfied 'when each shall be recognised in his reality and in his human dignity by *all* the others'. History, in short, will 'stop itself when man is perfectly satisfied by the fact of being a recognised citizen of a universal and homogeneous State, or, if one prefers, of a society without classes encompassing the whole of humanity'.[37] (Extraordinary — from an authentically Marxian perspective — to say 'universal State', *or* 'if one prefers', a 'society without classes': in Marx one would not say state 'or' society,[38] nor would one say 'if one prefers'.) If man is fully satisfied 'by what he *is*', the only desire left — on the part of a *philosopher* — is that of 'understanding what he is . . . and revealing it through discourse'. This 'understanding' and 'revealing' are provided by Hegel, standing at the end of time, who offers an 'adequate description of the Real in its totality'.[39] Hegel, in short, provides a satisfying account of a Reality which has (finally) become satisfactory.

This is about as far as most accounts of Kojève go. Thus Hannah Arendt, in her frequently stimulating last work, *Willing*, claims that Kojève was influenced above all by the closing lines of Alexandre Koyré's 'Hegel à Iena', which had argued that 'it is possible that Hegel believed' that history was at an end, and that 'this essential condition [for a philosophy of history] was *already* an actuality . . . and that this had been the reason why he himself was able — had been able — to complete it'. And Arendt goes on to speak of Kojève, 'for whom the Hegelian system is *the* truth and therefore the definite end of philosophy as well as history'.[40]

Unfortunately 'definite' is too definite a term at this point; for while Arendt is certainly essentially right about Kojève, she does not take into account some peculiarly Kojèvian additions to the *Ende der Geschichte* and to Hegel as 'the last philosopher' — additions which need to be attended to.

One might pardonably imagine — having been told that the future 'belongs' to 'the working slave' — that the 'universal and homogeneous state' would be produced precisely by these (former) slaves when they (finally) 'suppress' both the Master and their own slavery. But this turns out to be not quite the' case: if a 'Master' is not needed to usher in the 'end of history', a *hero* at least is. And this hero is Napoleon. Since this somewhat odd doctrine is peculiarly Kojèvian, but is not noticed by Arendt and many others, it requires some attention.

Hegelianism is true, for Kojève, because it stands at the end of time and 'knows' the whole or Reality; it is 'no longer the *search* for wisdom, but wisdom (= absolute knowledge) itself'.[41] Now truth is not 'truly true', *selon* Kojève, unless 'the reality which it reveals is *entirely* attained (all that was possible is effectively realised), thus "perfect", without possibility of extension or change'. This 'total, definitive reality is the Napoleonic Empire'; for Hegel in 1806 — the year of the composition of the *Phenomenology* — this Empire is a 'universal and homogeneous state' which 're-unites the whole of humanity ... and "suppresses" (*aufhebt*) in its womb all "specific differences": nations, classes, social groups, families'.[42]

Since this state — for Kojève-reading-Hegel — is 'perfect' and 'definitive', there will be no further change, no further 'negation' of the 'given'; 'this state changes no more because all its citizens are "satisfied" '. In a 'universal' state, according to Kojève, 'I am recognised by *all* men, who are all my *peers*'. And thanks to the 'homogeneity' of this state, 'it is truly *I* who am recognised, and not my family, my social class, my nation'.[43] True, in the Napoleonic state it is Napoleon himself who is best satisfied;[44] but apparently everyone is sufficiently satisfied. Hegel's role in the process is simply to 'understand' and to 'reveal': 'this Sage, who (through "knowledge") reveals Reality (incarnated in Napoleon), is the incarnation of Absolute Mind: thus he is, if one likes, the incarnated God of whom the Christians dreamed'.[45] And Kojève ends with a bold claim: 'the true, real Christ = Napoleon-Jesus + Hegel — Logos; the Incarnation thus takes place not in the middle but at the end of history'.[46] This claim, however, in Kojève's view, is no longer 'blasphemous' if one understands that Christianity, *qua* 'anthropology', is only 'symbolically' true: 'the life of Christ and his death symbolise the real course of history: Christ sacrifices his particularity (= Jesus) in order to realise the

Universal (= Logos) and the Universal (= God) recognises this particularity (= Man) which is God himself'. Christ, Kojève insists, 'works — he is a carpenter; he sacrifices his life — this is struggle and risk'. But it is not a true struggle, since Christ 'remains a slave' who 'dies on the cross'; thus He reveals 'the final atheism, the death of God'. And he is 'resurrected' — to the extent that one can say this at all — only 'as real Man, that is as Community, as Church (= prototype of the Napoleonic Empire)'.[47]

It is Napoleon — or rather Napoleon 'revealed' by Hegel — who is, according to Kojève, the 'revealed God' of Chapter VI of the *Phenomenology*; and the section of that work called 'Evil and Forgiveness' deals (again *selon* Kojève) with Napoleon's 'crime' in establishing a 'universal' state and Hegel's 'forgiving' him by 'understanding' the world-historical significance of his action).[48]

Why Kojève should have attached such weight to Napoleon is less clear in *Introduction to the Reading of Hegel* than in the article 'Hegel, Marx and Christianity'. In the article Kojève begins, familiarly enough, with the view that history 'ended' with the publication of the *Phenomenology;* that Hegelianism is true 'solely because history has ended, because man no longer negates, no longer transforms the Real revealed by the last philosophy, which, for that reason, is no longer philosophy or *recherche de la vérité*, but truth itself or Wisdom (absolute knowledge)';[49] that there is a 'man' who 'realised or incarnated' the end of history, 'that is to say Napoleon'; that 'Hegelian thought' gives 'an account of Napoleon'; that 'the Christ who exists empirically, the God who actually reveals himself to man, the Word truly become flesh — is the diad Napoleon-Hegel, is the man achieving the historical evolution through a bloody struggle, doubled by a man revealing the sense of his evolution through his discourse'.[50] It is a crucial footnote to 'Hegel, Marx and Christianity' which reveals *why* Kojève sees philosophy, history, Napoleon and Hegel in this light. 'In a famous letter,' Kojève urges, 'Hegel says that, having finished the *Phenomenology*, he saw at dawn the "soul of the world" on horseback beneath his windows.' This letter, Kojève insists, is a 'revelation': Napoleon, 'the conqueror at Jena, is called "world-soul" . . . he incarnates not the history of the French people, but that of the whole of humanity'. But Napoleon, taken by himself, is not 'mind', because he is not 'fully conscious of himself: by his action, he has in fact completed history, but he does not know that he does it and that by doing it he realises Absolute Mind'. It is Hegel who 'knows' this, and says it in the *Phenomenology*. Thus 'Absolute Mind or "God" is neither Napoleon nor Hegel, but Napoleon-understood-by-Hegel or Hegel-understanding-Napoleon'.[51]

(If one stresses 'the diad Napoleon-Hegel', it is because this theme is characteristically and peculiarly 'Kojèvian', and cannot be accounted for on a 'Marxian' view: after all, in the *18th Brumaire* Marx, while calling the reign of Napoleon III a 'farce' referred to the reign of the first Napoleon as a 'tragedy'.[52] And contemporary Marxists have continued to take an unsympathetic view of Napoleon: even Georg Lukacs, for all his appreciation of Hegelianism, says that Hegel's 'opting' for Napoleon and his making 'the French Revolution and the new bourgeois society it had created the climax of modern history' was nothing but 'Utopianism' and an 'ideological' defense of 'a wretched thing'.[53] But neither is Kojève's Napoleonism either 'existentialist' or 'Nietzschean'. It may come *closer* to being truly Hegelian; Hegel did, after all, write the 'famous letter' which Kojève makes so much of. But that Hegel himself saw Napoleon as the 'end' of history and as 'the word become flesh' — this one can reasonably doubt. That Chapter VI of the *Phenomenology* is, as Kojève insists, Hegel's 'forgiving' of Napoleon, seems to rest on the fact that in that chapter one finds the famous passage about no man's being a 'hero to his valet'[54] [valets are spiteful, not 'forgiving']; but this is necessarily 'about' Napoleon only if Hegel's 'famous letter' is a 'clue' to the [very abstract] language of Chapter VI.)

In any event, and whatever one makes of Kojève's Napoleonism, it turns out that it is not *simply* the case that 'the diad Napoleon-Hegel' has 'realised' (in the double sense) a 'satisfying' state: it may only have launched a state of affairs which might (yet) *become* satisfactory. For, after having said in *Introduction to the Reading of Hegel* that Napoleon and Hegel between them bring history to an end, Kojève backtracks a little: 'The perfect State . . .? No doubt possible, but one is far from it.'[55] Hegel himself, Kojève urges, knew quite well that the state 'was not yet actually realised in all its perfection', and therefore 'affirmed only the existence in the world of the *germ* of this State and the existence of the necessary and sufficient conditions of its flowering'.[56] Now no one, Kojève continues, can 'deny with certainty the absence of such a germ and of such conditions in our world'; thus the Hegelian 'universal and homogeneous state' is no 'error' and remains possible 'in principle'.[57] In an argument reminiscent of what Kant says about the 'possibility' of 'eternal peace',[58] Kojève goes on to insist that 'that which is neither an error nor [yet] a truth, is an idea, or, if one prefers, an ideal'. The idea or ideal of an Hegelian state 'will only be transformed into truth by negative action, which, in destroying the World which does not correspond to the idea, will create through this very destruction the world which conforms to the ideal'.[59] Thus the Hegelian state, though extant as a 'germ' since 1806, remains a *projet à realiser*. Or, as Kojève puts it in a note in *Pagan Philosophy,* 'Hegelianism is alone in translating itself into existence (at least insofar as history is not definitively completed) through social and political action properly speaking ("revolutionary" or "Marxist")'.[60]

It seems, then, that there is some uncertainty in Kojève whether history ended, and 'satisfaction' began, in 1806; or whether only the 'germ' of a future 'satisfaction' sprang up with 'the diad Napoleon-Hegel'. Kojève tries to cast a little light on this obscurity at the end of 'Hegel, Marx and Christianity' by saying that, if history did not (utterly) end with 'Hegel-understanding-Napoleon', it is at least the case that there has been nothing truly or wholly 'new' *since* Hegel: 'if there has been from the beginning a "left" and a "right" Hegelianism, this is also *all* there has been since Hegel' (leaving out of account the vestigial survival of liberalism, a pre-Hegelian thing).[61] And 'history', according to Kojève, has not yet awarded the palm to either 'left' or 'right'.[62]

In sum: however Kojève may vacillate, he vacillates within a narrow range of possibilities. Either history and philosophy ended in 1806, and universal 'recognition' and 'satisfaction' set in (the strong version); or at least the *germ* of all this began in 1806 (remaining a *projet à realiser*), and there has been nothing truly new *since* Napoleon-Hegel (the weak version). The 'end', then, or the 'beginning-of-the-end' — those are the possibilities; the vacillation is perhaps not as serious as it might at first appear to be.

III

The 'Napoleonism' apart, there are several ways in which it is reasonable to characterise Kojève's 'reading' of Hegel as (more or less) 'Marxist'. Most noticeably, it is no accident that Kojève begins his interpretation of Hegel with a quotation from Marx' *Economic and Philosophic MSS of 1844* ('Hegel . . . grasps labour as the essence of man — as man's essence in the act of proving itself')[63] and then places his own heavily-glossed version of the 'Master and Servant' chapter of the *Phenomenology* at the outset of *Introduction to the Reading of Hegel*, so that this chapter colours and indeed 'governs' the rest of the 'reading'. (Hegel, of course, does *not* begin with Master and Servant; and he gives no indication that this chapter is 'privileged' above other parts of the *Phenomenology*.[64]) Now if 'mastery' (in Marx' time, or our own) might mean something like owning the 'means of production', and 'slavery' might take the form of 'alienated labour' on the part of a 'proletarian', then Kojève's insistence on 'Master and Servant' as central and governing *could* certainly be viewed as a 'Marxian' reading of Hegel. (One says 'could', and not 'must', because it is noticeable that where one might expect Marx to mention Hegel as *the* theorist of Mastery and Slavery — above all in Book III, Chapter 23 of *Capital* — he in fact quotes Aristotle's discussion of the subject, at length, and in Greek, but fails to mention Hegel at all.[65] But as an example of Master — in this same passage — Marx mentions the 'capitalist'; and a wage-labourer serves as his 'slave'. And this supports Kojève.)

More clearly Marxian, perhaps, is Kojève's insistence that — for Hegel — 'real' history is 'political, social, economic', while 'the history of the sciences, or the arts and of religions is only . . . the history of "ideologies" which are born of the real historical process'.[66] The whole of 'ideology', according to Kojève-reading-Hegel, 'is a sort of ideal "superstructure", which has a sense and a possibility of being only on the basis of a real "infrastructure", formed by the totality of political and social struggles and of labours undertaken by man'. This 'aspect' of 'the Hegelian dialectic', he concludes, which is ' "materialist", if one likes', actually 'determined all of Marx' thoughts'.[67] (With this last claim it looks as if Kojève is purveying an 'Hegelian Marx', rather than a 'Marxian Hegel': if Hegel as 'materialist' 'determines' 'all of Marx' thought', and if Hegel in addition has something that Marxism lacks, or at least displays less fully — say, the notion of 'recognition' — then Marx is to Hegel as the part to a whole.)

But if there is a sense in which Kojève's 'reading' of Hegel is 'Marxist' — or at least stresses notions (work, struggle, history and ideology) which are 'also' in Marxism, and *congruent with* Marxism — there is an important sense in which the reading is less Marxist than (roughly) 'existentialist'. Now Marx is quite clear in *The German Ideology* that 'men can be distinguished from animals by consciousness, by religion or anything else you like. They themselves begin to distinguish themselves from animals as soon as they begin to *produce* their means of subsistence . . .'.[68] In Marx, then, it is 'production' which is distinctively and characteristically *human*. In Kojève, on the other hand, 'humanity' is distinguished from animal ('biological') life by the struggle for recognition: 'man is only human . . . insofar as he is "recognised" '.[69] Moreover, for Kojève, this 'recognition' is not something which springs up *after* 'production' (*qua* first human fact): in Kojève 'recognition' is not an 'epiphenomenon' of production or work — it is the *undetermined* expression of human freedom, and work ('production') comes *after* 'recognition', as something imposed by the Master on the Slave. ('In order to realise or "objectify" the unilateral recognition of the Slave,' Kojève argues, 'the Master obliges the latter to *work* for him. This forced work for the exclusive benefit of the Master is brought about in opposition to the natural instincts of the Slave . . . and it is this essentially human work which transforms the very essence of the natural world by creating, in the midst of nature, the technical world in which universal history unfolds.'[70]) The 'decision' on the part of the (potential) Slave to 'interrupt the struggle' for recognition, Kojève argues (above all in 'Hegel,

Marx and Christianity') is 'brought about as a function of the fear of death', but it is also as ' "free" (= unforseeable) or "non-natural" as the decision to engage in the struggle' in the first place. 'Nothing,' Kojève urges, 'predisposes the future conqueror to victory, as nothing predisposes the future vanquished [one] to his defeat. It is by an absolute act of liberty that the adversaries create each other, in and through the struggle for prestige, freely entered into.'[71] Since Mastery and Slavery are produced by 'absolute liberty', they are not things which exist 'in the natural or animal world'.;[72] but in Kojève it is 'freedom' and 'recognition' which depart from 'nature' and 'animality', while in Marx it is 'production' which does so. This is just as clear in *Introduction to the Reading of Hegel* as in 'Hegel, Marx and Christianity': in the *Introduction* Kojève insists that for Hegel 'Mastery and Slavery are not given or innate characteristics. At least at the beginning, man is not *born* slave or free, but makes himself (*se crée*) one or the other by free or voluntary action'. And he goes on to urge that Mastery and Slavery 'have not the slightest "cause", they are not "determined" by any *given*, they cannot be "deduced" or predicted in terms of the past that has preceded them: they result from a free Act'.[73] (Thus while Kojève, with Marx, views many moral ideas and philosophies as 'ideological' or 'epiphenomenal', he certainly does not view 'recognition' in that light: the struggle for recognition, at the risk of 'animal' existence, is the first characteristically human thing).

But recognition (and the struggle for it) is not only primary, not only not 'caused', not only not 'epiphenomenal'; it is the very 'key' to the whole of Hegel. 'In having discovered the notion of recognition', Kojève tells us, 'Hegel found himself in possession of the key-idea (*notion-clé*) of his whole philosophy. Also, it is through the analysis of this fundamental notion that one understands the role of the different aspects and elements of the Hegelian dialectic'.[74] And in the essay 'The Political Action of Philosophers' Kojève puts the matter just as plainly: 'the desire to be 'recognised' (by those whom one 'recognises' in return) in one's reality and eminent human dignity is effectively . . . the final cause of all *emulation* between men, thus of all political struggle . . .'.[75] In Kojève, then, it is the desire for recognition which 'explains everything'; and something like work or production is only the 'objectification' of a Slave's 'unilateral' recognition of a Master. Hence, despite the presence of 'work' and 'struggle', Kojève is not any sort of Marxist in a strict sense.

Just how far Kojève's 'reading' is 'Marxist' can be seen to best advantage in one of the (rare) passages in which Kojève actually *treats* Marx' own words. The most illuminating of these passages comes quite late in *Introduction to the Reading of Hegel*, and in it Kojève interprets Book III, Chapter 48 of *Capital* — the very important but fragmentary and unfinished chapter dealing with the 'trinity' of 'capital-profit, landground rent, labour-wages'.[76] Kojève begins his interpretation by invoking familiar themes: at the 'end of history', what will disappear is 'man properly speaking, that is to say negative Action . . . or in general the Subject opposed to the object'. Philosophy will disappear as well, because man, 'no longer essentially changing himself . . . no longer has any reason to change the (true) [i.e. Hegelian] principles which are at the root of his knowledge of the world and of himself'. But if philosophy and history will disappear, 'everything else can maintain itself indefinitely: art, love, play, etc., in short, everything which makes Man happy'.[77]

Now Marx, Kojève maintains, 'takes up . . . this Hegelian theme, among many others'. And he takes it up precisely in *Capital* Book III, Chapter 48. 'History properly speaking, where men ("classes") struggle between themselves for recognition and struggle against Nature through work,' Kojève argues, 'is called "the realm of necessity" (*Reich der Notwendigkeit*) by Marx; beyong (*jenseits*) is situated the "realm of freedom" (*Reich der Freiheit*), where men, recognising each other mutually without reserve, no longer struggle and work as little as possible (Nature being definitively subjugated).'[78] Kojève, as one would expect, mentions 'recognition' first of all — which is no surprise, given his view that recognition is the 'key idea' of Hegel's 'whole philosophy'.

But how closely does this reading of *Capital* correspond to what Marx actually said? One can judge only by 'reading' Marx for oneself:

In fact, the realm of freedom actually begins only where labour which is determined by necessity and mundane considerations ceases; thus in the very nature of things it lies beyond the sphere of actual material production. Just as the savage must wrestle with Nature to satisfy his wants, to maintain and reproduce life, so must civilised man, and he must do so in all social formations and under all possible modes of production. With his development this realm of physical necessity expands as a result of his wants; but, at the same time, the forces of production which satisfy these wants also increase. Freedom in this field can only consist in socialised man, the associated producers, rationally regulating their interchange with Nature, bringing it under their common control, instead of being ruled by it as by the blind forces of Nature; and achieving this with the least expenditure of energy and under conditions most favourable to, and worthy of, their human nature. But it nonetheless still remains a realm of necessity. Beyond it begins that development of human energy which is an end in itself, the true realm of freedom, which, however, can blossom forth only with this realm of necessity as its basis. The shortening of the working day is its basic prerequisite.[79]

How does Kojève read this magnificent passage? What one notices first is that the notion of 'recognition', which Kojève professes to find in Book III, Chapter 48, does not appear to be there at all — unless it is 'read into' Marx' phrase, 'conditions worthy of . . . human nature'. But at the very least, 'recognition' does not seem to be the 'key idea' of *this* passage. Next one observes that while Kojève-reading-Hegel invariably makes 'work' come *after* the struggle for recognition, as the 'objectification' of Mastery, Marx does not do this at all: Marx says flatly that the 'realm of freedom' begins only where 'labour which is determined by necessity and mundane considerations ceases'; freedom for Marx, then, begins not with the 'suppression' of the 'Master', but with going 'beyond' work which is 'determined by necessity'. But if work is 'determined' by 'necessity', then it is *not* something 'imposed' by a Master as an 'objectification' of 'recognition'. It is (again) *production* which is primary for Marx, whereas for Kojève-reading-Hegel it is secondary. And finally one notices that when Marx speaks of the 'true realm of freedom', 'beyond' work dictated by 'necessity', he continues to say that true freedom 'can blossom forth only with this realm of necessity as its basis', and therefore that the 'working day' can only be 'shortened'.[80] How sharply this contrasts with Kojève's 'art, love, play and happiness' in a 'definitively subjugated nature' — surely a fanciful 'reading' of Marx' 'development of human energy which is an end in itself', since Marx argues that under 'all *possible* modes of production' man must 'wrestle with Nature'.[81]

If a reading of *Capital* fails to turn up 'recognition' as something primary — even in the very passage which Kojève specially insists on — neither does one find that notion in the Marxian work from which Kojève borrows the phrase that he sets at the beginning of *Introduction to the Reading of Hegel* (as a kind of clue to his 'reading'). Kojève, as will be recalled, begins with Marx' saying that 'Hegel . . . grasps labour as the essence of man — as man's essence in the act of proving itself' ('Critique of the Hegelian Dialectic and Philosophy as a Whole', *Economic and Philosophic MSS of 1844*).[82] In Marx' *urtext*, however, what comes in the Kojève-created blank space between 'Hegel' and 'grasps labour' is crucial, though it is no wonder that Kojève prefers three dots. What Marx actually says is this: 'Hegel's standpoint is that of modern political economy. He grasps *labour* as the *essence* of man — as man's essence in the act of proving itself: he sees only the positive, not the negative side of labour. . . . The only labour which Hegel knows and recognises is *abstractly mental labour* . . . he is therefore able . . . to present his philosophy as *the* philosophy.'[83]

Obviously, when one looks at a full text of the *MSS of 1844*, Marx is not wholeheartedly praising Hegel as the discoverer of labour as the essence of man: Hegel's discovery, while real enough, is not co-extensive with Marxism, because Hegel's 'standpoint' is that of 'modern political economy' (above all Adam Smith and Ricardo), and because Hegel reduces labour to thought (ultimately to his own philosophy). Moreover, if one looks at the rest of 'Critique of the Hegelian Dialectic', it turns out that Marx complains of Hegel's 'one-sidedness and limitations' in the *Phenomenology*, and that (most importantly), while he refers to several of the great set-pieces in the *Phenomenology* (such as 'the Unhappy Consciousness' and 'Noble and Base Consciousness'), he does not refer, even *en passant*, to Master and Servant.[84] This is surely odd, to say the least, if, as Kojève asserts, the 'recognition' which arises from the 'master-slave dialectic' is the 'key notion' in Hegel, and if Hegelianism 'determines' the 'whole thought of Marx'. It

leads one to doubt whether Allan Bloom can possibly have
been right in calling Kojève a 'Marxist'.

IV

Whatever the degree of Kojève's 'Marxism' may be, it could
reasonably be argued that the central question to ask about
Introduction to the Reading of Hegel is not how 'Marxist' it is
but how *adequate* it is. And if this is the question, then it seems
clear that Kojève does best with parts of the *Phenomenology*
(though not equally well with the whole work), and considerably less well with the *Philosophy of Right*, which he mentions
little and very selectively — probably because that work does
not argue for the 'universal and homogeneous state' that
Kojève imagines as 'realised' (or at least made possible) by 'the
diad Napoleon-Hegel'. Indeed it might be argued that Kojève
ignores Hegel's actual theory of the state, and advances in its
place what Hegel's theory *would* have been if Mastery,
Slavery, recognition and satisfaction were the sole political
notions which he used. And in closing it will be noted that it is
only by systematically ignoring Hegel's *Philosophy of Fine Art*
that Kojève can claim that Hegel viewed art as an
'epiphenomenon' of the political 'infrastructure'. Kojève, in
short, truly illuminates some portions of the *Phenomenology*,
and this is welcome because the work is so difficult and often
so obscure. But he darkens some parts of Hegel whose bright-
ness can be restored by 'reading' them for oneself.

Kojève is most helpful, as one would expect, in elucidating
the Master and Servant chapter of the *Phenomenology* and the
few chapters which follow — those dealing with Stoicism,
scepticism, and 'the Unhappy Consciousness'.[85] Though he
alters Hegel a little by speaking of a 'fight to the death' for
'pure prestige' — 'pure prestige' is a Kojèvian addition — it
really is the case that the Master and Servant chapter argues
that 'self-consciousness . . . *is* only by being acknowledged or
"recognised" ', that men 'recognise themselves as mutually
recognising one another' (to quote Hegel's own words).[86]

Perhaps the finest thing in Kojève's illumination of 'recognition' is the contrast which he so successfully draws between
recognition and 'love' — above all in 'Hegel, Marx and Chris-

tianity'. Love, Kojève argues, is, like recognition, 'dialectical'; lovers are 'united', but their 'absolute unity is the union of two "separate" beings, essentially autonomous or different . . . their "totality" is the child'.[87] But Hegel, Kojève insists, finally 'abandoned (or, more exactly, transformed) the dialectic of love' because it could not 'account for the phenomenon of history'. And it could not offer this account because of an 'essential limitation'. 'Love is essentially limited,' according to Kojève, 'because it attributes an absolute value, not to the action (*Tun*), but to the given-being (*Sein*) of the loved one: one loves someone "without reason", that is simply because he *is*, and not because of what he *does*.' Love, which relates solely to 'given-beings', or what one *is* 'does not presuppose action and does not give rise to any truly active (= negating) behaviour'. Thus love is 'essentially passive', even 'ineffi-cacious'; at most it can 'found a human family . . . slightly enlarged by a "circle of friends" '. But love, as something 'static', does not generate historical movement.[88]

In order to account for history and 'historical man', Kojève argues, Hegel saw that one must 'replace the limited and passive dialectic of love with a universal dialectic of action'. While the lover wants to be 'recognised' only by the beloved, the historical man 'aspires to universal recognition of the absolute value of his particularity' — more exactly, universal recognition of what he has *done*. 'It is the ensemble of the negating actions of individuals, carried out with a view to universal recognition,' Kojève concludes, 'which constitutes the concrete content of universal history.'[89] The 'transfor-mation' of the 'dialectic of love' into that of recognition came to Hegel in about 1800, and in his mature philosophy he did nothing else but 'reveal . . . the dialectical whose general *schema* he discovered'.[90] Here, at the very end, Kojève approaches his (exaggerated) view that 'recognition' is the 'key' to all of Hegel, to the *Philosophy of History* as well as the *Phenomenology*; but up to this point the contrast between 'love' and 'recognition' is *mainly* helpful.

If the notion of 'recognition' casts a strong light on Master and Servant — it must at least do this much, obviously — it casts a certain amount of light on other important sections of the *Phenomenology* as well, above all on the part dealing with the notion of 'conscience', the final and 'highest' social or moral 'form' which Hegel treats in this work. Now while on occasion Hegel uses the terms 'moral self-consciousness' and 'conscience' almost interchangeably, in the *Phenomenology* he is extremely careful to draw a line between them. For since there is no theory of the state in this work — unless one agrees with Kojève that Chapter 6 is about the 'forgiven' Napoleonic Empire — Hegel wants to make 'conscience' the most universal, the most objective, the most *social* concept in his spiritual 'gallery of forms'.[91] He was, doubtless, all the more careful to be clear about 'conscience', in view of the significance attached to it since the Reformation; in a sense, Hegel was reclaiming the word from religious sectarians full of 'conscientious' convictions.

It is well-know that Hegel criticised 'moral self-consciousness' — exemplified in something like Kant's 'good will' — because it was completely self-contained: it 'willed' but never accomplished ('the laurels of mere willing are dry leaves that never were green').[92] Conscience, on the other hand, involved for him 'the *common* element of distinct self-consciousness', that is, recognition by others. 'Doing something,' Hegel says, 'is merely the translation of its individual content into that objective element where it is universal and is recognised.'[93] What is (actually) dutiful, what the 'content' of conscience is, one does not specify in the *concept* of conscience; conscience is simply whatever is 'universal for all self-consciousness', whatever is recognised or acknowledged, and thus objectively is. The essence of the act of conscience, Hegel says, is indeed in the 'conviction that conscience has about it',[94] but this is not merely private or personal or solipsistic, since conscience, by declaring itself and appealing for recognition, is universalised. Hegel tries to clarify this less-than-clear idea in a crucial passage: 'When anyone says, therefore, that he is acting from conscience, he is saying what is true, for his conscience is the self which knows and wills. But it is essential that he should *say* so, for this self has to be at the same time universal self.'[95]

This 'universality' cannot exist in the content of the conscientious act, since for Hegel content is derivative from the actual 'ethics' of a given society at a given time. The universality can lie, therefore, only in the form of the act of conscience. And this form, he urges, is the self, which is 'actual in language', which 'pronounces itself to be the truth, and just by so doing acknowledges all other slaves, and is recognised by them'.[96]

Obviously a great deal depends on Hegel's view of language, which permits selves to 'pronounce' themselves, to 'say' what they 'know and will'; and it is precisely his theory of language which makes his whole doctrine of conscience 'work'. 'We see language to be the form in which spirit finds existence. Language is self-consciousness existing for others . . . [it] . . . is self separating itself from itself. . . . The self perceives itself at the same time that it is perceived by others: and this perceiving is just existence which has become a self.'[97]

By concentrating, then, on what is 'universal in all selves', by insisting on the embodiment of personal conviction in language which can be understood because it uses 'universal' terms, any 'distinction between the universal consciousness and the individual self is precisely what has been cancelled, and the superseding of it *constitutes* conscience'.[98]

In the *Philosophy of Right* Hegel makes this even plainer. The 'objective system' of the principles and duties which constitute the 'content' of conscience, he says, 'is not present until we come to the standpoint of ethical life' — to an actual *ethos*. And he expands what he says in the *Phenomenology* by declaring that 'whether the conscience of a specific individual corresponds with the Idea of conscience . . . is ascertainable only from the content of the good it seeks to realise'.[99] Since this 'good' is most frequently defined in terms of the amount of rational freedom 'realised' in the Hegelian state, the state cannot 'give recognition to conscience in its private form as subjective knowing, any more than science can grant validity to subjective opinion'.[100] It may tolerate — rather than 'recognise' — less-than-universal forms of conscience, if it is strong enough to afford such toleration (and 'modern' states are, in Hegel's view);[101] but it need not, and in some cases it should not (if it is too weak).

These formulations involve, of course, a radical transformation of the idea of conscience: what is only 'private' in conviction is precisely what is bracketed out. Indeed, Hegel argues that 'actual conscience is not this insistence on a knowledge and a will which are opposed to what is universal', and that anyone who acts from a conscience 'of his own' is actually saying that he is 'abusing and wronging' others.[102] Doubtless this transformation was important to Hegel's purposes if he wanted to 'cancel and preserve' the Christian and Kantian 'realm of subjectivity':[103] to retain 'conviction' but to require it to 'universalise' itself through language, to appeal for recognition. On Hegel's view of conscience, whoever says 'here I stand' must find others to stand there *with* him: con-science, after all, stresses this 'with', this need of 'others'.

Interestingly Kojève, who might have found some authentic support for his 'reading' of Hegel in the 'conscience' chapter of the *Phenomenology*, says next to nothing about it: possibly because, though that chapter does indeed stress 'recognition' and 'universality', this recognition does not arise out of a 'struggle' between 'masters' and 'slaves': 'pronouncing' and 'saying' are not 'struggle', still less struggle for 'pure prestige'. A calm, measured, non-violent 'recognition' seems to be 'beyond' Kojève — except at the end of history.

So much for the light which Kojève sheds on parts of the *Phenomenology*; there is a less bright side as well. His 'reading' — at its weakest — forces him to view a large segment of the work, that which treats ancient Greek society and Greek ethics, as divided into two branches of false consciousness, Mastery and Slavery; whereas, as Judith Shklar shows in her splendidly even-handed *Freedom and Independence: The Political Ideas of Hegel's 'Phenomenology of Mind'*, Hegel was so devoted to Athens as a 'paradise of the human spirit'[104] that one falls into one-sidedness in seeing him as the exposer of Greek 'ideology'. That Shklar does better than Kojève in dealing with Hegel's limited but authentic 'Hellenism' is clear if one examines the way in which Kojève treats the chapter called 'the Ethical World' — Hegel's masterly re-interpretation of Sophocles' *Antigone*, in its way just as important a set-piece as Master and Servant.

Hegel, as Shklar reminds us, often found it useful to show what he thought the nature of ancient ethics had been by reminding his readers of certain Greek plays, particularly *Antigone* and *Oedipus*, which were ideally suited to a demonstration of the fact that strong individualism and insistence on personal will and conviction — Christian and (still more) Kantian notions — were foreign to Greek ethics. It was not exactly the case, however, that such an ethical system (in Hegel's view) was so integrated that there were no elements whatever which could fly apart; on the contrary, Greek ethical communities contained an inherent tension between what he called the 'divine law' of the family and its 'piety', and the objective 'universality' of the city.[105] This tension might break out into open conflict if, as in the case of Antigone, a woman — who for Hegel *embodies* family piety — defied the state in the service of the family; both the 'divine' command ordering the burial of her brother, and the state's command (issued by its monarch, Creon) to leave the body unburied were valid for Antigone, but the divine law took precedence. Be it ever so true, Hegel suggests, that 'the family . . . finds in the community its universal substance and subsistence', and that 'the community finds in the family the formal element of its own realisation',[106] this ideal unity can fly apart so long as minds can choose between different 'moments' of ethical life. It is true that, for Hegel, individuals in Greek life (as exemplified in Greek tragedy) do not choose *qua* individuals, putting forward their own conviction or intention; the content of choice is determined by the 'laws and customs of . . . class or station'.[107] Hence Antigone chooses as a sister and as a defender of the family, not as a particular self, just as Creon cared 'for the weal of the entire city',[108] not for his personal will: in antiquity, Hegel argues 'self-consciousness within the life of a nation descends from the universal only down as far as specific particularity, but not as far as the single individuality'.[109] Still, even though fully personal choice and personal will are not involved in a decision like Antigone's or Creon's, the Greek ethical consciousness 'cannot disclaim the crime and its guilt'. 'The deed consists in setting in motion what was unmoved, and in bringing out what in the first instance lay shut up as a mere possibility.'[110] Guilt is purer, Hegel suggests, if crime is knowingly committed; hence Antigone's 'ethical consciousness' is more complete than that of Oedipus because, though an agent of 'divine' law and family piety, she defied the city, whereas Oedipus was ignorant of his situation. Unlike modern men, however, Antigone does not dwell on the less than fully voluntary character of her 'choice' in an effort to justify herself; in acknowledging her error she indicates that 'the severance between ethical purpose and actuality has been done away', that 'the agent surrenders his character and the reality of his self, and has utterly collapsed'.[111] But this 'victory' of the ethical whole, which wants to prèserve permanently 'a world without blot or stain, a world untainted by any internal dissension' — is short-lived, because, according to Hegel, the opposition of ethical powers to one another 'have reached their true end only insofar as both sides undergo the same destruction'.[112] This destruction might take a merely external form, as when foreign forces attack the city to right the wronged divine laws of the family; but in a deeper sense the destruction is contained with the society itself, in the form of an individualism and self-consciousness which ethical choices help to bring into the light. It is this deeper *malaise* of subjectivity with which Hegel is really concerned, and which he knew Plato had been concerned with as well: the *Republic*, for Hegel, represented a monumental effort to refute the rising claims of individualism.[113] In any case, for Hegel *Antigone* serves to show in a stroke all of the implications of Greek ethical thought, all the facets of Athens as 'the Ethical World'.

But what does Kojève make of Greek 'ethics', and of *Antigone*? As one might expect, he stresses 'Mastery' — but here to less effect than sometimes. The Greek 'Ethical World', he argues, is 'the world of the Master' — though the Master is 'also' the 'citizen of a state' and the 'member of a family'.[114] (What Hegel represents as primary in *Antigone* — the collision between the city and the family — becomes a mere 'also' in Kojève's reading.) Kojève goes on to argue that, in the 'ancient Greek world', the 'family is a *human* family because the (male) members of the family struggle for recognition and have Slaves: thus they are Masters';[115] but this is certainly not what *Hegel* stresses in 'the Ethical World', and Kojève's effort to carry over into his reading of this chapter the notions which served him in Master and Servant can only appear strained. He only compounds this sense of strain by insisting that 'the inner enemy of the ancient state is the family which it destroys and the individual which it does not recognise';[116] here Kojève succeeds in drawing in 'recognition' only at the cost of distorting what Hegel says about the ancient family as the 'formal element' for the 'realisation of the city'. And the way in which Kojève introduces 'struggle' works even less well: 'the contradiction within the ancient state . . . is the separation of the sexes. Thus there is a struggle between the Universal and the Particular, the citizen and the woman . . .'.[117] This 'reading' of *Antigone* is simply crude, and the 'successful' introduction of 'contradiction' and 'struggle' does not offset the crudity. (This crudity was noticed by Tran Duc Thao, the orthodox Marxist reviewer of Kojève's *Introduction* for Sartre's journal, *Les Temps Modernes*; Tran Duc Thao complained that it is 'exaggerated to wish to interpret the whole content of the *Phenomenology* through the dialectic of Master and Slave', and that this works particularly badly in illuminating 'the Ethical World': 'the ancient city, though it implies the "moment" of slavery, is characterised in its spiritual structure by the opposition of the family and the city . . . here there is neither domination nor servitude, but an internal scission in the community of free men'.)[118]

The Kojèvian insistence on Mastery, Slavery, struggle and recognition, even where these notions are peripheral and thus distort and strain what Hegel actually says, points to a difficulty in Kojève which George Kelly has revealed better than anyone else. In his *Idealism, Politics and History: Sources of Hegelian Thought,* Kelly complained that Kojève takes the Master and Servant 'tableau' as 'the synoptic clue to a whole philosophy';[119] in his new *Hegel's Retreat from Eleusis* he offers the most searching criticism of Kojève available in English. While 'every student of Hegel is deeply enriched by Kojève', Kelly argues, *Introduction to the Reading of Hegel* is drastically one-sided: in it 'the master-slave relationship is made an unqualified device for clarifying the progress of human history'. The notion that 'the future belongs to the slave' — to the 'proletarian', perhaps, on a Marxist view — is, Kelly insists, an 'unwarranted romanticised refraction of Hegel's thought'. Though Kojève's 'original exegesis of Hegelian themes' is 'a profound work for our own times', a 'Marxian' *Phenomenology* 'does not make very good sense'. Such a reading, in Kelly's view, 'ignores the depth and passion of Hegel's Greek attachments; it ignores, too . . . his struggle with the Kantian split vision. These are the two combatants wrestling on the soil of Christian Europe for the possession of Hegel's own ego'.[120]

But Kojève's *Introduction* does not simply 'ignore', in Kelly's view; it also begets 'social hypotheses that do not square with Hegel's known conclusions'.[121] And one of the most important of these 'known conclusions' comes in the *Philosophy of Right*, which Kojève (largely) ignores. In paragraph 57 of the Philosophy of Right, Hegel insists that

The position of the free will, with which right and the science of right begin, is already in advance of the false position at which man, as a natural entity and only the concept implicit, is for that reason capable of being enslaved. This false, comparatively primitive phenomenon of slavery is one which befalls mind when mind is only at the level of consciousness. The dialectic of the concept and of the purely immediate consciousness of freedom bring about at that point the fight for recognition and the relationship of master and slave.

Here several things might be said. First, if slavery is a 'false' and 'comparatively primitive phenomenon', then one should not expect all 'recognition' in Hegel to be necessarily attached to 'slavery': the recognition of 'consience', for example, which involves no element of violence or domination or submission, would arise out of (what Hegel calls) 'free will' sooner than out of a 'struggle for pure prestige'. But if (secondly) 'free will' is, as Hegel says, what 'right and the science of right' begins with, and if this 'will' is 'in advance of' slavery as something 'false' and 'primitive', where is this 'free will' to be found in Kojève's 'reading' of Hegel?

If it is easy to exaggerate the 'place' of Mastery, Slavery, and recognition in the *Phenomenology*, it would be difficult to overstress the role of 'will' in the *Philosophy of Right*. The notion of will, indeed, is the *central* one in that work[123] (which is one reason that Kojève slights it). Most generally, Hegel characterises the difference between 'ancient' and 'modern' ethics and politics in terms of will (not Mastery and recognition):

Even in the beautiful democracy of Athens . . . we cannot help noticing that the Greeks derived their final decisions from the observation of quite external phenomena such as oracles, the entrails of sacrificial animals, and the flight of birds. They treated nature as a power which in those ways revealed and expressed what was good for men. At that time, self-consciousness had not yet advanced to the abstraction of subjectivity, not even so far as to understand that, when a decision is to be made, an 'I will' must be pronounced by man himself. This 'I will' constitutes the great difference between the ancient world and the modern, and in the great edifice of the state it must therefore have its appropriate objective existence.[124]

This 'I will' — which for Hegel entered the world with the advent of Christianity and reached its subtlest expression in Kant — assumes several forms of 'appropriate objective existence' in the *Philosophy of Right*'s theory of the state: monarchy, the 'constitution of developed reason',[125] involves a ruler who cuts short the 'perpetual oscillation' between mere possibilities and 'by saying "I will"', makes its decision and so inaugurates all activity and actuality';[126] the 'universal class' of enlightened civil servants, who have the 'deepest' and 'most comprehensive insight' into the state's 'organisation and requirements', are much more nearly aware than average citizens or popular assemblies of what should be willed for the state ('to know . . . what the absolute will, reason, wills, is the fruit of profound apprehension and insight, precisely the things which are not popular'[127]); and even ordinary citizens of the Hegelian state 'will' it by seeing it as 'the good become alive — the good endowed in self-consciousness with knowing and willing and actualised by self-conscious action'.[128] Everything, then, in Hegel's notion of the state — monarchy, the 'universal class', ordinary citizenship — turns on will (rather than on 'mastery' or 'struggle' or 'recognition'). But this is not surprising, since Hegel stands at the end of a modern tradition in which 'will' is always the central notion:[129] Hobbes, after all, says that wills 'make the essence of all covenants';[130] Locke that 'voluntary agreement gives . . . political power to governors';[131] Rousseau that 'the general will is always right';[132] Kant that a mature, rational people could never will something such as unmerited hereditary ranks.[133] The 'voluntarism' of modern political and moral thought is plain enough, and Hegel does not depart from it altogether — though he tends to reduce 'real' will to 'reason'.[134]

Kojève, in always stressing Mastery and struggle, finds little that is congenial in the voluntaristic *Philosophy of Right*; how far, then, can one expect this work to theorise the 'universal and homogeneous state' which Kojève hopes to find at the 'end of history'? The answer must be, not very far: for the state outlined in the *Philosophy of Right* is neither 'universal' nor 'homogeneous'. It is certainly not 'universal', for Hegel envisions a political world which continues to be divided into national states, belittles the Kantian notion of a universal *foedus pacificum*, and speaks of war as the preservative of the 'ethical health' of nations.[135] But neither is there 'homogeneity', since the 'universal class' is drawn from the middle class,[136] and since Hegel preserves a whole gradation of social classes from monarchs to an 'impoverished rabble' — not least in the ranks and orders of his 'civil society'.[137] It is no wonder, then, that Kojève ignores the whole *Philosophy of Right*, with the exception of the famous passage in the 'Preface' about philosophy as the 'thought of the world' arriving on the scene to paint its 'grey on grey' only after reality is 'cut and dried'[138] — since this passage seems to prefigure the notion of 'ideology'. This passage alone he quotes in full; but he ignores the rest of the 'Preface' — possibly because his own notion of an 'Hegelian' universal and homogeneous state, as a possible 'ideal', as a *projet à realiser*, would be dealt a fatal blow by the 'Preface's' animadversions against 'idealism'. After all, Kojève would find it exceedingly difficult to reconcile his notion of 'destroying the world which does not conform to the idea'[139] of a 'universal and homogeneous state' with Hegel's flat assertion in the 'Preface' that philosophy is 'the apprehension of the present and the actual' and that 'to recognise reason as the rose in the cross of the present and thereby to enjoy the present, this is the rational insight which reconciles us to the actual, the reconciliation which philosophy affords'.[140] To be sure, Hegel does not *always* say that 'what is actual is rational';[141] but in the *Philosophy of Right* he usually says it, and this doubtless accounts for Kojève's downplaying this work.

If Kojève minimises the significance of the *Philosophy of Right*, he also grants little weight to the politically important *Philosophy of Fine Art* — ostensibly because *Fine Art* is derived from student lecture-notes and hence is not 'rigorously authentic',[142] but possibly because a careful inspection of *Fine Art* would reveal that Hegel does not view art as an 'epiphenomenon' of the 'real' political and economic 'infrastructure'. This language, borrowed mainly from *The German Ideology*, does violence to Hegel. To be sure, Hegel views this or that *Kunstwerk* as the expression of the 'spirit of an age'; but this does not make him a 'materialist', nor a partisan of the view that art is a mere 'reflection' of social 'bases' and 'substructures'. Admittedly, Hegel recognises a social 'content' in a work such as *Antigone*; indeed in *Fine Art* he says plainly that 'the purest forces of tragic representation' involve the opposition between 'ethical life in its social universality and the family as the natural ground of moral relations'.[143] And he adds that *Antigone* is, 'among all the fine creations of the ancient and modern world . . . the most excellent and satisfying work of art'.[144] *Antigone* is 'excellent' and 'satisfying' partly because its 'content' is 'ethical' or social, in Hegel's view; whereas a play such as *Hamlet*, which he also admired, is an interior tragedy of 'the particular personality, the inner life', in which conflict is not between colliding *ethoi* but 'essentially abides within the character himself'.[145] The pages of *Fine Art* which contrast *Antigone* and *Hamlet* are incomparably insightful; but they do not treat art as an 'epiphenomenon' of the social 'infrastructure', as a 'reflection' of what is 'real'.

This is clear if one turns from Hegel's discussion of ancient and modern drama to his account of sculpture, architecture or painting, and most particularly to his account of post-Reformation Dutch painting. The Dutch people, Hegel argues, after overcoming 'the depotism of the Spanish Crown and Church', has contented itself with 'well-to-do and genial citizenship'. 'This intelligent and artistically endowed people,' Hegel goes on, 'seeks its enjoyment in the pictorial representation of its vigorous, justly coordinated, satisfying and comfortable existence; it is all for taking a renewed delight by means of its pictures in the cleanliness under all conditions of its towns, houses and domestic arrangements, of enjoying thus its household felicity.'[146] Dutch painting, by transforming the ordinary into the extraordinary, preserves a 'vital ingredient of every work of art', namely 'the observation of what generally concerns our humanity, the spirit and characterisation of man, in other words, what man is and what *each* individual is'. In the best Dutch painting 'we may study and acquaint ourselves with human nature and mankind', and so there is no room to regret Dutch artists' having abandoned 'Madonna pictures, crucifixions, martyrs, popes, and saints of both sexes'.[147]

Now in this discussion of Dutch art there is, assuredly, attention to social 'content'; but there is no notion of 'phenomena' determining 'epiphenomena', or of 'infrastructures' determining 'superstructures'. Such a crudely mechanical theory is alien to Hegel. Surely he thought that the *ethos* of an age got expressed in this or that work: Greek religion, for Hegel, is closely connected with 'nature', and therefore Greek temples are open to the natural world (whereas Gothic cathedrals provide a closed and largely dark space for spirits to 'ascend' to God);[148] Greek ethics, again for Hegel, is more collective and less individual than post-Christian ethics (hence a chorus, a *social* commentator on ethical action, is appropriate in *Antigone*, but not in *Hamlet*).[149] The leap, in art, from 'having' a social *content*, to being an 'epiphenomenon' of 'real' causes, is a leap that Hegel does not make; and Kojève's 'reading' of Hegel is a 'violent interpretation'[150] (to use Kojève's own phrase) when it intimates that Hegel's view of art is approximately the same as *The German Ideology's*.[151]

Kojève's 'reading', then, casts helpful light on some parts of Hegel, while distorting some other parts. But Kojève does not confine himself to Hegel: his aim is also to 'read' Hegel's greatest predecessors, Plato, Aristotle and Kant. It is to the last of these that Kojève devoted his final work, *Kant*; and it is to that work that one must now turn.

V

However far 'Mastery', 'Slavery', 'work', 'struggle', 'recognition', 'satisfaction', 'freedom' and even 'ideology' may go in illuminating (parts of) Hegel's *Phenomenology*, they are arguably *not* the notions which cast the strongest or the fairest light on philosophers who are not Hegelians. And this emerges clearly in Kojève's treatment of Kant: it is no accident that in his *Kant* Kojève argues that if one suppresses Kant's idea of the 'thing-in-itself' ('beyond' the empirical world, in a realm of 'transcendence') and treats freedom and purposiveness as *real* rather than as 'necessary hypotheses' (as Kant treated them), one can 'transform' Kantianism 'quasi-automatically' into the Hegelian 'system of knowledge'[152] — as if such a 'transformation' would necessarily be advantageous. (Kojève — to be fair — grants that this would be a 'violent interpretation'.[153])

Now Kant *did* treat freedom as a 'necessary hypothesis' whose reality could neither be demonstrated nor denied; in his *Groundwork of the Metaphysic of Morals*, indeed, he argues that 'freedom is only an idea of reason, and its objective reality in itself is doubtful'.[154] Nonetheless Kant urges that if the idea of a free will as a 'noumenal' or intelligent 'causality' is given up, all morality will become merely 'empirical', and concludes that every being which 'cannot act except under the *idea* of freedom' is 'from a practical point of view' really free; that while freedom cannot be proved to be 'actually a property of ourselves or of human nature', it must be pre-supposed 'if we would conceive a being as rational and conscious of its causality in respect of its actions, that is, as endowed with a will'.[155] Unless men *take themselves to be free,* that is, they cannot make intelligible to themselves their own notions of duty, responsibility, blame, and so forth. And this 'hypothetical' freedom has a very immediate bearing on Kant's politics, since he argues in *Eternal Peace* that if there exists 'no freedom and no moral law based upon it, and if everything which happens . . . is simply part of the mechanism of nature', then it is appropriate to manipulate men as natural objects in order to govern them; but that if 'right' is to be the 'limiting condition of politics', morality and politics must be conceded to be 'compatible', and politics must be capable of treating men as they ought to be treated — as 'ends-in-themselves'.[156]

What distresses Kojève is that the Kantian 'categorical imperative' of treating men as 'ends', as free beings who ought to be 'respected', is based on a freedom which is only *hypothetical:* one builds categorical moral requirements, which also serve as the 'limiting condition' of politics, on 'as if' foundations. Or, as Kojève himself puts it, 'one cannot effectively speak of "morality" without speaking of "freedom", and good sense would be scandalised by a "commandment" addressed to someone who would be materially incapable of following it'.[157] Kant, he goes on, succeeds only in talking about 'what one ought to do, *if* the will is free';[158] but this reduces the categorical to the hypothetical (with a devastating effect on the 'limiting condition' of politics). And since (according to Kojève), Kant failed to treat freedom as something *real*, he could not account for 'efficacious free action': 'he never wanted to admit the *efficacity* of free or conscientious human activity in the world and as a result refused to identify (discursive) truth with history' — a history characterised by work and struggle.[159] (For this reason, Kojève argues in *Introduction to the Reading of Hegel*, Kant 'accepts' the 'result' of the French Revolution, but rejects the 'means', which include 'bloody struggle and work by all'.[160])

Since at least a part of this criticism is a serious one, and since, at the same time, one cannot 'settle' the question of Kantian freedom at this juncture, it will have to suffice (for present purposes) to say that (a) even if freedom could be shown to be something more than a necessary 'idea of reason', Kant would have had no reason to 'identify truth with history', since he 'needed' freedom to account for the *conceivability* of common moral concepts (duty, responsibility, etc.), not to explain historical work and struggle; and (b) it is by no means clear that it is legitimate to reduce the Kantian notions of 'necessary hypothesis' and 'idea of reason' to a mere 'as if': Kant does not say that it is 'as if' men were free (but 'really' not), but that men must *necessarily* conceive themselves as free if their ordinary moral ideas are to be intelligible. (The philosophy of 'as if' is not strictly Kantian, and is, in fact, an invention of the 'neo-Kantian' Hans Vaihinger.[161]) Kant, after all, may have been perfectly right in thinking that freedom can be neither more nor less than a necessary hypothesis: if one makes it more one may go beyond what can legitimately be claimed, and if one makes it less common moral concepts may vanish.

The strengths and weaknesses of Kojève's insistence on the 'as-ifness' (so to speak) of Kant's philosophy emerge with particular clarity in his handling of the *Critique of Judgment*, which is Kant's greatest treatment of teleology or 'purposiveness'. Kojève begins by observing, correctly enough, that Kant undertook the *Critique of Judgment* 'with a view to looking for a connecting-point between the *given* natural world and man as possessor of a *free will*';[162] that connecting point was to be purposiveness', since the natural world has a 'purposive' structure and man *qua* free agent has 'purposes'. But Kant failed, according to Kojève, to talk about 'struggle' and 'work', which are the most 'striking' instances of a 'purposive' freedom operating on a purposively-organised nature; and this failure can be traced to the fact that in *Judgment* Kant treated purposiveness 'in the 'as-if' mode'.[163] Now there *is* something in this: Kojève is right when he says that Kant accounts better for (say) artistic *judgments* than for artistic *production*; hence Kant 'judges' that a work of art involves 'purposiveness without purpose'[164] (what a brilliant definition of the 'argument' of a sonata-movement!), but is hard-pressed to account for the work and struggle of *producing* that sonata-movement.

Even if what Kojève says in this connection is true, one can still complain that finding this truth has cost him another: namely the fact that in *Judgment* Kant was trying to link up nature, human freedom and art through the notion of purposiveness (plants have 'purposes' which men impute to them, men both *have* purposes and *are* the 'final purpose' or final 'end' of creation, and art is 'purposiveness without purpose'). But Kojève misses Kant's effort to achieve this tripartite linking-up when he says that Kant limits 'his teleology to natural and artistic beauty and to organic life', that he excludes purposiveness from 'the domain of human action, of struggle and work'.[165] This not only contradicts what Kojève himself earlier called Kant's effort to find a connecting point between nature and human freedom, but leaves wholly out of account the very section of *Judgment* which is most important for Kant's moral and political philosophy. And in that section (84), Kant argues that while the 'purposes' of things in the natural world are imputed by us to those things, man is the ultimate purpose of creation on earth because 'he is the only being upon it who can form a concept of purposes, and who can by his reason make out of an aggregate of purposively formed things a system of purposes'; that one cannot ask 'for what end' man exists, since 'his existence inherently involves the highest ends'.[166] Since the argument that only man can *conceive* purposes — let alone conceive of himself as the 'ultimate' purpose — constitutes Kant's most effective defense of the notion that men are 'ends-in-themselves' who ought never to be used merely as means to arbitrary purposes, and since that 'purposive' argument is the 'limiting condition' of rightful politics in *Eternal Peace*, it is difficult to understand why Kojève argues that Kant 'excludes' purposiveness from 'the domain of human action'. Even though Kant treats purposiveness, like freedom, as a necessary hypothesis, this involves no 'exclusion'; indeed Kant argues that teleology is the *one* concept which draws together nature, human freedom, and art.

If Kojève's 'Hegelian' emphasis on work and struggle permits him to see some parts of Kant clearly at the cost of slighting others, his insistence on 'satisfaction' leads to a difficulty with which one can reasonably conclude. Now Kant is famous for the asceticism of his moral philosophy, and is rightly celebrated as the enemy of eudaemonism and utilitarianism (hence of Aristotle and Bentham); 'the majesty of duty', he once observed, 'has nothing to do with the enjoyment of life'.[167] But Kojève makes Kantian morality turn on 'satisfaction' in a 'beyond'. To be sure, Kant sometimes argued that the 'supreme good' — happiness connected with *worthiness* to be happy — does not exist on earth, that there ought to be immortality in which God provides this connection[168] (and then, *selon* Kojève, those who have been *good* are 'satisfied'). But this interpretation, on which Kojève puts an enormous weight, is (to use a good Hegelianism) 'one-sided': it leaves out of account the fact that Kant increasingly doubted this 'moral proof' of God and immortality (as evidenced in his *Opus Posthumous*),[169] and it seems to make 'satisfaction' the *precondition* of morality. But if there was ever a philosopher who separated moral philosophy from psychology (with a vengeance), it was Kant; if, for him, one's motive in 'acting well' involves a hope for happiness ('satisfaction'), one doesn't have a 'good will' at all.[170] Kant's idea of the 'supreme good' is problematical enough without trying, *à la Kojève*, to make 'satisfaction' the pivot of Kantian morality — which is not, after all, just a Benthamism in which 'satisfaction' is maximised in a 'beyond' rather than on earth.

VI

If in Kojève's 'reading' Kant is refracted through an 'Hegelian' lens which partly distorts his shape, he at least emerges in tolerably 'recognisable' form; and this is perhaps more than can be said about the forms in which Plato and Aristotle issue from Kojève's *Attempt at a Reasoned History of Pagan Philosophy.* Plato, indeed, can rarely have been treated with less sympathetic understanding; he is said to have been 'blinded' by the 'brilliance of a self-styled ideal beauty of a pretended transcendent world bathed in the blind light which emanates from an ineffable and divine Good'.[171] (How much lighter, and therefore more effective, is Nietzsche's comparable onslaught in *Twilight of the Idols:* 'The true world — attainable for the sage, the pious, the virtuous man; he lives in it, *he is it.* The oldest form of the idea, relatively sensible, simple, and persuasive. A circumlocution for the sentence, "I, Plato, *am* the truth".'[172]) Plato's retreat into a 'beyond', into a Parmenidian Eternity of unchanging (timeless) Ideas, is for Kojève nothing but a flight from the historical reality of human social life.[173] 'What is absurd,' Kojève complains, 'is the negation, by Plato, of the creative (= negative) activity of Humanity and of men.' In declining — through sheer contempt of the merely temporal — 'to give a discursive account of the *creation* by man of the human, technical or historical universe', Plato also renounced 'giving an account of Discourse as such, including his own'.[174] Platonic other-worldliness, in Kojève's view, is at the root of all 'academies', which share 'the desire (and sometimes the fact) of separating themselves from the world in which men live'. Thus one can say that 'academies', 'today as in the time of Plato, are all living images of the Platonic *cosmos noetos,* itself regarded as separated . . . from the empirical world of phenomena'. And just like this *cosmos,* Kojève complains, 'the academies are regarded as being beyond geographical (or political) space and beyond time (their own included)'.[175] Thus for Kojève an 'authentic' Platonist 'reduces to a minimum his animal, social and political activity. He retires into a 'monastery' [or academy] and does not participate in the life of the State'.[176] At a stroke, then, Kojève 'writes off' the *Republic, Laws,* and

Statesmen (to mention only these three); as in the case of Hegel, Kojève offers not Plato's actual theory of the state, but what that theory 'would' or 'should' be if Platonic hankering after 'Eternity' dictates every line of Plato's works.

Kojève's reading of Aristotle is considerably more sympathetic, largely because (for Kojève) Aristotle 'was willing to be satisfied in the here-and-now'.[177] An 'authentic' Aristotelian, 'by definition a-religious', will leave to the Platonists 'the task of being preoccupied . . . with what may happen before birth or after death, and, in a general way, beyond the world in which men live'.[178] But if Aristotle's general perspective is far preferable to Plato's, that does not mean that Kojève approves of Aristotle's *Ethics* or *Politics*: on the contrary, for Kojève Aristotle makes the fundamental error of treating Mastery and Slavery as 'natural' or 'biological' phenomena, whereas the essential truth is that the struggle for Mastery is the 'negation' of everything merely natural or biological. While Aristotle's *Ethics* 'describes correctly' the distinction between Master and Slave, Kojève urges, it 'completely misunderstands' this relation by 'reducing it . . . to the effect of a *cause* properly speaking — that is to say *efficient* and therefore purely "biological" '.[179] For Aristotle, he laments, 'the Slaves constitute a *race*, in the biological sense of the word, "naturally" distinct from that of the Masters'. Aristotelian Masters, according to Kojève, are not 'created' by 'free' and 'voluntary' action which has recognition as its 'end'; they *are* Masters, 'by birth', and thus do not *become* Masters.[180] Since Aristotelian Mastery and Slavery are 'natural', and not chosen, Kojève urges, Aristotle cannot account for free choice at all; hence his *Ethics* is incoherent, though it claims to speak of 'freedom', 'responsibility', and the like.[181] In the end Aristotelian ethics, with its notion of 'moderation' and the *via media,* is a 'treatise of veterinary art' which only shores up *'l'Optimum vital general'*.[182] Aristotle's *Politics*, too, *selon* Kojève, has an essentially 'medical' function: it concerns itself with 'the maladies of the communal life and the means . . . of curing them.'[183] Kojève concludes by citing Aristotle, with his own gloss in brackets: 'For it is evident [sic] that the State is a creation *of Nature* [and not of Man who struggles to the death for Recognition] and that man is a political animal *by nature* [and not as a function of . . . the desire for recognition, which is "contrary" to "nature" and which can push a man toward behaving in such a way as to die a non-natural or "violent" death — i.e. precisely *pre-maturely*].'[184] Aristotle's fatal defect, in a word, is that of viewing social 'relations' as 'natural'.

Kojève's determination to write at length about Plato and Aristotle, even when he is evidently out of sympathy with them, is probably rooted in a wish to 'follow' Hegel: after all, two-thirds of Hegel's *History of Philosophy* is devoted to Greek philosophy. But this determination, which winds up attacking Plato for his transcendentalism, and Aristotle for his biologism, leads Kojève to neglect utterly the main thinker whom he *could* reasonably have treated in terms of Mastery, Slavery, struggle and recognition — namely Rousseau, who gets mentioned only *en passant* in *Introduction to the Reading of Hegel* and in *Kant* (probably because of Kojève's aversion to what he calls *'l'empirisme anglo-francais'*[185]).

Fortunately, one can see what Kojève *might* have made of Rousseau by looking at Guy Besse's fine essay, 'J.J. Rousseau: Maitre, Laquais, Esclave'; for what Besse has done is to read Rousseau in the light of the notions which Kojève found in his 'reading' of the 'Master and Servant' chapter of the *Phenomenology*. Taking up the Hegelian-Kojèvian notions of 'work', 'struggle', 'recognition', 'equality', 'mastery', and 'slavery', Besse claims that most of these ideas are 'central in Rousseau: in his life, his thought, his work'. He argues effectively that in Rousseau a notion such as 'friendship' involves 'recognition based on equality'; he shows that the rule of the poor by the rich in *Inequality* involves mastery and slavery, and the total absence of recognition *of* equals *by* equals.[186] (Besse is fortunate, of course, that Kojève singled out as the essence of the *Phenomenology* an ensemble of notions which can be applied to much of Rousseau's work with *comparatively* little distortion.)

Surely the most striking and useful part of Besse's essay is the last, in which his ensemble of Kojèvian ideas is applied to Rousseau's unfinished 'sequel' to *Émile*, entitled *Émile et Sophie ou les Solitaires*. In *Émile et Sophie* Émile, without family or country, is finally enslaved by 'barbarians'; and

Besse quotes a long passage in which Rousseau reflects on Émile's enslavement. 'Émile a slave! But in what sense? . . . What have I lost of my original liberty? Was I not born the slave of necessity? What new yoke can men impose on me? Work? Did I not work when I was free? . . . There is no real servitude save that of nature. Men are only her instruments. Whether a master knocks me down or a rock crushes me, it is the same thing in my eyes.' And in connection with this passage Besse remarks, *à la Kojève*: 'One sees here how the master-slave relationship is internalised and "cancelled" in *le mode stoïcien*.'[187] Ultimately, however, Besse claims, the Stoic 'ideology' no longer persuades Émile, who urges his fellow-slaves to withhold their labour at the possible cost of their lives: 'this "life" which, according to Hegel, the master was willing to risk, and which the slave kept at the price of his liberty, Émile the slave will throw into the balance in order to force the master to change his attitude'.[188] Or rather Émile will *seem* to risk his life; but since his aim is only to 'enlighten' his master about his 'true interest', and not to 'break the master-slave relation', Émile will be 'recognised' as a 'sensible' man who knows how to make slavery work more effectively. There will be no recognition of equals by equals.[189] And so Besse ends his treatment of *Émile et Sophie* with the cryptic remark, 'In these pages, so 'modern' in many respects, the old "wisdom" guards its rights'.[190] (This seems to mean: which is the 'real' Rousseau? The 'Stoic' who is resigned to the 'old wisdom' of 'necessity', and who views a human institution such as slavery as just as 'necessary' as death or pain?[191] Or the rebel who hates injustice in the *Discourse on Inequality*?)

If Kojève's aversion to 'Anglo-French empiricism' leads him to neglect Rousseau, it is perhaps this same distaste which accounts for his ignoring of Hobbes — who is, after Rousseau, the main modern theorist who might reasonably have been given a Kojèvian treatment. And this ignoring is the more striking in view of a footnote which is to be found in Leo Strauss' *The Political Philosophy of Hobbes*: 'M. Alexandre Kojevnikoff [Kojève] and the writer [Strauss] intend to undertake a detailed investigation of the connexion between Hegel and Hobbes.'[192] Evidently, by the time he produced his mature works Kojève no longer thought this 'connexion' very important, no longer agreed with Strauss' insistence that Hegel, in stressing the 'fight to the death' for 'recognition', in effect 'tacitly recognises the superiority of Hobbes' philosophic basis'.[193] For by the time he published 'Hegel, Marx and Christianity' — a year before *Introduction to the Reading of Hegel* — Kojève was not tracing Hegelian 'struggle' and 'recognition' to any 'philosophic basis', in Hobbes or anyone else; by then he was stressing the total originality of Hegel's 'discovery' of the dialectic of Master and Slave: 'the evolution of Hegel's thought is completed at the very moment when he discovers (1800) the dialectic of Recognition'.[194]

Hobbes, of course, in both *De Cive* and *Leviathan*, had discussed 'mastery', 'slavery', 'submission' and (above all) the 'war of all against all' — and in a way that Hegel would have found partly 'satisfying'. In his treatment of conquest and submission, for example, Hobbes stresses the importance of 'free' action, and downplays all notions of 'natural' or 'biological' necessity. 'It is not therefore the victory that giveth the right of dominion over the vanquished,' Hobbes says in Chapter 20 of *Leviathan,* 'but his own covenant. Nor is he obliged because he is conquered . . . but because he cometh in, and submitteth to the victor.'[195] Or, as Hobbes puts it in a passage from *Liberty, Necessity and Chance* which has the incidental merit of showing that death is not invariably (though it remains usually) his *summum malum*, some people believe that 'conquerors who come in by the sword, make their laws also without our assent', that 'if a conqueror can kill me if he please, I am presently obliged without more ado to obey all his laws'. But, Hobbes asks, affirming freedom and rejecting 'biology', 'may not I rather die, if I see fit?'. And he concludes that 'the conqueror makes no law over the conquered by virtue of his power; but by virtue of their assent, that promised obedience for the saving of their lives'.[196] Hobbes stresses 'assent' equally in his account of 'mastery' and 'slavery', arguing in chapter 15 of *Leviathan* that it 'is not only against reason, but also against experience', to hold that 'master and servant were not introduced by consent of men, but by difference of wit'.[197] (This view he aims against Aristotle in a way that Hegel would have found half-pleasing, half-distressing: 'I know that Aristotle in the first book of his *Politics* . . . maketh men by nature, some more worthy to command, meaning the wiser sort, such as he thought himself to be for his philosophy; others to serve, meaning those that had strong bodies, but were not philosophers as he'; what Aristotle failed to see, Hobbes complains, is that nature has 'made men equal'.[198])

If Hobbes, in his account of Mastery, Slavery, struggle and submission, has rejected 'biology' and 'natural' inferiority, and insisted on free acts of 'assent' and 'consent', why, then, does neither Hegel himself nor Kojève (*pace* Strauss) see the Hobbesian 'war of all against all' as the 'basis' of Hegelianism? Probably precisely because of the terms 'assent' and 'consent', which, though they avoid nature and 'biology', are *contractarian*; Hegel, after all, was very much hostile to any contractarian view of social relations.[199] 'Recognition' is, for Hegel, a psychological and moral notion, a facet of 'consciousness'; to convert all this into the legal ideas of 'covenant' and 'consent' would constitute an unacceptable reductionism. While Kojève, then, might well have pointed out that Hobbes does indeed discuss 'mastery' and 'slavery', and in non-biological, anti-Aristotelian terms, and that Hegel himself treats Hobbes' social thought in the *History of Philosophy*,[200] Kojève seems to have been right not to follow Strauss' suggestion that Hegel prefaced 'his analysis of the pre-modern forms of self-consciousness . . . by the analysis, based on Hobbes' philosophy, of mastery and servitude', that Hegel 'recognised that Hobbes' philosophy was the first to deal with the most elementary form of self-consciousness'.[201] However wrong Kojève may have been in ignoring Hobbes (and Rousseau), arguably the greatest political philosophers of the seventeenth and eighteenth centuries, he at least did not fall into 'finding' Hegel in Hobbes.

VII

If one sets a bit of distance between oneself and the particular details of Kojève's 'reading' of the history of Western political and moral thought (above all Hegelianism), what conclusions of a quite general character seem to be almost irresistible? Two seem most striking: first, that it is exceedingly difficult to determine what counts as a 'Marxist' reading of the history of philosophy; and second, that one should avoid treating something like 'Mastery' and 'recognition' as a 'synoptic clue' to that whole history unless one is certain that one is operating with a light that illuminates (almost) everything and distorts (almost) nothing.

On the first point nearly enough has been said. It seems clear, on a full inspection of Kojève's whole *oeuvre*, that Allan Bloom cannot have been too close to the truth in styling Kojève a 'Marxist'.[202] Certainly the Marxists themselves have declined to accept him as orthodox. Jules Vuillemin, in his review of Kojève's *Introduction* for the *Révue Philosophique,* complained that 'the reality of work' fails to appear in Kojève's 'exegesis' of the *Phenomenology*, that 'the existential attitudes' which Kojève describes 'are not interpreted in terms of the situations which constitute the development of the economy'; hence Kojève's *Introduction,* for all its 'brilliance', must yield to 'the true commentary on Hegel's *Phenomenology*, which is Karl Marx' *Capital*'.[203] Roger Garaudy, in his *Dieu est Mort: Étude sur Hegel*, finds that while Kojève has spoken 'justly' in characterising Mastery as an 'existential impasse', he has completely misunderstood the 'dialectic'; this, for Garaudy, would disqualify Kojève as a writer able to illuminate Marx (though at least Kojève does not make Lukacs' mistake of transforming Hegel into *'un marxiste avant la lettre'*).[204] Jürgen Habermas, who is *some* sort of Marxist, does not think Kojève's work worth mentioning — even in a footnote — in his remarkable article, 'Arbeit und Interaktion: Bemerkungen zu Hegels Jenenser "Philosophie des Geistes" ', which attempts to relate Hegel's earliest writings on Mastery, Slavery and work to Marx' *1844 MSS* and *The German Ideology*.[205] But the strongest (though only tacit) opposition to viewing Kojève as any sort of 'Marxist' would surely come from Louis Althusser's reading of Marx — as is clearest in the paper which Althusser delivered at the 1974 Hegel-Congress in Moscow, 'Sur la dialectique de l'évolution intellectuelle du jeune Marx'. Marx, Althusser argues, far from being Hegel's successor, 'replaced the old notions . . . of the philosophies of history with absolutely new, unprecedented concepts, not "findable" in the old conceptions'.[206] While figures such as Hegel spoke 'of man . . . of the juridical subject, of the political subject, of the social contract, of civil society, of theft, of injustice, of alienation, of freedom of mind' — in a word, of 'society' — Marx spoke 'of the world of production, of the means of production, of the relations of production . . . of infrastructure, of superstructure, of ideologies, of classes, of class-struggle, etc.'. One must conclude, in Althusser's view, that there is 'no relation of continuity . . . between the system of Marxist conceptions, and the system of pre-Marxist notions'; instead what one finds is an 'epistemological severing' between Marx and his predecessors, above all Hegel.[207]

Certainly there is something in this view (as the analysis of *Capital* and *The German Ideology* in part III showed); and it is a view which (if correct) would obviously rule out Kojève's reading of Hegelian 'materialism' as 'determining' the 'whole thought of Marx'. But if the Hegel-Marx connection is sometimes made too close by Kojève — often by declining to 'read' portions of both writers' work — it is doubtless made too distant by Althusser, who attempts to explain away even Marx' famous acknowledgement of (limited) indebtedness to Hegel in the second preface to *Capital*. In that celebrated acknowledgement, as is well-known, Marx criticises the 'idealist' and 'mystifying side of Hegelian dialectic', which views 'the Idea' as 'the demi-urgos of the real world'; and he insists that 'the ideal is nothing else than the material world reflected by the human mind, and translated into forms of thought'.[208] But at the same time he excoriates the 'peevish, arrogant, mediocre' anti-Hegelians who treat Hegel like 'a dead dog', and argues that Hegel was the first true theorist of dialectic, 'the first to present its general form of working in a comprehensive and conscious manner'. Though in Hegel the (idealist) dialectic is 'standing on its head', and 'must be turned right side up again, if you would discover the rational kernel within the mystical shell', nonetheless in its 'rational' form Hegelian dialectic 'includes in its comprehension and affirmative recognition of the existing state of things, at the same time also, the recognition of the negation of that state, of its inevitable breaking up'. De-mystified Hegelian dialectic 'is in its essence critical and revolutionary', because it 'regards every historically developed social form as in fluid movement, and therefore takes into account its transient nature not less than its momentary existence'.[209] Kojève's 'reading' of Hegel, for all its one-sidedness, preserves a glimpse of what Marx admired in Hegelianism; whereas Althusser, in reducing Marx' acknowledged indebtedness to Hegel to the bare notion of 'process without a subject',[210] files that debt down to something between transparency and non-existence. If Kojève, without every being a strict Marxist, finds it rather too easy to 'relate' Hegel to Marx, Althusser finds it rather too hard.

All of this simply supports the first general conclusion — that it is difficult to know what counts as a 'Marxist' reading of . . . anything. Whether Hegelianism is a 'clue' to Marxism, or something separated from it by an 'epistemological' gulf — on that, Marxists disagree profoundly. (Here much depends on what one chooses to 'read': those who, like Habermas, wish to see continuity between Hegel and Marx, often stress early Hegel [*Jenenser Realphilosphie*] and early Marx [*1844 MSS*];[211] while those who, like Althusser, wish to find a gulf between them, insist on late Hegel [*Philosophy of Right*] and late Marx [*Capital*].[212] But there is no irresistible 'necessity' in either procedure.) Perhaps Jean Hyppolite, a left-Hegelian with some Marxist leanings, was right (or at least prudent) to take refuge in a measure of vagueness in characterising the Hegel-Marx *rapport*: the '*struggle for life and death* . . . is the root of history for Hegel, while the *exploitation of man by man* is only a consequence of it, this consequence serving on the other hand as Marx' point of departure'.[213] (This much could be supported by the quotation from George Sand with which Marx closes *The Poverty of Philosophy*: 'Struggle or death; bloody war or nothing. It is thus that the question is inevitably posed.' And Marx adds that this will be 'the last word of social science' until 'there are no more classes and class antagonisms'.[214]) But even Hyppolite does not employ 'struggle' to illuminate the *Philosophy of Right*[215] — here one recalls what Hegel says about Mastery and Slavery as 'primitive'; nor does he ask just how far Marxian 'exploitation' resembles Hegelian 'struggle'. A purposeful abstractness saves him from this.

In any case, 'reading' Kojève and his Hegelianising contemporaries forces one to re-think what counts, or should count, as an Hegelian, or Marxist, or Hegelo-Marxist view of anything. And such a reading also forces one to the second general conclusion that can be drawn, namely that if one wishes to characterise and interpret Western political thought from Plato to Hegel one should probably resist making something as *particular* as the 'dialectic of Recognition' the 'key' to that whole tradition — particularly if, as in Kojève's case, one adds in further personal peculiarities which keep one from undertaking analyses that one *could* have made. (A perfect example in Kojève's case would be Leibniz, who argues in his *Meditation on the Common Concept of Justice* [c. 1703] that Aristotle *would* be quite right about slaves *deserving* to be enslaved — when masters will govern them better than they could govern themselves — were it not for the Christian notion of 'rational souls which are naturally and inalienably free';[216] Christianity, for Leibniz, overrules Aristotle. Now Kojève, had he treated Leibniz, might have pointed out — plausibly enough — that Leibniz was a 'literal' but 'imperfect' Christian, whereas Hegel was an 'anthropological' but 'perfect' one. Since, however, Kojève seems to have believed that in the history of Western philosophy there are 'really' only six philosophers of genuine stature — Parmenides, Heraclitus, Plato, Aristotle, Kant and Hegel[217] — he was forced, if he wanted to say anything about a figure of Leibniz' eminence, to treat Leibniz' philosophy as a 're-statement' of Stoicism, and to treat Stoicism, in its turn, as a 're-statement' of Aristotle.[218] And to shore up this rather peculiar and personal method, Kojève speaks of 'monads' *in Aristotle*[219] — the more easily, evidently, to 'find' Leibniz 'in' Aristotle. So even where his insistence on Mastery and Slavery might have been turned to good effect — as in Leibniz' case — other Kojèvian idiosyncracies rule this out.)

The essential Kojèvian thing, however, remains Mastery, Slavery, struggle and recognition; and the simple fact is that this ensemble of notions fails to do perfect justice to anybody, even Hegel. Among the six philsophers (only) that Kojève 'recognises', this ensemble does substantial violence to Plato, a little less to Aristotle, a bit less still to Kant (though still enough). But it is in connection with Kant that an irony in

Kojève's 'reading' of Western philosophy emerges — an irony with which one can conclude. That is that while Kojève reads Kant as standing in need of 'quasi-automatic' 'transformation' into the 'Hegelian system of knowledge', the 'Hegel that emerges from Kojève's 'reading' may 'preserve' more of Kant, and 'cancel' more of Hegel,[220] than it imagines: for the goal of history in Kant is assuredly a state of affairs in which there will (finally) be universal 'respect' for all persons as 'ends in themselves';[221] and this Kantian aim seems to be realised more nearly in Kojève's 'universal and homogeneous state' (in which every man is 'recognised in his reality and in his human dignity by *all* the others') than in the state 'understood' by Hegel in the *Philosophy of Right*. One could, perhaps, call this irony 'Kant's revenge', were it not for the fact that revenge is so very un-Kantian a notion. But Kojève's reading of Hegel, particularly when it ignores the *Philosophy of Right*, seems to involve some 'quasi-automatic' 'transforming' of Hegel into Kant. Kojève's refurbished Owl of Minerva 'recognises' Konigsberg, even if it doesn't land there.

NOTES

All translations from French are my own, unless otherwise indicated.

1 A. Kojève, *Introduction à la Lecture de Hegel: Leçons sur la Phenomenologie de l'Esprit* (Paris, 1947) (hereafter referred to as *Lecture de Hegel*).

2 A. Bloom, 'Introduction' to Kojève, *Introduction to the Reading of Hegel*, trans. J.H. Nichols, Jr. (New York, 1969) p. viii. (hereafter referred to as *Reading of Hegel*).

3 A. Kojève, 'Hegel, Marx et le Christianisme', in *Critique*, (Paris, August-September 1946) p. 352, (nominally a review of Henri Niel's *De la Médiation dans la Philosophie de Hegel*).

4 Kojève, *Lecture de Hegel*, op. cit. pp. 494–5.

5 F. Nietzsche, *The Twilight of the Idols*, in *The Portable Nietzsche*, trans. W. Kaufmann (New York, 1954) Section 34, p. 535: 'The "beyond" — why a beyond, if not as a means for besmirching *this* world?' (Kojève, to be sure, would not endorse a politics 'derived' from Nietzschean aestheticism; he and Nietzsche share mainly *enemies*.)

6 A. Kojève, *Essai d'une Histoire Raisonnée de la Philosophie Païenne*, Vol. 2, (Paris, 1972). Plato, *selon* Kojève, indulges in the 'absurd' wish to 'define objective reality as something Transcendent, that is, as something which is "above" or "beyond" the extended duration of empirical

Existence' (p. 36); he 'has recourse to myth when he speaks of objective reality, which for him is the Ideal world' (p. 37). (Hereafter referred to as *Philosophie Païenne*.)

7 A. Kojève, *Kant* (Paris, 1973), particularly pp. 67ff.

8 Kojève, *Philosophie Païenne, op. cit.* Vol. 2, p. 40.

9 *Ibid.* p. 42.

10 Kojève, *Lecture de Hegel, op. cit.* p. 262; cf. p. 570, where Kojève argues that 'Hegelian anthropology is a laicised Christian theology'. Cf. Kojève, 'Hegel, Marx et le Christianisme', *op. cit.* p. 340: 'One often finds theological formulations in Hegelian philosophy. But, in the deepest sense, this philosophy is nonetheless radically atheistic and areligious.'

11 Kojève, *Philosophie Païenne, op. cit.* Vol. 2, p. 71ff.

12 See note 3.

13 Kojève, 'L'Action Politique des Philosophes', in *Critique* (Paris, October 1950) p. 46ff. (nominally a review of Leo Strauss' *On Tyranny: An Interpretation of Xenophon's 'Hieron'*).

14 Term borrowed from Judith N. Shklar, *Freedom and Independence: The Political Ideas of Hegel's Phenomenology of Mind* (Cambridge, 1975).

15 Kojève, *Lecture de Hegel, op. cit.*, pp. 19ff., 172ff.

16 *Ibid.* p. 173.

17 *Ibid.* p. 20.

18 *Ibid.* p. 174.

19 *Ibid.*

20 *Ibid.* pp. 173–7.

21 *Ibid.* p. 178.

22 *Ibid.* p. 179.

23 *Ibid.* pp. 179–80.

24 Kojève, 'Hegel, Marx et le Christianisme', *op. cit.* p. 356.

25 Kojève, *Lecture de Hegel, op. cit.* p. 180.

26 *Ibid.*

27 *Ibid.*

28 *Ibid.*

29 *Ibid.* pp. 182ff., particularly p. 260.

30 *Ibid.* pp. 190–1.

31 *Ibid.* pp. 184–5.

32 *Ibid.*

33 *Ibid.* p. 494.

34 Kojève, *Reading of Hegel, op. cit.* p. 20.

35 *Ibid.* p. 23.

36 Kojève, *Lecture de Hegel, op. cit.* p. 465.

37 Kojève, 'Hegel, Marx et le Christianisme', *op. cit.* pp. 355–6.

38 Cf. K. Marx, 'Critique of the Gotha Program', in *Marx and Engels: Basic Writings on Politics and Philosophy,* ed. L. Feuer (New York, 1959) Section IV. The German workers' party, Marx complains, has made the mistake of treating 'the state . . . as an independent entity that possesses its own *intellectual, ethical and libertarian bases*' (Marx' italics).

39 Kojève, *Lecture de Hegel, op. cit.* p. 465.

40 H. Arendt, *The Life of the Mind: Two: Willing* (New York, 1978) p. 47. In her notes, Arendt mentions only the (abridged) English translation of Kojève's *Introduction*; it is thus impossible to say whether she knew (particularly) 'Hegel, Marx et le Christianisme' — the essay that might have modified her view that, for Kojève, history and philosophy have 'definitely' ended.

41 Kojève, *Lecture de Hegel, op. cit.* p. 145. Unfortunately this entire section (IV) — crucial to an accurate view of Kojève — is omitted in the Nichols-Bloom English edition of the *Introduction*.

42 *Ibid.* p. 145.

43 *Ibid.* pp. 145–6.

44 *Ibid.* p. 146: 'To be sure, only the head of the universal and homogeneous state (Napoleon) is *really* "satisfied" (= recognised by all in his personal reality and value).'

45 *Ibid.* p. 147.

46 *Ibid.*

47 *Ibid.* p. 262. This very important passage is omitted in the Nichols-Bloom English edition.

48 *Ibid.* p. 152: 'Evil = the Revolution and its realisers: Napoleon. Forgiveness = Justification of the Revolution and of Napoleon by Hegel in and through the *Phenomenology*.' And on p. 153 Kojève adds, *à la* Nietzsche, that Napoleon was 'beyond good and evil'. (All these passages are omitted in the English edition.)

49 Kojève, 'Hegel, Marx et le Christianisme', *op. cit.* p. 360.

50 *Ibid.* pp. 362–3.

51 *Ibid.* p. 363n.

52 K. Marx, *The 18th Brumaire of Louis Bonaparte,* in *Basic Writings, op. cit.* p. 320.

53 Georg Lukacs, 'In Search of Bourgeois Man', in *Essays on Thomas Mann,* trans. Mitchell (New York, 1964) pp. 27–8.

54 Hegel, *The Phenomenology of Mind,* trans. Baillie, (New York, 1971) p. 666ff. It is by no means obvious that this section is 'about' Napoleon (rather than about 'the beautiful soul').

55 Kojève, *Lecture de Hegel, op. cit.* p. 290.

56 *Ibid.*

57 *Ibid.*

58 Kant, *Rechtsphilosophie,* in *Political Writings,* ed. H. Reiss, (Cambridge, 1970) pp. 173–4: 'If a person cannot prove that a thing [e.g. eternal peace] exists, he may attempt to prove that it does not exist. If neither approach succeeds . . . he may still ask whether it is in his interest to assume one or the other possibility . . . We can have a duty to act in accordance with the idea of such an end [peace] . . . provided there is no means of demonstrating that it cannot be realised. . . .'

59 Kojève, *Lecture de Hegel, op. cit.* p. 290.

60 Kojève, *Philosophie Païenne, op. cit.* Vol. 2, p. 400.

61 Kojève, 'Hegel, Marx et le Christianisme', *op. cit.* p. 365.

62 *Ibid.* p. 365–6.

63 Kojève, *Reading of Hegel, op. cit.* p. 3.
64 The term 'privileged' is borrowed from John Heckman's helpful essay which introduces Jean Hyppolite's *Genesis and Structure of Hegel's Phenomenology of Spirit,* trans. Cherniak and Heckman (Evanston, 1974).
65 K. Marx, *Capital,* trans. Moore and Aveling (New York, 1967) Vol. 3, p. 820.
66 Kojève, 'Hegel, Marx et le Christianisme', *op. cit.* p. 356.
67 *Ibid.*
68 K. Marx, *The German Ideology,* ed. R. Pascal (New York, 1947) p. 7.
69 Kojève, 'Hegel, Marx et le Christianisme', *op. cit.* p. 352.
70 *Ibid.* p. 354.
71 *Ibid.* p. 353.
72 *Ibid.*
73 Kojève, *Lecture de Hegel, op. cit.* p. 494.
74 Kojève, 'Hegel, Marx et le Christianisme', *op. cit.* p. 352.
75 Kojève, 'L'Action Politique des Philosophes', *op. cit.* p. 52.
76 Marx, *Capital, op. cit.* Vol. 3, p. 812ff.
77 Kojève, *Lecture de Hegel, op. cit.* p. 435n.
78 *Ibid.*
79 Marx, *Capital, op. cit.* Vol. 3, p. 820.
80 *Ibid.* Cf. *Capital, op. cit.* Vol. 1, pp. 183–4: 'The labour process . . . is the necessary condition for effecting exchange of matter between man and Nature; it is the everlasting Nature-imposed condition of human existence, and therefore is independent of every social phase of that existence, or rather, is common to every such phase.' Had Kojève attached sufficient weight to Marx' 'everlasting' and 'every', he might not have stressed 'art, love, play and happiness'.
81 *Ibid.*
82 K. Marx, 'Critique of the Hegelian Dialectic and Philosophy as a Whole', in *Economics and Philsophic MSS of 1844,* trans. Milligan, ed. Struik (New York, 1964) p. 177.
83 *Ibid.*
84 *Ibid.* pp. 176–7.
85 All of these are treated by Kojève as 'slave ideologies', as epiphenomena of Master-imposed labour.
86 Hegel, *Phenomenology, op. cit.* p. 231.
87 Kojève, 'Hegel, Marx et le Christianisme', op. cit. p. 349.
88 *Ibid.* pp. 350–1.
89 *Ibid.* p. 351.
90 *Ibid.* pp. 351–2, Cf. Kojève, 'L'Action Politique des Philosophes', *op. cit.* p. 52ff., where this idea is enlarged: political men, Kojève argues, even tyrants, seek 'recognition' rather than 'affection', and 'the man who has satisfied this desire through his action is, in effect, "satisfied", whether he is happy or not, loved or not'.
91 Hegel, *Phenomenology, op. cit.* p. 644 ff.
92 Hegel, *Philosophy of Right,* trans. Knox (Oxford, 1942) p. 252.
93 Hegel, *Phenomenology, op. cit.* p. 650.

94 *Ibid.* p. 651.
95 *Ibid.* p. 663.
96 *Ibid.*
97 *Ibid.* p. 660.
98 *Ibid.* p. 662.
99 Hegel, *Philosophy of Right, op. cit.* p. 91.
100 *Ibid.*
101 *Ibid.* p. 168.
102 Hegel, *Phenomenology, op. cit.* p. 670.
103 Hegel, *Philosophy of Right, op. cit.* p. 84ff.
104 Shklar, *Freedom and Independence, op. cit.* p. 103 ff.
105 Hegel, *Phenomenology, op. cit.* p. 466ff.
106 *Ibid.* p. 478.
107 *Ibid.* p. 489.
108 *Ibid.*
109 *Ibid.*
110 *Ibid.* p. 490.
111 *Ibid.* p. 491.
112 *Ibid.* pp. 481 and 492.
113 Hegel, *Philosophy of Right, op. cit.* p. 124.
114 Kojève, *Lecture de Hegel, op. cit.* p. 98ff. Kojève's entire treatment of 'the Ethical World' is omitted in the Nichols — Bloom English edition.
115 *Ibid.* p. 98.
116 *Ibid.* p. 105.
117 *Ibid.* Kojève adds that 'the woman [i.e. Antigone] is the concrete realisation of crime'.
118 Tran Duc Thao, review of Kojève's *Lecture de Hegel,* in *Les Temps Modernes,* ed. J.-P. Sartre, No. 34 (Paris, July 1948) p. 492ff., particularly p. 494.
119 G. Kelly, *Idealism, Politics and History: Sources of Hegelian Thought* (Cambridge, 1969) p. 338.
120 G. Kelly, *Hegel's Retreat from Eleusis* (Princeton, 1978) p. 31ff.
121 *Ibid.* p. 53.
122 *Ibid.* pp. 51–2.
123 In this work Hegel urges that 'right and the science of right begin' with 'the position of the free will'; and the opening quarter of the book is taken up with elucidating the notion of 'will'.
124 Hegel, *Philosophy of Right, op. cit.* p. 288.
125 Hegel, *Encyclopedia,* Part III, trans. W. Wallace as *Hegel's Philosophy of Mind* (Oxford, 1894) p. 139.
126 Hegel, *Philosophy of Right, op. cit.* p. 181.
127 *Ibid.* p. 196.
128 *Ibid.* p. 105.
129 Cf. Arendt, *Willing, op. cit. passim.*
130 T. Hobbes, *Leviathan,* ed. Michael Oakeshott (Oxford, 1957) Chapter 40, p. 307. For a full treatment of 'will' in Hobbes' moral and political thought, cf. the author's 'Will and Legitimacy in the Philosophy of Hobbes', in *Political Studies,* Vol. XXI, No. 4, December 1973.

131 J. Locke, *Two Treatises of Government,* ed. P. Laslett (New York, 1965) para 173, p. 430, Cf. the author's 'Locke on "Voluntary Agreement" and Political Power', in *Western Political Quarterly,* March 1975.

132 J.J. Rousseau, *Du Contrat Social,* Book II, Chapter 6, in *Rousseau: Political Writings,* ed. Vaughan (Oxford, 1962). Cf. the author's 'A possible explanation of Rousseau's General Will', in *American Political Science Review,* March 1970.

133 Kant, *The Metaphysical Elements of Justice,* trans. J. Ladd (Indianapolis, 1965) p. 97.

134 On this cf. Michael Foster's splendid *The Political Philosophies of Plato and Hegel* (Oxford, 1935) pp. 131–40, which argues that in the *Philosophy of Right* the 'ethical will' which relates to the state is 'imperfectly differentiated from reason'.

135 Hegel, *Philosophy of Right, op. cit.* p. 208ff.

136 *Ibid.* p. 198ff.

137 *Ibid.* p. 150ff.

138 *Ibid.* pp. 12–13; quoted by Kojève in *Lecture de Hegel, op. cit.* p. 437.

139 See note 59.

140 Hegel, *Philosophy of Right, op. cit.* pp. 10–12.

141 *Ibid.* p. 10.

142 Kojève, 'Hegel, Marx et le Christianisme', *op. cit.* p. 352n.

143 Hegel, *Philosophy of Fine Art,* trans. Osmaston (London, 1920) Vol. 4, p. 318ff.

144 *Ibid.* p. 324.

145 *Ibid.* p. 334ff.

146 *Ibid.* Vol. 3, pp. 335–6.

147 *Ibid.* p. 336. Hegel knew many of the art-works of which he spoke at first hand, having made trips to the Netherlands and Belgium in the 1820s, where he saw works of Van Eyck, Rubens, and others; he also knew the great cathedrals of Antwerp, Ghent, etc. On all this cf. Albert Chapelle, SJ, 'Quand Hegel Passait aux Pays-Bas', in *Hegel-Jahrbuch 1972,* ed. W.R. Beyer (Meisenheim am Glan, 1972) p. 1ff. (In 1976–77, the author went to see the art-works in Belgium, France and Italy which Hegel describes in *Philosophy of Fine Art;* this will be the subject of a forthcoming article.)

148 *Ibid.* p. 25ff, particularly 98ff.

149 *Ibid.* Vol. p. 315ff.

150 Kojève, *Kant, op. cit.* p. 10.

151 Marx, *The German Ideology, op. cit.* p. 14: 'The phantoms formed in the human brain are also, necessarily, sublimates of their material life-process. . . . Conceiving, thinking, the mental intercourse of men, appear . . . as the direct efflux of their material behaviour.'

152 Kojève, *Kant, op. cit.* p. 10.

153 *Ibid.*

154 Kant, *Fundamental Principles of the Mataphysics of Morals,* trans. T.K. Abbott (Indianapolis, 1949) pp. 10–11.

155 *Ibid.* p. 65.

156 Kant, *Eternal Peace,* in *The Philosophy of Kant,* ed. C.J. Friedrich (New York, 1949) p. 459ff.
157 Kojève, *Kant, op. cit.* p. 30.
158 *Ibid.*
159 *Ibid.* p. 39; cf. p. 197: '*Kant ne veut pas admettre l'éfficacité de l'Action-libre dans la durée-étendue de l'Existence-empirique et c'est pourquoir il a consciement et volontairement exclu la Sub-Categorie de la Téleologie (= Liberté) de son Système categorical developpable discursivement sans contra-diction dans le mode de la Vérité.*' (This is a fair example of Kojève's style.)
160 Kojève, *Lecture de Hegel, op. cit.* p. 150. There is, of course, something in this objection, as one can see by reading Kant's *The Conflict of the Faculties.*
161 Hans Vaihinger, *The Philosophy of 'As If',* trans. C.K. Ogden (London, 1935) p. 319: 'The As-if view plays an extraordinarily important part in Kant.' Cf. p. 293, where Vaihinger calls 'the dignity of man' and 'the realm of purposes' in Kant 'concepts . . . without any reality', 'heuristic fictions', 'something unreal', etc.
162 Kojève, *Kant, op. cit.* p. 87.
163 *Ibid.*
164 *Ibid.* pp. 86–89.
165 *Ibid.* p. 90.
166 Kant, *Critique of Judgment,* in *The Philosophy of Kant,* ed. Friedrich, *op. cit.* p. 354.
167 Kant, *Critique of Practical Reason*, trans. T.K. Abbott (London, 1923) p. 180.
168 Kojève, *Kant, op. cit.* p. 35ff.
169 Cf. the passages on the 'moral proof' cited by N.K. Smith in Appendix C of his *A Commentary to Kant's 'Critique of Pure Reason',* (London, 1923) p. 636ff. (The same passages are treated by Vahinger, *op. cit.* but with less judiciousness.)
170 Kant, *Fundamental Principles,* trans. Abbott, *op. cit.,* p. 10ff.
171 Kojève, *Philosophie Païenne, op. cit.* Vol. 2, p. 197.
172 Nietzsche, *The Twilight of the Idols, op. cit.* p. 485.
173 Kojève, *Philosophie Païenne, op. cit.* Vol. 2, p. 17.
174 *Ibid.* p. 117.
175 *Ibid.* p. 143.
176 *Ibid.* p. 399.
177 *Ibid.* p. 224.
178 *Ibid.* p. 204.
179 *Ibid.* p. 320ff., particularly, p. 332.
180 *Ibid.* p. 332.
181 *Ibid.* p. 333ff.
182 *Ibid.* p. 335.
183 *Ibid.*
184 *Ibid.*
185 *Ibid,* Vol. 1, pp. 26–7. Anglo-French 'empiricism', according to Kojève, 'predicted' the 'inevitable, definitive elimination of philoso-

phy'; and it was Kant who 'succeeded in saving philosophy *in extremis'*.

186 G. Besse, 'J.-J. Rousseau: Maître, Laquais, Esclave', in *Hegel et le Siècle des Lumières*, ed. J. d'Hondt (Paris, 1974), p. 71 ff.

187 *Ibid.* p. 94.

188 *Ibid.* p. 97.

189 *Ibid.*

190 *Ibid.* p. 99. Unlike Kojève, Besse is a fairly orthodox Marxist. But he declines to view philosophy as merely 'epiphenomenal' as is clear in his 'Lénine et la Révolution Culturelle', in *Lénine: La Philosophie et la Culture*, (Paris, 1971) p. 166: 'Marx and Engels could not have erected scientific socialism if they had not . . . assimilated the history and the substance of the great philosophies, from Epicurus to Diderot, from Aristotle to Hegel.'

191 On Rousseau's understanding of 'necessity', the best modern treatment is John Charvet's remarkable *The Social Problem in the Philosophy of Rousseau* (Cambridge, 1974), p. 48ff.

192 Leo Strauss, *The Political Philosophy of Hobbes*, trans. Sinclair (Oxford, 1936) p. 58n.

193 *Ibid.* p. 57.

194 Kojève, 'Hegel, Marx et le Christianisme', *op. cit.* p. 351.

195 Hobbes, *Leviathan, op. cit.* Chapter 20, p. 132.

196 Hobbes, *Liberty, Necessity and Chance*, in *English Works*, ed. Molesworth (London, 1841) Vol. 5, p. 180.

197 Hobbes, *Leviathan, op. cit.* Chapter 15, p. 100.

198 *Ibid.*

199 Hegel, *Philosophy of Right, op. cit.* pp. 156–7.

200 Hegel, *History of Philosophy*, trans. Haldane (London, 1892) Vol. 3, pp. 316–8. In Hobbes' *Leviathan*, Hegel urges, one finds 'no idle talk about a state of natural goodness': in this respect Hobbes is an improvement on Rousseau.

201 Strauss, *The Political Philosophy of Hobbes, op. cit.* pp. 57–8. (This view is dropped — or at least not mentioned — in Strauss' *Natural Right and History*, Chicago, 1953.)

202 Bloom, 'Introduction' to Kojève, *Reading of Hegel, op. cit.* p. viii.

203 J. Vuillemin, review of Kojève's *Lecture de Hegel* in the *Révue Philosophique* (Paris, 1949) p. 200.

204 R. Garaudy, *Dieu est Mort: Étude sur Hegel* (Paris, 1962), pp. 191–2n.

205 J. Habermas, 'Arbeit und Interaktion: Bemerkungen zu Hegels Jenenser "Philosophie des Geistes" ', in *Technik und Wissenschaft als Ideologie* (Frankfurt am Main, 1968), p. 9ff.

206 L. Althusser, 'Sur la Dialectique de l'evolution intellectuelle du Jeune Marx', in *Hegel-Jahrbuch 1974*, ed. W.R. Beyer, (Köln, 1975) p. 130.

207 *Ibid.* In his opening paragraph (p. 128), Althusser makes this even sharper: 'Marx founded a new science, the science of the history of social formations. I should add: this scientific discovery is a political and theoretical event which is without precedent in the whole of human history. And I should sharpen this: this event is irreversible.'

208 Marx, *Capital, op. cit.* Vol. 1, p. 19.

209 *Ibid.* pp. 19–20.

210 Althusser, 'Marx' Relation to Hegel', in *Politics and History: Montesquieu, Rousseau, Hegel and Marx,* trans. B. Brewster (London, 1972) pp. 181–2.

211 Habermas, 'Arbeit und Interaktion', *op. cit.* p. 9ff.

212 Althusser, 'Jeune Marx', *op. cit.* p. 128ff.

213 J. Hyppolite, 'Marxisme et Philosophie', in *Etudes sur Marx et Hegel* (Paris, 1955) p. 133.

214 Marx, *The Poverty of Philosophy,* in *The Marx-Engels Reader,* ed. R. Tucker (New York, 1978), p. 219.

215 Hyppolite, *Etudes sur Hegel et Marx, op. cit. passim.*

216 Leibniz, 'Meditation on the Common Concept of Justice', in *The Political Writings of Leibniz,* trans. and ed. P. Riley (Cambridge, 1972) pp. 62–3.

217 Kojève, *Philosophie Païenne, op. cit.* Vol. 1, p. 158ff.: 'Now, instinctively, in a way, these names (and these alone) have always been counted among the Greats of philosophy.' Kojève then indulges in an extremely peculiar 'justification' of omitting all other philosophers, ancient and modern: 'It would be easy to add a half-dozen names. But how to designate the chosen ones without being 'unjust' towards the other candidates, who are also "possible"?' The real question, of course, is why one has to 'designate' anybody at all. And it may be Kojèvian peculiarities such as this 'election' of 'Greats' which led Dominique Janicaud, in her review of Volume 2 of *Philosophie Païenne (Les Études Philosphiques,* Paris, April-June 1975, p. 218), to observe that Kojève's work 'is a sort of philosophical "one man show"', which some will find suggestive and fascinating, and which many others will judge sterile, narcissistic and conceited'.

218 Kojève, *Philosophie Païenne, op. cit.* Vol. 3, p. 149.

219 *Ibid.* Vol. 2, p. 323: 'Now, as Leibniz said in re-stating Aristotle, the monads . . . etc.'

220 On 'cancelling' and 'preserving', cf. Hegel, *Phenomenology, op. cit.* p. 223ff.

221 Kant, *Eternal Peace,* op. cit. *passim.*

Judicial Discretion, Legal Positivism and Democratic Theory
DAVID ROBERTSON

I

FOR more or less a century the prevailing theory of law in Anglo-American democracies has been legal positivism. In recent years this theory has come under severe attack, despite having been put on sounder foundations in 1961 by H.L.A. Hart.[1] The most notable criticisms have come from Ronald Dworkin, ironically Hart's successor to the Oxford chair of Jurisprudence. Dworkin's attack is part of the anti-utilitarian movement in political philosophy that he has centred round Rawls. Indeed Dworkin not only acknowledges Rawls' leadership, but expresses himself as seeking, against Bentham, for a 'liberal' theory of law. It is Bentham's characterisation of human rights as 'nonsense on stilts' that he quotes, for to Dworkin the key to the new jurisprudence is that it must be a 'rights' jurisprudence.[2]

To Dworkin the key to understanding law is to see it as a system of rights and duties that pre-exists legal phenomena, and not, as in positivism, to see law as a system of rules constituting a legal system which alone can create rights.

To establish the superiority of his rights-jurisprudence, Dworkin concentrates on the presence of judicial discretion in the positivist system. He tries to argue that positivism does, but rights-jurisprudence does not, involve a major element of judicial discretion, and thus rights-jurisprudence is both a better description, and a preferable norm, for law.[3]

In this paper I shall attempt to show that Dworkin is mistaken in his claim that rights-jurisprudence, or his special theory of decision-making in hard cases,[4] removes discretion. I shall then argue that positivism is correct in insisting on the presence of discretion, and is a correct description of, and a desirable norm for, a legal system. Finally I shall argue that the problem of discretion is insoluble within legal theory, and that the solution must be sought in a developed political theory of the nature of legislation and legislative machinery.

It is useful first to review what legal positivism has become since its origins with Bentham[5] and Austin. According to its greatest modern exponent, H.L.A. Hart,[6] a legal system consists (only) of rules, which are of two kinds. The vast mass of rules are *primary* rules, directly binding on individuals, whether they cover criminal law, property and inheritance, contract, liability for negligence or whatever. These are binding not because they are backed by force, but also not because people believe in them or accept them. They are binding because they can be shown to be derived from one or more of the other sorts of rules, the *secondary* rules. A secondary rule is one that grants to someone or some body the right or duty to make a primary rule. They are best described as 'rules of recognition', and they cannot ultimately be discovered by logical analysis of interconnection between rules, but only by observing the practice of officials, above all judges, in the system. It is the pedigree of a primary rule, demonstrating its dependence on a secondary rule empirically verifiable, that differentiates between a rule that is, and one that turns out not to be, a genuine member of the legal system.

Rules of recognition are ultimately constitutional and Hart's system, though it deals with rules that are binding without necessarily being backed by will and force, is at heart positivistic. Only when and to such extent as officials in a system do in fact obey or follow some ultimate rule of recognition that validates primary rules, will a rule be a binding primary rule. Hart leaves out the question of why any rule of recognition is in fact accepted and followed by officials, just as he leaves blank what the rule of recognition is.

Two things must be emphasised. The legal system is a system of rules, specific, hard, clearcut, and definitely binding. A rule, as both Hart and his critics see it, has the logical form 'If X, Y, Z, then A', and not 'If X, Y, Z, then perhaps A but maybe not'.

Second, legal positivism in all its guises insists on a clear distinction between rules of law, and other rules of behaviour, as in rules of morality, decency, or good taste. The rule of recognition enforces this distinction. One is only *legally* obligated by a rule that can be traced to a rule of recognition authorising courts and judges to tell one to obey.

Another, and very important way of saying all this is that the content of a rule never tells one whether it is a binding law or not. There is nothing that a rule can order or provide that is so right that it is binding, and nothing so wrong that it is not binding. Only the pedigree tells one something which has been handed down in keeping with the ultimate secondary rule of recognition is valid (whether approved of, or morally right or not), that which has not is not, however popular or decent.[7]

This theory works adequately as long as a rule exists covering a legal problem, as long as the rule is clear and unambiguous, and as long as there is no contradictory rule. Legal positivism is fine for the ordinary case. The problems arise in what the critics of Hart call 'hard cases'. Suppose a problem arises for which there does not appear to be any valid rule, or suppose one does not quite know what the relevant rule actually implies because of an ambiguity, or, finally, suppose a case crops up where there appear to be two or more incompatible rules. How then can there be a legal solution? If the system contains only fixed secondary rules, validated by a rule of recognition, it lacks the creative capacity to deal with new or unforeseen problems.

Here positivism has to admit that there is no legal solution, and judges must therefore use their discretion, are not bound to give the victory to either side, but allowed, indeed obliged, to decide for themselves what the answer ought to be, rather than determining what the correct answer is.

Austin accepted this, and built it into his system by a notion of delegated command. When a judge comes across such a situation he must decide for himself; his decision will either be repealed by the sovereign, in which case the repeal will give the new answer, or not. If the sovereign does not repeal the decision, then the judge's decision is taken to be retrospectively commanded, and is thus new law. Hart, though he doubts the frequency or extent of 'hard cases',[8] would say something roughly similar. Indeed a very similar version actually is the working theory of the English judiciary. For if a statute has been found confusing and received judicial interpretation, later the argument is accepted that Parliament must have been aware of the judicial gloss on the statute, could have done something about it, has not, and thus must be taken to have ratified it.[9]

Now this acceptance of the necessity of judicial discretion has been the target for a series of very serious attacks on positivism, attacks furthermore which are directly aimed at what I would claim is democratically necessary in any legal system, the passivity of the law.

The trouble with discretion is obvious; it sounds rankly undemocratic to admit that fairly often cases crop up where the legal system, or for that matter the political system, has provided no right answers, and socially unrepresentative, non-elected officials are entitled to decide the case any way they like.

We are used to the idea that, in a democratic system, we all have our rights, and we probably accept the legal philosopher Dworkin's characterisation of law cases as granting and enforcing pre-existent legal rights and obligations. To be told 'you ain't got any rights, 'cos Parliament messed things up, and a man in a red robe can decide for himself what to do to you', is alarming.

Dworking makes two different, though related, attacks on legal positivism.

II

PRINCIPLES VERSUS RULES
Dworkin's first attack on positivism involves three steps, only the last of which is *prima facie* fatal to Hart. First, he claims that rules are not the only elements in the legal system, but that there exist also logically different entities he calls 'principles'. From this he argues that the presence and use of principles removes the need, and therefore the legitimacy, of judicial discretion. Finally he claims that these principles cannot be identified by some 'rule of recognition'. The consequence is that there can be no firm distinction between the legal system

and the general moral beliefs of a society. Thus the primary aspect of legal positivism, ensuring the supremacy of the legislative aspect of the state, is destroyed. In itself, no positivist need particularly object to the inclusion of 'principles', and most welcome the apparent disappearance of discretion. There have been several attempts to modify Dworkin so as to accept most of his argument but to keep it positivist, by showing that the principles he incorporates can be contained within a rule of recognition.[10]

I believe they fail to have their cake and eat it, but have no space to argue this here. However, even had they succeeded in this limited objective, positivism would still be destroyed, for the acceptance of principles into the system does not, as Dworkin claims, abolish, but increases and disguises discretion. Before arguing this I try to show that principles do not in any case exist as elements logically different from rules.

Principles, for Dworkin, are general standards by which a judge can come to a conclusion about the rights of litigants, but they are logically different from rules because they do not determine a result, but only incline towards one. Principles, unlike rules, are not applied automatically whenever a given set of circumstances exists. Deciding a case contrary to a principle, or ignoring it in some situations where it might *prima facie* apply, does not involve abandoning or repealing or breaking it. If a rule says X, then Y, failing to decide Y involves breaking or altering it, and is not legitimate in a positivist world. Principles on the other hand one can apply in one case and not in another, roughly identical, case without giving up or altering them.

He gives two examples of principles at play. In Riggs v Palmer, a New York case from 1889,[11] a man due to inherit under his grandfather's will had his otherwise safe inheritance disallowed by a court because he had murdered the grandfather. The court claimed that there was a common law principle, 'No man may profit from his own wrongdoing', although the court admitted: 'It is quite true that the statutes regulating the making . . . of wills and the devolution of property . . . if literally construed, and if their force . . . can in no way be controlled or modified, give this property to the murderer.'

He tries to show that to forbid profit from wrongdoing is a principle, only applicable sometimes, and not a rule always binding, by giving several examples of situations where people do benefit from doing wrong. If a man breaks an employment contract with one employer and goes to work for another at a higher salary, he may have to pay damages for breach of contract, but will be allowed to keep his new salary.[12] Similarly, if a man breaks bail, crosses to another state, and there makes a brilliant investment earning him millions, he will be deported and imprisoned, but the fortune will not be confiscated.[13]

In failing to apply the principle in these two cases we are not being inconsistent, or altering the principle, as we would were there to be a rule about the matter, claims Dworkin. Principles are not like that, they are just 'good reasons' in some contexts, for doing X which might not be good enough reasons for X in other contexts.

Principles have a dimension of 'weight' that rules do not. If two or more principles intersect in a case, the judge chooses the one with the greater 'weight', or, presumably, contextual importance, but in so doing does not cause the rejected principle to be invalid. One the other hand, if two rules clash, only one can be valid, and the other must be rejected or reformulated.

One might point out that rules too have exceptions but Dworkin does not think this relevant. A full statement of a rule includes a mention of all the exceptions to it, though for convenience we use a shorthand that omits them.[14] One could not, even in principle, give a list of exceptions to a principle, because it is not possible to know ahead of time what they are.

Others have argued, and I think correctly, that this logical difference is mistaken.[15] It is not clear that principles do exist in this form. It is interesting that though his example of the principle being applied comes from a real case, he quotes no actual example of a principle being considered and rejected, or given an insufficient weight. We know that (especially in the common law) courts do introduce new exceptions into rules, and there is no obvious reason to treat the murder inheritance case as one that shows the application of a principle not elsewhere applied. We could just as easily treat it as an example of a new exception being made in the specific law of inheritance. This would have the virtue of removing the problem of the imaginery cases; there would then be no reason to expect Dworkin's principle of not profiting from wrong to be applied to a contract law case or a case of bail-jumping if it is not in fact an independent principle but a special clause of the law of inheritance.

Nor is it true that one can list the exceptions to a rule in a way that one cannot list the exceptions to a principle. Of course rules cannot be rules if they can be applied or not as a judge wishes given the context of a case. The exceptions must be specifiable in some sense ahead of the context. But exceptions to rules are not, and cannot easily be, context-descriptions, but are rather generalised statements of the sorts of situations in which, or the sorts of reasons for which, courts need not apply a given rule.

The law that forbids assault, for example, has a series of exceptions. One can do what would normally be assault and get away with it, if one is protecting one's life, arresting a suspected criminal, saving someone from suicide, carrying out medical aid.[16] In all of these one may use too much force, and therefore still be guilty of assault. I could list the exceptions to the law forbidding assault in this sense, but I could not give an exhaustive account of what actions, in detail, in any conceivable circumstance, would lead a court to acquit on a charge of assault, and this is a necessary inability, not a contingent one.

Unless principles have at least this degree of definiteness, it is hard to see how they can be justified, or even identified. How can a judge be justified in overthrowing a clear law of inheritance if he adduces a principle which is so indeterminate that he can give no general account of when else it might be binding? How can one indeed know that a principle exists as part of the law, or even choose words in which to express it, if one can give no general account of when and why it applies?

Suppose we accept the existence of principles with varying weights. It now follows that judges may (indeed for Dworkin, must) 'balance' two of them together to come to a conclusion in a case, rather than applying a rule to a set of facts and determining the result.

How can the 'balancing' of two principles fail to be an

exercise of discretion? Surely the wildest positivist who believes that unclarity in a rule requires judicial discretion is attributing to the judge no more extensive a power than is Dworkin in saying that the judge must decide for himself whether, in the context, something may be allowed or not? Indeed Dworkin allows, as a positivist will not, that a clear rule may be ignored because of a conflicting principle. Does this not allow more discretion?

Dworkin needs to defeat this criticism, for the main argument in favour of his theory of law is that it removes troublesome discretion from the legal system.

III

TWO SENSES OF DISCRETION?

He does it by an analysis of the meaning of discretion. There are two important senses of discretion he differentiates. One, the weak sense, is where a judge has discretion because a rule is not so clear, or the factual situation so given, that no exercise of thought and judgment is needed to decide how to carry it out, though the rule is still binding on the court despite its vagueness.[17] This he dismissed as being obvious and unimportant.

His strong sense of discretion implies that the judge has no duty to find for either litigant, that there are no pre-existent legal obligations in the situation. Thus whatever the judge decides he cannot be criticised (unless he is manifestly arbitrary, unreasonable, or whatever). Dworkin thinks that positivists attribute discretion in this strong sense, that to use the weak sense would be uninformative and even tautologous, and that in this strong sense the positivist 'rule only' model does, but the 'principles' model does not, involve discretion.[18]

Dworkin's 'ordinary language' example of the two senses of discretion may make the point clearer. If a sergeant was told[19] to take five men on patrol, he would have discretion in the strong sense, for no indications by authority are given about how he should select. Were he told to take his five most experienced men, he might still have difficulty deciding whom he should take, the notion of experience being 'fuzzy', but the fact that he would have to use his judgment would still not imbue him with discretion — except in this weak sense. The difference, in Dworkin's terminology, is that in the second example some men have a right not to be chosen, because they are inexperienced, though it might be difficult to know precisely who they were. In the first example, with the strong sense of discretion, no one has such a right.

If only rules exist in the model of law, says Dworkin, then there are times where litigants have no rights at all, for where no rule exists, or where the 'rule' runs out there is nothing else at all in the system that can give a litigant a right. But under the model that includes principles, there will be available some general standard, from a social stock of moral precepts, that can be brought to bear. There must always be a 'right' answer. One or other of the litigants must always have a 'right' to win the case, even if it is difficult, or controversial, to decide which one.

There are a series of assumptions buried in this argument:

(1) that rules do run out, or cease to exist in this way;
(2) that the general morality of the society contains an infinite capacity for generating moral precepts so that there cannot exist a dispute to which there is no correct answer;
(3) that rights exist even when they are essentially contestable;
(4) that the 'judgment' used in deciding upon conflicting principles from outside a system of rules is essentially similar to the weak sense of discretion always with us because of the fuzziness of concepts inside rules.

It seems to me that each of these four assumptions is wrong in one way or another, but I shall here concentrate on the last. Sergeants told to pick the five most experienced men may have difficulty about what constitutes 'experience'; judges *do* have difficulty in deciding what a phrase in a statute means. Both, however, have access to techniques of solving their problems, partly because they only have to find a 'workable' solution in a special sense. As long as the sergeant knows, as he ought to, why the patrol is being sent out, what is supposed to be achieved, he ought to be able to come up with a working definition of 'experience', in that he can pick the soldiers most likely efficiently to achieve the given aim and he, as a mere sergeant, has no business to do anything but accept that aim without question. Judges, provided they are presented with statutes that make it clear what the whole aim of the legislation is, ought, at least in principle, to be able to select a definition of the contested phrase that best fulfils the purpose. Again this purpose they must simply accept as deemed desirable by the legislature. They have done this in Britain for several hundred years under the rubric of the 'Mischief' rule, nowadays sometimes known as 'teleological' interpretation.[20] Of course this is not always easy, or even possible, but the fault is the legislature's, and does not follow from some inescapable fact about rules.

This is categorically different from the situation where a judge, finding no rule to guide him, consults general principles of morality. In this latter case, there is no externally-given purpose to be consulted. Consider Dworkin's own example, an American case from 1960, Henningsen v Bloomfield Motors,[21] where Henningsen sued the car manufacturers to recover the costs of an automobile accident, despite having signed a contract that explicitly limited the manufacturer's liability to 'making good defective parts'. Despite the rule of common law, that 'one who does not read the terms of a contract he signs cannot afterwards ask a court to remove a clause he has agreed to', the court found for Henningsen, saying: 'Is there any principle which is ... more firmly embedded in the history of Anglo-American law than the basic doctrine that the courts will not permit themselves to be used as instruments of inequity and injustice?'[22]

Well, yes there are several principles more firmly embedded. One such is that if there is no rule of law by which a plaintiff can demonstrate that he has a right to X, the defendant should not even be put to the trouble of arguing that he need not provide X. The judges in Henningsen clearly considered general socio-political principles of morality, and used their discretion in judging that Henningsen should be protected against manufacturers of shoddy cars. They may even have been, in some cosmic sense, right to do so. But there is no comparison at all here with judges having difficulty in deciding what a particular law means, because there is no externally given and unarguable general social purpose against which the court could make its decision. Any sense in which Henningsen 'had a right' to a particular decision in this case must follow from a very general social or political or economic theory, one that is clearly not capable of demonstration as a given. No judge could be *mistaken* in not recognising it. Henningsen's case is two things: if it is an example of Dworkin's principles at work, it demonstrates an extreme use of discretion never sanctioned by positivism. It is also a clear and flagrant example of judges misbehaving. For it is in fact not true that positivists force judges to use discretion. The Henningsen case calls for no discretion at all, and therefore none is allowed. There is one correct answer, to find for the defendant, however much some of us might regret that.

The very notion of discretion in positivism is misunderstood by Dworkin, because he imports another argument, without mentioning it; this is the assumption that any conflict between citizens is justiciable, and therefore courts must always find a solution. In fact positivism does not pretend, and only a strange pseudo-liberal political theory would expect, that the state has devised an all-embracing code that can deal with all emerging conflicts. It has done no such thing, and most legal philosophies have never thought it had.

After all, the common law descends today from the old English doctrine that there is no right without a remedy. This doctrine did not mean that wherever anyone had a moral right the courts would find a way of protecting it. On the contrary, it meant that unless the courts already had a remedy at hand, they would refuse to find that someone had a right they should protect. There are plenty of cases exhibiting this attitude today, and they are far more characteristic at least of the 'Anglo-' part of 'Anglo-American' law than is 'Henningsen'. An example is the recent case of the Banaban Islanders,[23] where the presiding judge made it quite clear that he felt the Crown was responsible for the destruction of their homeland, publicly called upon the Crown to do something, *and* found against the islanders for want of jurisdiction.

Dworkin makes much of the point that one is not free of an obligation to do what is right just because what is right is a matter of obligation in an extra-legal sense. Of course, in this sense, judges never have discretion. It is never the case that there exists no argument against which their decisions may be criticised. He adds that it will not do to say that this is 'only' a moral obligation, unless one can show how this sort of obligation differs from the obligation to follow rules.

I hope I have done something to demonstrate in what way it is a different form of obligation. It is worth pointing to something that the abandonment of a tougher Austinian positivism allows one too easily to forget. Judges may not be the transmitters of the command of a powerful sovereign, but they certainly exercise the sovereign's coercive power.

What makes the law of contract important, after all, is that even if the contract itself cannot be seen as the will of the sovereign, litigants who lose a contract case and refuse to pay damages can be put into prison indefinitely for contempt of court. When a man is wielding the power of the state, it makes a vast difference if he is bound by a rule deliberately created by that state, or bound only in the sense that there exists some controversial code against which his actions may be criticised.

The essential difference between law and morality, which Dworkin ignores, is that law covers a *subset* of moral arguments in which the state has decided to step in and back a particular side.

Consider, if I have not yet given good enough reasons to doubt the place of principles in a legal system, Dworkin's strange notion that judges characteristically decide cases by balancing principles which intersect (i.e. conflict). How? There are several general approaches to such problems in moral philosophy; some resort to an ordering of principles, *à la* Rawls, some to basic notions of desert of the parties, and most frequently a utilitarian maximum-good criterion is advocated. This latter would seem to be Dworkin's preference, as at one stage he accepts that an earlier distinction he drew between principles and policies can be collapsed 'by adopting the utilitarian thesis that principles of justice are disguised statements of goals (securing the greatest happiness of the greatest number)'.[24]

They must surely reach for criteria to resolve conflict that come from some very general moral philosophy. Let us suppose that judges are all utilitarians, as the safest answer.

Utilitarianism itself, in its commonest modern form would prohibit them from doing what Dworkin wants them to do. It is generally understood that while rules may be best defended by utilitarianism, acts ought not to be given individualised utility calculations, but should *follow* from rules. Certainly the notion that we set up courts to come to fresh and separate utilitarian decisions on cases coming before them would be sharply rejected by most political thinkers, or politicians for that matter. It would also be sharply rejected by legal theorists in general, because one of the most sacred, and logically necessary virtues of law is supposed to be certainty. It is supposed to be vital that a man can know ahead of time whether his proposed action is lawful or not. If all he can know is that it will be judged lawful or otherwise depending upon the balance of utilities between him and anyone who brings him to court, law can be no guide to action at all.

Some defenders of positivism against Dworkin have tried to argue that the law as a system contains a determinate ordering of priority between goals. Unfortunately as Dworkin insists that principles are not restricted to those passing some test of recognition-pedigree, this hardly helps, even if true.[25]

Concluding this section, I would suggest that Dworkin is right in a special way. He has not provided another model of law, either prescriptive or descriptive, to replace the rules model, which abolishes discretion. Principles do not exist in the way he wants them to, and would indeed render more discretion to the system were they to exist. Furthermore he is mistaken in over-emphasising the extent and nature of discretion required to make the positivist model work, when he assumes that all claims made on a court must be answered.

What he has done, I think, is to point to some of the ways that discretion itself works when it has to. It is not that legal systems consist of principles rather than rules and thus do not need discretion, but that they consist of rules and not principles and thus require discretion which is handled through principles.

The need for discretion is certainly present in any imaginable legal system, though Dworkin's two main concerns, discretion occurring because of the conflict of principles or rules, and discretion arising because of the absence of rules, are

rather unimportant. Rules very seldom conflict in practice
(though rules and general moral principles may often do so),
and where they do they can usually be handled by simple
procedures, themselves impeccably positivistic.[26] As to rules
being absent, the rather obvious doctrine, that what is not
illegal is legal, virtually removes this problem.

Discretion arises overwhelmingly because of unclarity or
ambiguity in an existent rule, though it is typically considered
a trivial problem. Hart, for example, admits that the concepts
used in rules are 'open textured', but insists that the vast
majority of cases fall into the clear core of the concepts.[27]

It is to Dworkin's credit that he has attempted to develop his
theory of principles, or what he sometimes disingenuously calls
the 'rights' thesis, into a complex theory of interpretation to
deal with this crucial area of discretion, especially in his recent
book *Taking Rights Seriously*.[28]

IV

DWORKIN'S THEORY OF INTERPRETATION

I now discuss his argument about how judges should engage in
interpretation. Though I think it must finally be rejected for
much the same reasons as his 'principles' model of the overall
legal system, it highlights the political nature of statutory
interpretation in a way positivism tends to ignore.

Take a problem of interpretation — does a statute that
forbids racial discrimination in any establishment offering
'services to a sector of the public' prevent a Conservative Club
refusing to serve a black, given that clubs only offer service to
members?[29] Or does a similar statute forbidding racial discrimination prevent a local authority refusing to give a council
house to a permanent resident of the UK who is of Polish
nationality?[30]

I dealt with this sort of problem earlier by suggesting that
courts had a simple method of solving such discretionary
problems, in that they only need consider what the statute was
aiming at to know how to define the words, just as the platoon
sergeant only has to know the battle plan in order to be able to
decide which of his men should be considered experienced.

Generally English judges follow positivist lines and believe that such questions should be answered by trying to work out what Parliament intended in the clause in question. Legal effect should then be given to this intention. A slightly different thesis is that 'teleological' interpretation should be used; that is, rather than the specific intention of Parliament in a particular clause, the general purpose of the statute should guide one.[31] Much of the time this method works well enough. But not infrequently it is very hard to see what Parliament did intend, and the act itself gives no clear idea of what its basic purpose was.

Here positivism has problems; often the resulting necessity for discretion has been described as requiring the court to act as deputies to the legislature, or to 'legislate interstitially'.

Dworkin leaps in again, to show that a proper regard to how judges use general political and social principles not only explains how such problems are and should be handled, but that discretion again is illusory, and that the judge does not legislate.

He dismisses the psychological attempt to decide what Parliament actually intended. He also dismisses the argument that when careful reading of the statute fails to dictate a result, the 'force' of the statute lapses and can no longer apply. In his own words,

The act of a legislature is not an event whose force we can . . . measure so as to say it has run out at a particular point; it is rather an event whose content is contested. [The Judge] constructs his political theory as an argument about what the legislature has, on this occasion, done. The contrary argument, that it did not actually do what he said, is not a realistic piece of common sense, but a competitive claim about the true content of that contested event.[32]

And, of course, he argues that where litigants have a conflict not foreseen in the act, judges are not deciding *ex nihilo* what their rights are to be, but simply giving recognition to pre-existent rights whose ontological status is in no way affected by parliamentary oversight.

Dworkin arrives at this entertaining conclusion by an extended analogy between law and the rules of a game, which I will short-circuit, but cannot leave out altogether. He asks this question: suppose the rules of chess include a provision allowing the referee to stop a game, and give victory to one player, if the other intimidates him. What if one grandmaster continually smiles in an unnerving way at his opponent; does this count as intimidation? The only way to solve this is for the referee to ponder on the character of the game. He will quickly arrive, for example, at the idea that it is an intellectual game, and not a game of chance, by comparing the implications of different characterisations against the known rules. Going further, chess cannot be intellectual in any sense that involves physical grace, as ballet might be, because the rules do not penalise clumsily knocking over the board. This comparing of characterisations may not get one all the way: it might not allow one to decide between two types of intellectual game, one, like poker, where ability at psychological intimidation is part of the skill, another, like mathematics, where it is not. The referee, after this process of elimination, would be left finally having to decide by considering the notion of intellect itself and choosing one 'which offers a deeper or more successful account of what intellect really is'.[33]

The extension to judicial interpretation is direct. In place of the idea of the character of the game, the judge must create a general political theory where the statute is best justified. From that political theory and the justified statute he deduces the answer to his puzzle. Any judge who accepts the rules constitutive of his legal institution accepts the general political theory of his state. It should be noted that the political theory the judge uses is something he creates inductively to justify the given material (the particular statute) from other statutes, the constitutional framework, or anything else germane. So the judge is neither taking some existent general ideology and solving the problem *de nove*, nor simply giving reign to his own preferences. One does not decide whether discriminating against Poles is in keeping with bourgeois liberalism, nor whether one likes Poles oneself.

Dworkin's example is this: a statute in an American state forbids anyone from abducting or carrying away by any means another person, and makes it a federal crime so to do. A man converted a young girl to a freak religion and persuaded her to run away and consummate a 'celestial marriage'. Is this covered by the statute? Dworkin suggests the judge might work it out this way:

> *Question one;* Why does *any* statute have the power to take away liberty?
>
> *Answer one:* From democratic theory, legislatures are the right arena to make collective decisions about criminality. But the same constitutional doctrine imposes duties to act for the public good.
>
> *Question two:* What interpretation of the statute best ties the language of it to the legislature's duties?
>
> *Answer two:* The construction, not of some hypothesis about the legislator's minds but of a special political theory that justifies this statute in the light of their more general responsibilities better than any alternative theory.
>
> *Question three:* What principles and policies might properly have persuaded the legislature to enact that statute?
>
> *Answer three:* Well, for example, not the policy of making all crimes federal, because that would deviate from known constitutional rules; but perhaps either the desire to make all serious crimes federal, or to make all those involving possible crossing of state lines federal.
>
> *Question four:* But which?
>
> *Answer four:* Well, the statute sets such high penalties that only the policy of federalising serious crimes makes sense. Therefore the interpretation that appears justified by the general given features of the state is the one that frees the man.[34]

The details of Dworkin's theory are not clear, but the general line is. A doctrine he calls the 'thesis of political responsibility' requires a basic degree of consistency in legislation, so that constitutional principles and detailed statutes form a logical whole, and any interpretation can be tried out against an induced generalisation from these rules, until only one of the possible explanations fits.

It may not be possible to exhaust all alternative justifications for a statute this way. Discussing a statutory problem of religious liberty, Dworkin suggests that a judge might be left with two different versions, each equally in keeping with all other constitutional principles. Then only treating it as an issue in political philosophy, deciding for himself which is the better definition of religious liberty, will yield the judge an answer.

This theory of interpretation genuinely does ignore legislative intent, by taking the legislature to have done an open-ended thing when they passed a statute. The judge discovers what it is the legislatures have done, rather than trying to find out what they meant to do. He agrees, naturally, that any such account will be contestable. He is right that an enterprise such as this calls for different, though not less, discretion.

The approach is not absurdly far fetched. There are traces of it already in modern judicial interpretation where the nature of other, not directly related, statutes constitute reasons for adopting a particular interpretation of a troublesome clause. In common law much progress in the past has been made by drawing analogies from a rule contained in one set of precedents to a quite different area of law.[35]

However, judicial creation of political theory by induction has to be rejected, or at least reformulated, until it is too weak to help much. It rests ultimately on one extremely strong assumption, that of the internal coherence and compatibility of statutes and constitutional rules. The analogy to chess misleads, for chess has two characteristics lacking in a legal system. It is a *whole*, deliberately created as an entity, and has not developed over time by accretion and deletion of separate rules. Second, it aims at one specific end. Given these characteristics it follows that there is no possibility of its rules and characteristics conflicting — any such conflict inside the rules of chess would make the game unplayable.

The political complex of statutes and rules is not a single creation, and it has no single identifiable aim. Take the three aims of the US Constitution — guaranteeing 'life, liberty, and the pursuit of happiness'. It consists of pieces of legislation passed at various times over two centuries. Even then it is an infinitely simpler complex than the body of English legislation and constitutional conventions. There is no guarantee or likelihood that any political complex will be internally consistent. Indeed it is most certain that it will not be, because half the process of politics is of pursuing incompatible goals by optimisation, because maximisation is impossible. The sort of political theory needed to justify any one interpretation is one that involves a series of substantive judgments precisely about how to reconcile incompatibilities. As such, creating the justifying theory to aid interpretation involves an essentially legislative activity, even more than guessing the intention of legislators, or making up one's own mind in the absence of any such clue.

Dworkin actually recognises this, because elsewhere he draws a distinction between arguments of principle and arguments of policy. Policy decisions involve no compulsion to treat equals equally, whereas decisions of principle do.[36] However, the theoretical justification of a statute is not a matter by itself of principles, but equally of policy choices.

Perhaps an example from recent English law will help. In 1976 Daymond v SW Water Authority involved a disputed clause where water authorities were given power to levy any rate they thought fit on anyone in their area to cover the costs of their varied services.[37] Mr Daymond, not being connected to mains drainage, objected to having to pay a levy for sewerage, because he did not benefit from this service, and contended that the true interpretation of the clause must be more restrictive than it appeared. The split court in the Lords gave conflicting decisions, both based on contitutional/statutory principles that anyone would have to admit were full and equal aspects of the political complex. On the one hand it was contended that it was an absurd negation of basic tax powers to allow a non-elected local body such freedom;[38] on the other that there was a long tradition of legislation dealing with public health that allowed people to be taxed to provide facilities they did not benefit from directly.[39]

It is hard to see how the political complex could engender any single justifying theory here without a primary value judgment about which of these two principles should prevail in this case.

A second major problem with Dworkin's theory here is that games of induction are notoriously infinite — given a set of facts or statutes, one can *always* come up with an overall framework that embraces them, as long as it is allowed to be sufficiently complex; indeed, one can always come up with several! Again Dworkin partially notices this, in admitting that the political complex may not rule conclusively between two different justifications. This is where he says the judge would have to shift to political philosophy and decide what was the more satisfying or adequate definition of the troublesome concept. Unfortunately this argument rapidly becomes circular. There do not exist correct, or 'most satisfactory', versions of concepts. Conceptual definition involves the purpose for which the concept is to be applied. Dworkin wants his judge to decide the best definition of a concept in order to decide the purpose of a statute. This is simply the wrong way round.

V

CONCLUSION: POSITIVISM, PARLIAMENT, AND INTERPRETATION

Dworkin's theory of interpretation is a brave attempt to admit the essential political nature of statutory construction, rather than to dismiss it as trivial, and at the same time to make it compatible with a democratic theory where only an elected body may take political decisions. His general aim in both the theories I have discussed is stated explicitly in the introduction to *Taking Rights Seriously*, when he claims that he is trying to assert a distinctly liberal legal theory which is opposed to the ruling Benthamite utilitarian theory. The vehicle for this is the idea of 'human rights'. He seeks to set up a model, both descriptive and prescriptive, of a legal system based on the fundamental concept that basic human rights pre-exist legislation, and the basis of judicial activity is giving effect to these rights through the use of general political theories and moral principles. There is little wrong with the aim itself. As a *prescriptive political* theory of how we might prefer to organise our legislative and judicial institutions it may well command much respect. But as a theory either about how the legal system in a liberal democracy can best be characterised, or how it ought to work, it is very awkward in as much as it clashes head-on with the fundamental value of popular sovereignty as expressed in elected legislatures. More than that the actual strategy, which is to argue for his 'rights-jurisprudence' by showing it to be a critical improvement on an impossible positivist jurisprudence, fails abysmally.

This is inevitable. Positivism is geared to be compatible with legislative supremacy, and where it fails, mainly with problems of interpretation, no alternative theory which has at its core a rejection of this value can hope to supercede it.

Dworkin fails because he is trying to synthesise the two logically opposed beliefs of liberal-democracy, liberalism and democracy. The only tactics open to someone of his persuasion are to demonstrate the fact, if it be a fact, that *even* positivism cannot do without discretion, and thus argue that it is better to adopt a 'rights-jurisprudence' which acknowledges the impossibility of non-discretionary law, with all its costs, than to pretend that one can avoid it. Better, that is, admit the creative aspect of law and thus control it for liberal aims, than deny it and risk illiberalism creeping in by the back door one keeps one's eyes closed to.

We can however take a different tack on the problems of positivism. Dworkin's theory of interpretation shows rather clearly how the job of statutory construction calls for a political decision. He marks out clearly for us the open-ended, rather than the open-textured, nature of a rule. His mistake is to try to solve what he shows to be a political problem by non-political means. If the creation of a political theory is required to make sense out of difficult statutes, that is a clear sign to us that no *legal* or *curial* argument or technique is going to avail. No one can pretend, where a judge constructs a political theory, that he is not using discretion.

If positivism is to survive, a political means that is democratically justifiable has to be found to replace illegitimate political activity forced on judges by what Dworkin would want to see as a failure in the 'rules' model, but which I argue is a *consequence* of the rules model.

The problem to which Dworkin addresses himself I would suggest is not one for jurisprudence at all. There can be no alternative to the 'rules' model of a legal system that is compatible with majoritarian democracy. Discretion does exist, and cannot be spirited away by jurisprudential tinkerings.

The presence of discretion, and the embarrassment of judicial coping with it, arises from a failure of the 'rules' model, not a failure of it in describing the judicial process, but its inadequacy in describing the legislative process.

The truth is that the tripartite distinction 'legislation', 'execution', 'judging' has not for some time, if it ever did, described the process of governing. We have got the wrong canonical form of a parliamentary statute. It is not at all a rule, which says 'Do X unless Y or Z'. Rather is it a statement of purpose 'Achieve as much X as possible without getting too much Z or too little Y'. The 1971 Race Relations Act never really said one could not discriminate in supplying a service to a section of the public. It said, rather, avoid race riots and protect human dignity without changing established social patterns, threatening property rights or extending council house waiting lists more than is absolutely necessary, and absolutely without losing too many votes for the incumbents.

Dworkin is right in saying that we should not see legislation as an event that runs out. It is an on-going event, but not one that can be delimited by the application of a political theory, because the theory is written in the process of the event. Parliament does not have a purpose, it has purposes, most of them not internally compatible, because in the end the incrementalist idea of policy-making is at least empirically, and maybe normatively, correct.[40] Why no-one has before pointed out that incrementalist policy-making could not be applied by a legal system at all is not known. It is a pity that the first man to see it should misunderstand the consequences.

Practical politicians have known this subconsciously for years; in Britain the attempt to deal with the problem by the dual creation of administrative tribunals and parliamentary-delegated legislation has been imperfect, and in the first aspect, hotly fought by the courts. We desperately need an entirely new institutional framework to cope with the actual nature of government. Legal positivism has problems, but they are not its own fault. Attempts to make Dworkin compatible with positivism do no one any good at all because they deny the basic problem.[41] Dworkin himself seems to understand neither the inevitable process of government, nor the passivity of law in its face.

But then no lawyer could, because they cannot accept that law is a feeble mechanical assistant to government. Oddly, Aristotle knew it, when he preferred the rule of men to that of law.

NOTES

1 H.L.A. Hart, *The Concept of Law* (Oxford University Press, 1961).
2 R.M. Dworkin, *Taking Rights Seriously*, (Duckworth, London, 1977)
   (a) Introduction, Section 4, *passim*.
3 R.M. Dworkin, 'Is law a system of rules?', in *The Philosophy of Law*, ed.
   R.M. Dworkin (Oxford Readings in Philosophy, Oxford University
   Press, 1977) (b).
4 Dworkin, (a), *op. cit.* Chapter 4.
5 For example, J. Bentham, *The Limits of Jurisprudence Defined*, ed.
   C.W. Everett (Columbia University Press, 1945); or J. Austin, *The
   Province of Jurisprudence Determined*, ed. H.L.A. Hart (Weidenfeld &
   Nicholson, 1954).
6 Hart, *op. cit.* Chapters 5 and 6.
7 Hart, *op. cit.*
8 Hart, *op. cit.* Chapter 7.
9 This is particularly the case, for example, when a statute is a consolida-
   tion act, as is often the case in areas like Landlord and Tenant law.
10 For example, R. Sartorius, 'Social Policy and Judicial Legislation',
   American Philosophical Quaterly 8 (1971), pp. 151–60.
11 Dworkin, (b) *op. cit.* p. 44.
12 Dworkin, (b), *op. cit.* p. 46.
13 *Ibid.*
14 The best discussion of this is Hart's early article 'The Asciption of
   Responsibilities and Rights', in *Logic and Language*, ed. A. Flew,
   (Oxford University Press, 1960).
15 S.C. Coval and J.C. Smith, 'Some Structural Properties of Legal
   decisions', 32 *Cambridge Law Journal*, (1973) p. 81. Also see C.F.H.
   Tapper, 'A Note on Principles', *Modern Law Review*, (1971) p. 628.
16 A glance at any textbook on criminal law, under the 'assault' heading
   demonstrates how impossible the writer has found it to reduce the law of
   assault to a comprehensive account. Yet no one could seriously claim
   that, Cross, for example, in pages 155–58 of his *Introduction to Criminal Law* (Butterworth, 1968, 6th edition) thought he was only
   describing a general principle of law that might be 'balanced' against
   another of equal weight.
17 Dworkin, (b), *op. cit.* p. 52.
18 *Ibid.* p. 54.
19 This example of Dworkin's follows immediately upon an example
   drawn from the favourite area of umpires in sports. It is odd that he does
   not appear to notice how radically different the two domains are, and
   how misleading it is to extrapolate from either to a curial context. It
   would be instructive to know which of the two domains Dworkin thinks
   the better example; one suspects he sees judges as more akin to umpires
   than NCOs, while as a positivist I would reverse that ordering.
20 The phrase is perhaps as yet most commonly found in the jurisprudence
   of the European Court of Justice. A glance at such a theory of interpretation shows how little some practising judges anyway see themselves as
   operating by principles rather than rules, even when engaged in dis-

tinctly creative judging. For example: H. Kutscher, 'Methods of interpretation as seen by a judge at the court of justice', in *Judicial and Academic Conference Reports* 27–28 September 1976, of the *Court of Justice of the European Communities,* Luxembourg.

21 32 N.J. 358 (1960).

22 Quoted by Dworkin, (b) *op. cit.* p. 45.

23 Tito v Waddell (no 2) 1977 3 All ER 129–323.

24 Dworkin, (b), *op. cit.* p. 44.

25 Dworkin, (b), *op. cit.* p. 63.

26 After all, federal constitutions necessarily have to face this problem, and they solve it perfectly easily unless their supreme courts *choose* to find conflict between guiding constitutional rules. But as is well known in the history of the United States Supreme Court, the very act of talking in terms of balancing conflicting constitutional dogma, say between 5th amendment rights and Congressional investigation powers is a political act and is seen to be controversial.

27 Hart, *op. cit.* Chapter 7.

28 Dworkin, (a), *op. cit.*

29 Race Relations Board v Charter (1973) 2 W.L.R. 299

30 Ealing LBC v RRB (1972) A.C. 342

31 See fn 20

32 Dworkin, (a), *op. cit.* p. 109.

33 Dworkin, (a), *op. cit.* p. 103.

34 Dworkin, (a), *op. cit.* p. 107–8.

35 This is very well demonstrated in E.H. Levi, *An Introduction to Legal Reasoning* (Chicago University Press, 1949), in which such reasoning by analogy is held to be constitutive of legal thought.

36 Dworkin, (a), *op. cit.* p. 82–3.

37 Daymond v South West Water Authority (1976) 1 All E.R. 39.

38 Daymond, *op. cit.* Lord Dilhorne, especially p. 49.

39 Daymond, *op. cit.* Lord Diplock, especially p. 54.

40 C. Lindblom and D. Braybrooke, D., *A Strategy for Decision,* (The Free Press, Glencoe, Illinois, 1963).

41 See notes 14 and 15.

DATE DUE

GAYLORD			PRINTED IN U.S.A.